STOLEN YEARS

STOLEN YEARS

BEFORE AND AFTER GUILDFORD

PAUL HILL

WITH RONAN BENNETT

Doubleday

LONDON · NEW YORK · TORONTO · SYDNEY · AUCKLAND

TRANSWORLD PUBLISHERS LTD
61-63 Uxbridge Road, London W5 5SA

TRANSWORLD PUBLISHERS (AUSTRALIA) PTY LTD
15-23 Helles Avenue, Moorebank, NSW 2170

TRANSWORLD PUBLISHERS (NZ) LTD
Cnr Moselle and Waipareira Aves,
Henderson, Auckland

DOUBLEDAY CANADA LTD
105 Bond Street, Toronto, Ontario, M5B 1Y3

Published 1990 by Doubleday
a division of Transworld Publishers Ltd

British Library Cataloguing in Publication Data
Hill, Paul
    Stolen years: before and after Guildford
    I. Title   II. Bennett, Ronan
    364.131

    ISBN 0–385–401256

Printed in Great Britain by
Mackays of Chatham PLC, Chatham, Kent

To my grandparents, Charlie and Margaret Cushnahan,
who died during my years in prison

ACKNOWLEDGEMENTS

Fifteen years in prison do not pass lightly. They would have weighed more heavily without the support of my family. My grandparents, my mother, brothers, sisters, aunts, uncles and cousins stood by me, and they have my undying gratitude. In their search for justice, they were, over the years, joined by others – strangers at first, now, many of them, friends. Many of our supporters are mentioned by name in the pages that follow: to all, the named and unnamed alike, I give my thanks. I would also like to express my gratitude to those who helped directly with this book: Sister Sarah Clarke for her kindness and assistance; Vince Stevenson for suggestions with the manuscript; Deidre Ellis, Gina Clarke, Tom Barron, Martin Walker, Errol, Theresa and Janet Smalley for their valuable help with background detail; Maggie Morrissey for her work on the transcription; Eithne Bennett for picture research; and to Henry Bell, the Linenhall Library, Belfast, the Ulster Museum, Falls Community Council & Belfast Exposed, and Lensmen for their kind permission to reproduce photographs.

CONTENTS

	Principal Characters	xi
ONE	'This Unhappy Matter'	1
TWO	One of Our Own	5
THREE	Photographs in My Head	16
FOUR	A Memory of Repression	29
FIVE	In England, August–November 1975	45
SIX	'Placed in the Cells'	57
SEVEN	'One On'	78

EIGHT   'I Never Met It So Easy'   **98**

NINE   Trial   **115**

TEN   'May They Rot in Hell'   **132**

ELEVEN   The End of the Line   **147**

TWELVE   Appeal   **169**

THIRTEEN   A Citizen of Prison   **189**

FOURTEEN   Mutiny   **205**

FIFTEEN   Changes   **225**

SIXTEEN   Among My Own Again   **241**

SEVENTEEN   Stolen Years   **259**

Chronology   **266**
Index   **275**

PRINCIPAL CHARACTERS

Paul Hill
Gerry Conlon
Carole Richardson
Paddy Armstrong

The Guildford Four

Paul Colman
Sean McGuinness
Brian Anderson

Charged with Guildford bombings but released

Sean Mullin

Charged with explosives offences but released

Annie Maguire
Paddy Maguire
Vincent Maguire
Patrick Maguire
Patrick O'Neill
Sean Smyth
Giuseppe Conlon

The Maguire Seven

Hector Young	Paul's co-defendants in the Shaw
Martin Monaghan	trial
Joe O'Connell	The Balcombe Street men.
Eddie Butler	Members of IRA active service unit
Hugh Doherty	in London, August 1974-December
Harry Duggan	1975, responsible for Guildford
Brendan Dowd	and Woolwich bombings.
	Part of London active service unit.
	Took part in Guildford and
	Woolwich attacks
Elizabeth (Lily) Hill, *née* Cushnahan	Paul's mother
William Norman Hill	Paul's father
Elizabeth	Paul's sister
Patrick	Paul's brother
Marion	Paul's sister
Martin	Paul's brother
Katrina	Paul's sister
Charlie Cushnahan senior	Paul's grandfather
Margaret Cushnahan, *née* Hamill	Paul's grandmother
Charlie Cushnahan junior	Paul's uncle
Theresa Smalley, *née* Cushnahan	Paul's aunt
Errol Smalley	Theresa's husband
Anne Keenan, *née* Cushnahan	Paul's aunt
Frank Keenan	Anne's husband
Gina Clarke	Paul's girlfriend
Kara	Paul's daughter
Marion Serravalli	Married Paul in Long Lartin Prison, 1988
John Clarke	Gina's brother in Southampton
Cathy Crosbie, *née* Clarke	Gina's sister in Southampton
Malcolm Crosbie	Gina's brother-in-law in Southampton

Mary Hammond, *née* Clarke	Gina's sister in Greenwich
Yvonne Fox	Friend of Anne and Frank Keenan, alibi witness for Paul
Brian Shaw	Former British soldier killed by IRA, 1974
DCI Albert Cunningham DC John McCaul	RUC detectives involved in Shaw murder inquiry, 1974
Christopher Rowe	Assistant Chief Constable of Surrey, 1974
DCS Walter Simmons DS Anthony Jermey Det. Supt Ronald Underwood DI Timothy Blake DI Brian Richardson	Surrey police officers investigating Guildford pub bombings, 1974
Chief Supt Jim Nevill Det. Supt Peter Imbert	Officers of the Metropolitan Police's Bomb Squad. Imbert later Metropolitan Police Commissioner
Douglas Higgs Donald Lidstone	Principal scientific officers, Royal Arsenal Research and Development Establishment (RARDE)
Sir Michael Havers QC	Senior Crown counsel in trial and appeal of Guildford Four. Later Attorney General and Lord Chancellor
Michael Hill QC	Junior Crown counsel in Guildford trial and appeal
Roy Amlot QC	Senior Crown counsel in Guildford appeal court hearing, 1989
Sir John Donaldson	Judge in trial of the Guildford Four. Now Lord Donaldson, Master of the Rolls

Mr Justice Cantley	Judge in trial of Balcombe Street men, 1977
Lord Lane	Lord Chief Justice, 1980-
David Melton	Paul's solicitor, 1974-77
Alastair Logan	Solicitor for Paddy Armstrong, and later for Carole. Acted for Paul and Gerry, 1977-87
Mike Fisher	Paul's solicitor, 1987-
Gareth Peirce	Gerry's solicitor, 1987-
Michael Lavery QC	Paul's counsel, Belfast, 1975
Arthur Mildon QC	Paul's counsel, Old Bailey, 1975
Lord (Tony) Gifford QC	Paul's counsel, 1989
James Still	Retired police Superintendent who assisted Alastair Logan interview Dowd and Balcombe Street men
Det. Supt Ronald Sagar	Humberside detective in charge of investigation into brutality in aftermath of Hull prison riot
Jim Sharples	Former Deputy Chief Constable of Avon and Somerset. Headed inquiry set up in 1987 into Guildford case
Mickey Williams	Prisoners met by Paul, 1974-89
Jake Prescott	
Jimmy McCartney	
Martin Brady	
Bertie Coster	
Frank Conteh	
Marty Clifford	
Noel Jenkinson	
Graham Little	
Billy Power	

Johnnie Walker	
Hugh Callaghan	
Dick McIlkenny	
Gerry Hunter	
Mick Sheehan	
Conor Foley	Founding members of the
John McDonald	Guildford Four Relatives
Gerry Fitzpatrick	Committee along with Errol and
Tom Barron	Theresa Smalley
Richard Wize	
Sister Sarah Clarke	Campaigners for Guildford Four,
Fr Raymond Murray	Maguire Seven and Birmingham Six
Fr Denis Faul	
Jeremy Corbyn	Labour politicians who
Joan Maynard	campaigned for the Guildford Four
Cardinal Basil Hume	Archbishop of Westminster
Lord Devlin	Former Law Lord
Lord Scarman	Former Law Lord
Merlyn Rees	Former Home Secretary
Roy Jenkins	Former Home Secretary
Robert Kee	Author of *Trial and Error* on Guildford Four and Maguire Seven cases
Grant McKee	Makers of Yorkshire Television
Ros Franey	documentaries on Guildford and Maguire cases and authors of *Time Bomb*
Charles Haughey	Irish Taoiseach (Prime Minister) 1979-81, 1982, 1987-

Neil Blaney	Irish politicians who campaigned
Brendan Ryan	for the Guildford Four
Paschal Mooney	

Douglas Hurd   Home Secretary, 1985-89

Chapter One

'THIS UNHAPPY MATTER'

We must have appeared pathetic. I looked along the dock as the foreman of the jury read out the verdicts. Paddy had his head down and Gerry had his head down. Carole was distraught, her face in her hands. I wanted to say something to tell them that they were making a mistake. I wanted to jump up and scream at them, and be dragged away shouting that they were sending innocent people to prison. But I was unsure of myself. I thought, 'What do you do? What should I say?' Would my protest be misconstrued – the defiant parting shot of an unrepentant terrorist?

So I stayed quiet, too numb to take much in. I recall Donaldson, the judge, castigating us, each in turn, but I could not hear all he said. I do remember him saying that there was no word in the English language to describe the barbarity of what we had done. Not for the first and not for the last time I began to think that maybe I was guilty after all. For almost a year, the time we had spent on remand awaiting trial, it had been drummed into us by police, by lawyers, by prison officers, by newspapers, radio and television: we were

1

the Guildford Four and we were guilty; we were the 'warped dregs of humanity'. All of this had an effect: I felt shabby, ashamed to be where I was.

But I also felt anger. As the judge praised the police and thanked them for the skill with which they had performed their duty, there came into my mind images of an interrogation during which I sat, handcuffed, as police officers circled me, shouted at me, called me a bastard, and then knocked me to the floor. During the trial, the police had given their evidence calmly and persuasively. All denied that they had used violence and threats against us, or that they had concocted our 'confessions'. They maintained throughout that we had freely admitted responsibility to mass murder. In the witness box policeman after policeman lied to the court, and did such a good job of it. And our witnesses, who were made to look shifty, confused and stupid, had told the truth, and had done such a bad job of it.

As the judge continued, I could see several policemen in the well of the court just below the dock – Peter Imbert, then a Bomb Squad officer, now Commissioner of the Metropolitan Police, stands out in my mind – congratulating themselves on a job well done. They were nodding and smiling to each other, occasionally glancing up at the dock to remind us of their triumph.

To my left and up by the bench, I saw Sir Michael Havers, the prosecuting barrister who later went on to become Attorney General and Lord Chancellor, exchanging jokes with Michael Hill, his junior. They, too, were pleased with themselves and would now and then look over to us, sneers on their faces. I thought, 'What kind of victory is it they are celebrating?' For the five weeks of the trial Havers and Hill had pummelled and ridiculed our witnesses – ordinary people, mostly Irish, all from poor backgrounds, with little education or the confidence to stand up to men like them. They had dismissed our assertions of innocence and our witnesses' testimony. Now, in their moment of glory, they sat smug and grinning: they had beaten us, four pathetic and naive young people.

The judge started the sentencing. There had been little in the way of mitigation; Gerry's counsel had not even attempted to say anything. Carole, who was seventeen at

2

the time of the Guildford pub bombing, was sentenced to be detained at Her Majesty's pleasure. I heard Carole sobbing as Donaldson read out her sentence, and the sound of my mother's own crying reached me from the back of the court. At that moment all that could be heard was the judge's dry voice endlessly repeating, it seemed, 'murder, murder, murder', and the crying of the two women.

Donaldson finished with Carole and turned to Gerry, to whom he gave life with a recommendation that he serve a minimum of thirty years. Then he gave Paddy life, with a minimum recommendation of thirty-five years. It seems odd that my mind was working in this way, but on hearing Gerry and Paddy's sentences I assumed the judge was working on some kind of scale, and that I would get life with a recommendation to serve forty years. I remember thinking, 'So that's it, forty years. I am going to get forty years.' But the judge's scale went haywire. He said in my case, life should mean life. I was to remain in prison, he said, unless, as an act of mercy, I was to be released in case of extreme old age or infirmity. I did not realize it then, but I had just received the longest prison sentence handed down in English judicial history.

At that moment, what I felt most was anger at the viciousness of the system that was allowing this to happen. Against us were men of standing, titled men, men who had decorations and commendations, who pointed their fingers at us and accused us of things we had not done. They condemned us. They ran rings around us and made fools of our witnesses. They mocked us when we told them that we were innocent, and that the police had manufactured the evidence against us. They pointed their fingers at us and said we were liars, and convinced the jury and the country that we were guilty. They were believed and we were not.

The judge said it was unlikely that we would be released from prison during his lifetime. Lord Donaldson, now the Master of the Rolls, is still alive; so are most of the others who played their part in condemning us. Now we are out. And what we said at our trial, that we were innocent, has at last been shown to be true. Policemen lied to implicate us in offences we did not commit; the prosecution tampered with evidence; and the judges, in the trial and later in the appeal,

3

went along with it all, without, it seems, smelling the most obvious rat. Fourteen years after our trial, fifteen years after first being arrested, Crown counsel were forced to stand up in court and admit that what we had been saying all along was true. No one apologized. The judges referred to our stolen sixty years as 'this unhappy matter'. It seemed to me that they almost expected us to be grateful to them.

But I had no thanks for them. I felt vindicated and strong, and for those in the court, apart from our lawyers, families and friends, I felt only contempt. They had lied and cheated, and we spent fifteen years in prison. They got away with it because they were powerful, and because we were ordinary people, without influence or money or education, and because we were Irish.

Chapter Two

ONE OF OUR OWN

One night, not long after coming out of prison, I was driven through the streets of Belfast Docks. The Docks, so alive when I was a child, now are dark and ghostly. The orange lights of the multi-lane motorway, a long, wide asphalt scar in the district's heart, illuminate no people. The people and the houses they once lived in are gone. All I could see were empty building lots littered with untidy piles of bricks and breeze blocks, rectangles of decaying concrete cracked up by grasses and weeds pushing through to the light. Now and then, we passed strange survivors of old Sailortown: clusters of little houses that seemed to huddle together while they awaited the re-opening of the developers' offensive.

My family had warned me about what was happening, but I had not understood its scale. They had told me, 'The Docks, you know, is all changing. You would hardly recognize it now.' But after a decade and a half in prison how do you appreciate 'change' in a city? What scale do you use to gauge it? The warnings had not prepared me. Driving past that night, I was shocked. What I saw was abandonment. I was sad. I thought of the rows and rows of terraced houses outside which the women in their headscarves used to sit while they knitted and gossiped. They sat in the middle of the carefully scrubbed arc of pavement that was the badge of every well-tended home. In my mind's eye there were men coming home from work, and grannies in their black boots, dresses and shawls. I could see the girls walking in droves, in their big green aprons, to the red-brick sprawl of Gallagher's tobacco mill, the different parts of which were connected by mysterious pipes and tubes. And children, children everywhere, running and running around the streets.

In the car window I caught sight of my own reflection, my own face as a grown man who has spent his adult life in jail. But in the Docks, even the spectral Docks of today, my face changes and becomes the face of a child. For a moment I feel as if I could pass through the reflection, and step back into the Docks of my childhood.

I do not mean to be sentimental about Sailortown as it was when I was a child. Like the Docks area anywhere in the world it was a hard place, and the people were rough. Their language and humour were harsh, and to outsiders who knew no better the people could appear dangerous and unpredictable. Friendly banter, or 'slagging', often contained the most wounding of jibes. There was no false politeness here. Physical, personal and moral defects, even among the closest of friends, were considered fair targets for ridicule, with conceit, pomposity, cowardice and meanness singled out for the most scathing attention. Arguments were fierce. It was common to hear neighbours, families, friends and enemies exchange loud and angry words. These people had Belfast tongues and could lash with them. Quarrels could lead to fights and men did fight. It was important to stand up for yourself. The man who did not know how to handle himself was looked down on and taken advantage of. So, even if it meant taking a hiding, it was necessary to attempt to hold your own. Having so little, the people placed a high value on their integrity, which had to be defended against whatever form of insult or slight with all the ferocity of an army defending a citadel. Still, arguments, if they tended to flare up almost without warning, were quickly quenched, and people recovered their good humour with ease.

I look back on my childhood in the Docks not with nostalgia but still with a feeling of warmth because I belonged to a place where I knew and understood the people and their ways, and they knew and understood me. People from Sailortown, and from all parts of working-class Belfast, referred to those they knew and trusted as 'one of the people' or 'one of our own'. Roaming the streets as a child, our backdrop the silhouettes of battleships, tankers and steamers and the cranes and winches that served them, for all the harshness of the place, I was 'one of the people', and completely safe.

William Norman Hill was my father, and he was on the boats. He had served in the Royal Air Force but later joined the Royal Navy, and was wounded in Korea. After that he went into the Merchant Marines, and during most of my infancy was away on deep-sea runs. He met my mother, Elizabeth Cushnahan, in the Continental, a cafe in Castle Street, which runs off the city centre towards the Falls Road. At that time, my mother worked as a waitress in another cafe, the Chalet d'Or, and my father, dressed in his Navy suit, must have made quite an impression.

Belfast people, whose ears are attuned to the slightest nuances of sectarianism, will instantly understand that it was a mixed marriage. The name William Norman Hill will be immediately recognizable as that of a Protestant, just as the name Elizabeth Cushnahan will ring out as that of a Catholic. My mother came from Cairns Street, off the Falls Road, the heart of Republican West Belfast, while my father's family lived in Matilda Street, near Sandy Row, a staunchly Protestant area. My grandfather on my father's side had served in the 'Skins', the Royal Enniskillen Fusiliers, and years later, when I was brought to Crumlin Road Prison, I saw a photograph of him on a wall in the governor's office (the Governor had held a commission in the Enniskillens). Granddad Hill used to work as a commissionaire at a bank in Lord Street, and I used to go to look at him in his uniform, sash and white gloves, and would proudly point him out to my friends. Although as a child I was not often in their house, I got on well with my father's family, and at Christmas they would always send toys.

The Catholic Church insists that the children of mixed

marriages be brought up in the Faith, and so I and my brothers and sisters were baptized Catholics. As a child, I was puzzled at seeing in Granddad Hill's house huge portraits of the Queen, something, even as a child, it was simple to grasp was inimical to the pictures of the Sacred Heart I was more used to seeing at home. Mixed marriages are not easy, and often encounter parental opposition, but it seems that my parents' marriage, for all the troubles that later enveloped it, did not have to contend with sectarian feeling among the in-laws. The Hill family attended the wedding, which was held in St Peter's pro-cathedral, and afterwards went to the Cushnahan house for the reception. I have no memory of sectarian things being said by either side of the family, and I know that in difficult times the Hill family was good to my mother. But still, children always manage to sense apartness and difference. In Belfast, they pick up and devour, like sweets they find on the pavement, the careless words and curses that litter the conversation of adults who live in a society of such mysterious and stern divides.

The Docks was a mixed area, but for the most part the territorial boundaries separating Catholic and Protestant were to us children as invisible as they were to the birds in the sky. Except during July. Before 1969, before the outbreak of what is euphemistically termed 'the Troubles', there was a cyclical side to sectarianism. It bubbled to its threatening peak on 12 July when the Orange Order held its parades. It was on that day in 1690 that William of Orange defeated James II at the Battle of the Boyne, and every year the Orangemen celebrated the rout of 'papacy' and the triumph of the Protestant Ascendancy. On 12 July adults would give out fearful warnings. They said that streets we were used to playing in were now dangerous. They would say, 'Don't you go down there, don't go down that street!' Do I remember being bewildered by this? Oddly, no. Perhaps because the alterations to our physical world were highly visible, and simple to grasp. The streets proclaimed their enmity with flags and banners, or with kerb stones painted red, white and blue. More difficult to comprehend were the changes in the people. Neighbours and friends became Orangemen, as alien to us marching along to the flute and drum in their sashes, bowler hats and white gloves as beings from another planet.

Sectarianism's other focus in those days was football. The fortunes of Glasgow's two great teams, Celtic and Rangers, were followed with intense interest, and their supporters in Belfast used to organize weekend trips to go over by ferry to watch their champions. Here on the pitch was played out a confrontation whose history and meaning went far beyond football. For both sides it had to do with identity, and the survival of that identity in the face of insidious and unrelenting assault; and the players were a symbolic vanguard, standard-bearers of a people. The Celtic–Rangers encounters were a powerful source of sectarian legend. In Belfast itself, the game also fed sectarian feeling, and if the stories about Crusaders, Linfield, Belfast Celtic and Glentoran lacked the Glasgow battles' heroic proportions, they were no less powerful for that. I remember my granddad Cushnahan telling me that when he went as a boy to watch games, Catholics would be marked with an 'X' in chalk on their backs without their knowing it so that Protestant supporters would know to get them on the way home.

I used to go down to support Crusaders, a Protestant team, whose ground was on the Shore Road and in a Protestant area. To support Crusaders was not a normal thing for a Catholic boy to do, but at that time I had but a hazy awareness of sectarianism and, possibly because I was the son of mixed parents, had little sense of religious antagonism.

Perhaps because of the course of recent Irish history, sectarianism occupies a larger place in my memory of the Docks I grew up in than in reality it deserves. Its presence was, for most of the time, latent. As a child, I was more concerned with doing things and getting things, and the feelings I have for the Docks are not ones of fear or threat but of warmth.

I was born on 13 August 1954, the first of my mother's five surviving children, and was christened Paul Michael in St Joseph's church in Pilot Street. The house in which we lived was in Nelson Street. It was small, and we shared it with another family. We had three rooms – a kitchen, bathroom and bedroom. There were two beds: my parents had one and for the first couple of years I had the other to myself; later I shared it with my sister, Elizabeth.

The house, like all the little houses in the district, was

full of the paraphernalia of the Docks – bill hooks and so on. The people pilfered relentlessly, and their houses were littered with useless plunder. The men used to take things from the sheds around the Docks, or directly off the boats. Or they would wait at traffic lights to open up the backs of Northern Ireland Carrier lorries and make off with the boxes. Sometimes, the dockers broke open crates or had them 'accidentally' dropped by the winch drivers. Granddad Cushnahan, Charlie they called him, drove a winch, and they would say to him, 'Smash this one, Charlie!' He would let the crate drop and everyone would help themselves. People came home with all sorts of things. Once, I recall, our house filled up with washboards. We had about forty of them. These were not for sale for people did not think to make money out of the plunder. Neighbours would come in and take a washboard or whatever else, though the chances were that they already had what you had: the area suffered from gluts in certain commodities. I remember the washboards being in our house for a long time.

People pilfered from the boats, but real crime was rare. Burglaries and house-breakings were almost unheard of, although it would have been easy to gain access to the houses, for the doors were always open; the few people who turned their locks were considered odd by their neighbours. So, for the most part, doors were left open, and people entered and left as they would their own houses. Often I remember setting out with my mother to go somewhere and, as we were passing a neighbour's house, my mum saying, 'We might as well call in here for a wee minute.' The women used to gossip over a cup of tea, then it would be up and out and on our way again, only to stop at another house around the corner to repeat the process. We might visit half a dozen houses on our way.

On the rare occasion when someone was robbed, it was a great scandal. If the thief was caught, no one bothered with the police; retribution was private, swift and violent. Known thieves in the area were disliked, and the people drew a firm distinction between their activities and those of the dockers who took from the boats. Muggings were unknown, mugging an unknown crime. Later, when I lived in Cairns Street, off the Falls Road, Granddad Cushnahan

10

sometimes arrived home, having picked up his week's wages, and would fall down on the floor dead drunk. He walked in his stupor all the way from the Docks and his wages were still in his pocket.

Crimes against children, like abduction, were equally unknown, and we roamed the district until late at night in perfect safety. We boys wore almost identical clothing: T-shirts and pullovers, short trousers, big leather boots with great hobnails all over the soles and long, rough, serge-like grey socks with elastic bands at the top to keep them up. I had a snake belt, I remember, green and red with the catch in the form of a snake. I also had a tie held by elastic which I wore to mass and to school. Left to roam the streets we explored the sheds and quaysides and played football, emulating our Celtic heroes. When George Best came to the height of his powers he and Manchester United, for whom he played, attracted many supporters, although I was not one of them. Arsenal was the English team I supported.

The Docks provided other entertainments for children. Harland & Wolff was building some of the world's biggest super-tankers, and we would go to admire them and be awed by their vastness. Battleships, usually American, were another attraction. When they put into port there were hundreds of sailors in the streets. Sailors from Eastern European countries, however, were not allowed off the boats. They used to throw mailbags onto the quayside for us to post their letters, and watched through binoculars to make sure we posted them. Our payment for this service was cartons of cigarettes, and these we took to sell in the American Bar. We used to get a big silver halfcrown for two packets. After my first transaction of this sort, I remember walking away from the bar, holding the coin in both hands and staring at it, marvelling at its size and weight. It was the first time I had earned money. It had been quite easy; it was obvious I was going to be rich.

The children of the Docks were largely free from the interference of adults. It was not that parents did not love their children, but they did not pander to them or spoil them. Children were so numerous and riotous that adults took no special notice of them, and welcomed their absence. As a child, you were expected to look after yourself to a certain degree, and learn responsibilities quickly. These included

11

'going the messages'. Adults used to summon children over and send them to buy milk, lemonade or fish suppers for which we might be presented on return with a big chip 'piece' (sandwich).

Similarly, at school there were so many children in each class, forty or more, that there was little individual attention. When the teachers looked into their class what did they see? Forty noisy, restless, impatient children who would be distinguished only by whether or not they took free school dinners. Beyond that they were just an excited, gabbling mass. Still, I rarely 'went on the beak' (such consistency in attendance among my classmates was almost unheard of in those days). School I liked well enough and enjoyed history in particular. We also played football and Gaelic football and I used to look after the team's kit.

On the whole, I got on reasonably well with my teachers, and one or two of them were so odd that they fascinated me. One deputy headmaster exhibited a sort of stoic amazement at the behaviour of his pupils and their constant screaming and fighting. He had developed a theory that Irish children were mad. According to his theory, it went back to the Great Famine of the 1840s. He would say, 'You know why you are all mad? Because during the potato blight the people could not eat the potatoes so they made poteen out of them. The poteen got into the bloodstream, and was passed on from generation to generation. And now you are all mad.' In his funny way, he was trying to absolve us. It was as if he was saying, 'It's not your fault. You can't help it.' This deputy headmaster was Michael McLaverty, renowned in Belfast for his novels about life in the North. It was not until many years later that I discovered his beautiful and haunting books; at school he was just another of the strange potentates whose rule we had no option but to put up with.

Occasionally, missionary priests came to visit the schools and told us stories about Africa and the work they did there. They told us of the terrible poverty the people endured, that children would have to walk five miles to get a jug of water. I thought of the tap in the sink at our house, and tried to imagine what it would be like to live somewhere you had to walk five miles just to get a drink. It did not sound too good. And, anyway, how long was five miles? Pretty far.

Every Friday at school they took up a collection for the Black Babies, and it was expected that everyone put a silver sixpence in the box. Before the collection I used to go to the shop and change the sixpenny bit into two Irish threepenny bits, which were silver and to the teacher's uncunning eyes looked like a sixpence. I gave one of these to the Black Babies and kept the other for myself. Years later, a party of soldiers was raiding a house near my mother's. One of the soldiers was black and my mother, who had been screaming at the soldiers, saw him and shouted, 'I fed you when you were a baby!' I said to my mother, 'You only half fed him. He only got threepence a week from us.' The soldier, of course, had no idea what we were talking about and looked at us as though we were crazy.

Other priests used to visit the school. They were from the parish and came to prepare us for our first confession and communion. For Catholics these events, together with confirmation, are important reference points in their memory of when they were young. They are remembered, I suppose, because of all the fuss. For my first communion, my mum took me to get my first suit which she paid for with a Provident cheque. This was a cheque that clothes shops accepted, and the money was paid back to the Provident at so much a week. My first confession, which preceded communion by a day or two, I remember because it was so frightening. The darkness of the confessional scared me, and I imagined all sorts of things on the other side of the grill. When I realized it was the priest, so concerned was I to find out how he got in there that I almost forgot to tell him the sins I had memorized for the occasion. I was seven years old, and the concept of sin was new and only vaguely understood. The priests had assured us apprentice sinners that they were used to hearing the most terrible things, and that we were to hold nothing back. I tried to think of something that would impress my confessor. As part of our preparation in school we had had practice sessions during which the priests had helpfully listed some sins that we might choose from when the moment came. But these, disappointingly, consisted entirely of acts of extremely minor delinquency, mostly concerned with failure to obey parental commands and acts of wilful unkindness towards smaller siblings.

13

Confirmation held neither terrors nor confusion: it was well known among the lads in my class the confirmation was a time of legendary riches. It was also time for another suit, though to my horror and after many arguments with my mother, this turned out to be a short-trousered number. Absolute humiliation: to be seen by my classmates wearing a suit with short trousers when some of them were bound to have prevailed over their mothers. Still, compensation came in the form of money. Mother, grandparents, aunts and uncles all contributed. The booty was more than I used to get from a couple of trips to the American Bar laden down with Eastern European cigarettes.

My memories of when I was small are fond memories, of being loved and feeling secure. The only confusion I felt was when my father came home from the boats. Increasingly, he was a stranger, and the sense I had of him as a stranger was made worse by his inability to be warm and affectionate towards me. He never took me anywhere, and I cannot remember him picking me up to hold me, although I do remember that he did so with my other brothers and sisters. Here, perhaps, my memory is unreliable for I cannot decide what impact, if any, the lack of a real father has had on me. Sometimes I think it has damaged me, at other times not. There are times when I decide that he played no important part in my life, and am unwilling to concede even to myself that any emotional exchange, however slight, took place between us. But perhaps it did; I cannot be sure.

My parents argued frequently; and I remember that after one row Granddad Cushnahan came round to talk to my father about the way he was behaving. My father was standing at the top of the stairs, shouting abuse. My granddad started up the stairs and my father lashed out and kicked him in the face. His boot caught my granddad across the bridge of his nose. My granddad bore the scar for the rest of his life.

At first, my father was no more brutal than anyone else in the area in the way he treated his wife. Belfast men of his generation assumed that women should be kept barefoot, pregnant and in the kitchen. They assumed it was the woman's role to keep house and wait hand and foot on the man. But later his ill-treatment of my mother went beyond what was considered acceptable at that time. As his visits home became less frequent, he became increasingly withdrawn, moody and unpredictable. What money he sent home arrived in fits and starts, and the lack of regular income worried my mother. It was at these times that my Uncle Bobby, my father's brother, would unexpectedly arrive in his van, talk to my mother for a few minutes and be gone. After this, my mother was always happier. I was for years to remain puzzled by Uncle Bobby's sudden visits and the relief they brought in their wake, not just to my mother but to the whole house. I did not realize that what uncle Bobby was bringing was money.

One day, when I was ten or eleven and on my way to the Ardoyne to play football, my mother came and told me to come with her. She said we were going to visit my father. I had known he was in Belfast and asked where he was. She said, 'He's in the Crum.' She took me by the hand. I had my football boots with me, and we went off. To a child, Crumlin Road Prison was forbidding, and I was upset at the clash of the steel doors, the bars and the long corridors with gates at each end, and at the sight of prison officers in their black uniforms. Most of all, I was upset at seeing my father in such a place. Many years later, I was to worry when my young daughter came to visit me in prison, wondering what impact it would have on her, thinking back to that dreadful day I saw my own father in jail.

It turned out that my father and another fellow had been convicted of drunk driving. By this time, my father was a heavy drinker and had been treated a number of times in different clinics for his alcoholism. He and the other man had been stopped in a car in Portsmouth after running a woman down. They put my father first in Wormwood Scrubs and later transferred him to Belfast. On his release he did not return to sea. He lay around the house and drank. Then he left.

Chapter Three

PHOTOGRAPHS IN MY HEAD

When I was five or six years old, we moved out of the Docks and went to live in Greenisland, a district on the road from Belfast to Carrickfergus where new housing estates were then being built. In the late 1950s and early 1960s, people from all over Belfast were being taken from their overcrowded little homes and moved to places like Greenisland. The old houses were bad, and some people were so desperate to be rehoused that they deliberately made themselves homeless. The families living in the squalid prefabs along the Shore Road used to set them on fire after hauling out their bits of furniture. You used to pass by on buses and see the people standing by their few belongings, children perched on dressers and wardrobes, watching as the flames ate up the homes they hated.

On the new estates the houses were more modern and had inside toilets, but, like us, people arrived knowing no one. I think it is because the sense of community is so strong in me that I have almost no recollection of living in Greenisland. My memories of my childhood and youth are bound up with *where* I was, the place I belonged to and the people in it, so much so that my remembrances do not again become vivid until I went to live in my grandparents' house in Cairns Street, in the Lower Falls, and once again became part of a community. This period of my life – when I lived in Cairns Street – was to be the happiest: I can almost see photographs in my head of the streets I lived and played in.

We did not stay in Greenisland long. My mother managed to get a house in Turf Lodge, another new estate, practically on the edge of the countryside. The estates that subsequently sprang up around Turf Lodge – New Barnsley and Dermott Hill – had not been built when we arrived there. However, it felt less remote than Greenisland. It was near the top of the Falls Road, and reasonably close to my grandparents and the district my mother grew up in. Now it is one of West Belfast's most deprived areas: the houses are decayed, and black fungus spreads over the walls inside and out; three out of every five men have no job. But when we went to live in Turf Lodge it was considered a big step up in the world.

Such a step required some manipulation of the bureaucracy. My mum made the necessary alterations to the application form, but the Corporation found her out. The Corporation, whose control over housing was removed in 1971 after complaints that throughout its history it had discriminated against Catholics, evicted us. By then, my father had deserted us, and the authorities wanted to put the children (me, my sisters Liz and Marion, and my brother Patrick) into care. My granddad told them that they would break up the family over his dead body. So, the five of us went to live with the Cushnahans in Cairns Street where we stayed for about seven years. My mother then got another house in Turf Lodge, and we went to live there once more. However, soon afterwards I returned to Cairns Street, where I continued to live, apart from visits to England to fin'. work, until 1974, and I was always to think of Cairns Street as home.

The tight-knit, boisterous community of the Falls was just like that of the Docks. The Falls is a long road that runs more or less west from Castle Street in the city centre past Divis Street, Beechmount, Broadway, St James, Whiterock and up to Milltown Cemetery, where it forks into the Glen Road to the right (off which lies Turf Lodge) and the Andersonstown

Road to the left. But the real Falls, the 'Lower Wack', the area in which I lived, is the stretch from Divis Street to the junction with the Grosvenor and Springfield Roads.

In the early 1960s, the Falls was a bustling, exciting place. The road was served by old and very slow Corporation trolley buses that lumbered, to the sound of electrical crackle, to the terminus at Milltown Cemetery. The trolley buses were forever breaking down. It was common to see the driver and conductor beside their inert vehicle trying to manipulate with long poles the rods that ran to the overhead cables and the uncertain sources of the bus's meagre power. On the right-hand side as you went up the Falls from the city centre, there was mill after mill – Ross's Mill, Andrew's Mill, Conway Mill, Greeves's Mill – and every morning on the way to school I would pass hundreds of men, women and girls going to work. Many of the men walked with a 'Belfast dander', fists pushed deep into jacket pockets, feet pointing slightly out, shoulders swinging cockily.

The girls who worked in the flax mills were called a variety of names after the jobs they did – spinners, doffers, scutchers, rovers and so on. Some of them wore big rubber aprons from which hung the long needles they used to pick the flax with. Some went barefoot because they had to work all day standing in tepid water; the mill owners did not provide rubber boots. My mother, before she was married, had worked as a spinner in one of these mills. The scene seems out of another, long-past age; the photograph in my head is sepia-tinted and curled at the edges. But the memory is not just visual. There are other things demanding to get at other senses: the clatter of the girls' shouting and laughing; and the singing, for they used to sing going to and from the mills. And there were smells: rich, dark smells that were the grain mills' own special atmosphere.

Opposite the mills were long streets of terrace houses, and in the mornings on my way to school I would pass the women on their knees in the hall of the little houses busily scrubbing the crescent outside the door. As in the Docks, the doors were open day and night, a light left on in the hallway after dark. There was constant coming and going, with neighbours in and out of each other's houses, perhaps to borrow something, or just to enjoy the 'crack', the name given by Belfast people

18

to lively and witty conversation. The crack had to do with the district and the characters in it, for in general people, the older ones at least, did not like to go out of the neighbourhood, and they knew little of what went on outside it. A trip to the city centre, only a mile or two away, was an excursion, and there were people who died never having seen the sea beyond Belfast Lough.

The Cushnahan house in Cairns Street had a living room and scullery, two bedrooms upstairs and an outside toilet. When we went to live there, after our eviction from Turf Lodge, there was already a family of five in Cairns Street: my grandparents, my uncle Charlie, and two aunts, Theresa and Anne. Our arrival brought the numbers up to ten; when cousins came to stay we slept five to a bed. The rooms were small, and the overcrowding caused some strain, particularly to my granny.

Nevertheless, it was, by the standards of the time, one of the better-off houses in the district. There were four wages coming in: Theresa and Anne worked in Inglis Bakery in Eliza Street, and my granddad and uncle worked on the Docks. They were able to give my mother help to bring up the family. It is a measure of our affluence that at secondary school I had a uniform; most of my classmates did not. We could also afford holidays, something almost unheard of in the district. We used to go down to a cottage in Waterfoot to stay with relatives of my granddad whose family originally came from there. Waterfoot is only thirty-odd miles up the Antrim coast, but to me then it seemed to be at the ends of the earth. It seemed strange that a town like Belfast could exist in the same world as Waterfoot and the beautiful Antrim Glens.

In spite of the overcrowding, I loved living in the Cushnahan house. My granddad, who was long and thin with quick, nervous movements, was a warm man. As a young seaman, he had earned several fortunes on the well-paid, deep-sea tanker runs. These he squandered without a thought, for he was a man who loved a good time, a song and a dance, the crack and a drink with his friends. He was the kind of man who took pleasure in spending what he earned. But, like many Belfast men, he thought his wife demanded too much for the running of the house. On pay days I remember

19

my granny following him round the house, even into the toilet, to get him to give her what she needed.

My granny, who was ten years older than my granddad, came from a well-to-do family on the Falls Road, and older people used to tell me that as a little girl they saw her wearing velvet and lace. It was said that her marriage to my father, when she was thirty, was a comedown in the world for her. But the marriage was a happy one and after she died, in 1976, my granddad missed her badly. She was a very lady-like woman, and more serious than my granddad. She never went to take a drink in a bar and had great pride in her home. She bore seven children (one of whom died of meningitis at eighteen months), and although she did everything she could for her husband and her family, there was a part of her that wondered at woman's lot in communities like the one she lived in. Her advice to her daughters was always to stand up for themselves and not to have so many children that their lives would end in exhaustion and disappointment.

My uncle Charlie, who was quiet and gentle, spoke Gaelic fluently and had a gold fáinne, the small badge in the shape of a ring worn by Irish speakers in the lapel of their jackets to let other speakers know that they preferred to converse in Irish. Every year he used to go to the Donegal Gaeltacht, a native-speaking area in the Republic. Other Gaelic speakers would often drop in to talk to Charlie.

Charlie was fascinated by chess and would sit for hours over a board, spellbound by the pieces and their subtle patterns. He used to take part in competitions in bars, and in the Botanical Gardens where the participants sat at tables set out among the Gardens' glasshouses and exotic flowers. The house boasted several trophies commemorating his victories. Charlie tried to teach me chess and failed; then draughts and failed in that, too, for I had neither the patience nor the aptitude to learn.

The women of the house spoilt me. When I was small they bought me sweets, chocolates and toys. Theresa and Anne would take me to the zoo at Bellevue, and down town to the Co-op to see Father Christmas. But although I used to look forward to getting toys at Christmas – Lego, a cowboy rifle with silver bullets, a toy policeman on a motorbike – I remember no magic about Christmas itself. Perhaps it was because a Belfast upbringing was tougher, more realistic, and left little room for the comforting fantasy of reindeers and sledges. Or, perhaps, it was because there were other, more highly charged seasons. For me, Easter always had more meaning and held greater excitement. It was at Easter that Republicans used to hold parades up the Falls Road to Milltown Cemetery to commemorate the Rising of 1916. In 1966, on the fiftieth anniversary of the Rising, when I was eleven years old, the parade was particularly big and colourful, and almost everyone wore pinned to their lapels an Easter Lily (the flame-like flower in the Republican colours of green, white and orange that symbolized the sacrifice of the Rising). I have heard a Protestant playwright from the Ardoyne saying that for her 12 July was more important than Christmas. The communal and political loyalties of Belfast, I suppose, made a greater impression on us both than did the Christmas story.

Theresa and Anne, who were only nine or ten years older than me and more like big sisters, used to listen to Radio Luxembourg, and I used to stay up late in the living room listening to the music with them. We also watched late-night television, films in the *Tales of Mystery and Imagination* series. It was in this series that I saw my first X-rated horror film, an important event, almost one of the modern rites of passage.

To see more appropriate films – like *Mary Poppins*, which I remember being very popular with all the kids of the district – I used to go with my granny to the Clonard at the top of Leeson Street, to the Arcadia in Albert Street and to the Diamond at the bottom of Cooper Street. We would go sometimes two or three times a week. These were pretty rough cinemas, but they were always packed. Every Saturday there were matinees for the kids, usually John Wayne films, which inspired us to run through the streets shooting at our pals through pointed fingers, our thumbs the frantically working hammers of imaginary six-shooters.

One night, coming back from the pictures where I had been with my granny, I was confronted by my grandad. Some lads had thrown bangers into the hall of a neighbour's house, and the neighbour had gone to my granddad and told him that I was one of them. I swore to him that I wasn't, that I had been with my granny at the pictures. I had run on ahead so she was not there to bear me out. My granddad did not believe me, and as there was nothing I could say to convince him I got a hiding. It is the only time, though I am sure there must have been others, that I remember being disbelieved as a child, and I was to think of this incident on many subsequent occasions – when I was first questioned by the police about Guildford and Woolwich, during my cross-examination in both the Belfast and Old Bailey trials, and periodically during my imprisonment – so powerful were the feelings of anger, frustration and impotence caused by my granddad's refusal to believe me.

In the picture house my granny and I had been that evening I had seen a man called Tommy Simpson. Tommy was often found in the pictures. He was a kind of village idiot, well known in the district. His only two activities were watching films and prowling the dumps and digging holes in them. We used to bring potatoes with us to the pictures and when the lights dimmed we bombarded Tommy who would go berserk and scream at us.

The Falls was full of characters like Tommy, mild nuisances who were tolerated, more or less good-humouredly by the local people, if not by the kids. Joe Walsh was another one. Then, he was in his fifties and had long, dirty buck teeth. He wore a permanent idiot grin and dribbled out of the side of his mouth. He was known for turning up at funerals and wakes. Anyone that was buried, Joe, whether he knew them or not, would go to the funeral and the wake. Joe would wail and cry and bite his hands as if he was the dead person's best-loved brother. Everyone in the district knew Joe, and no one paid him any mind. After the funeral, they brought him to the bar, put him down on a seat, bought him a drink, and he used to sit there in the corner crying his eyes out. But people were always kind to him, in the rough way of the people there, and tolerated him because he was a simpleton. I often used to hear people, referring to Joe or others like him, say in sympathetic voices, 'Ach, look at that poor aul' eegit, God help him.'

Bunny Rice was another oddball. It was hard to tell if he was drunk all the time or just mad, or a combination of both. He used to stagger around the streets throwing punches and would hit anyone who came within striking distance. People, naturally enough, tried to avoid him. Some kids would bait him though, as matadors would a bull, and it was funny to watch Bunny trying to get hold of them. Mad Vinty, Vinty Loughran, was a well-known sight in the district. He used to push a handcart all day long. He was a collector; his passion was for cardboard. He lived alone in a house only four doors from where I lived in Cairns Street, and all he had in his house was cardboard. Apart from the time, that is, when his mother died. Vinty neglected to tell anyone, and the body was in among the cardboard for a week.

Then there were characters known only by their nicknames: like Forty Coats. He used to wear, if not forty, at least ten coats, old ragged coats, at the same time, coat after coat after coat. Or the Whistler, who just went about all day whistling, a long shabby overcoat tied with string about his middle.

I had many friends at school and in the district – John Donaghey, Joe McKinney, Danny McAreavey, Martin Skillen, and the Quigley brothers. One of our favourite activities used to be going to the houses of people who had recently died. In those days the open coffin was kept in the parlour. A black wreath or tie used to be hung on the door so word spread fast about where a body could be seen. We would go to the house and into the parlour where the family would be praying along with neighbours who had come in to pay their respects and join in the rosary. We would go in and say the prayers, but we were really there to get a glimpse of what a dead person looked like. Outside, we would excitedly discuss what had impressed or frightened us most.

Death was not covered up the way it tends to be in England, where people seem hardly able to bring themselves to say 'die' or 'death'. In Belfast, people were more realistic and discussed it naturally. It was also the subject of much superstition. There was a widely held belief that one death in the street presaged two more in quick succession, and there was always lively speculation about the likely candidates. But, superstition aside, death provided people, particularly the older ones, with much to talk about. When the daily paper, almost always the *Irish News*, came into the house, my granny turned straight to the death notices. In their own way the notices served as a kind of 'court circular' for the people of the district. Each death announced two very important social events: the funeral and the wake which everyone would attend and would talk about for some time.

The death notices were a reminder of how close-knit the community was. There were few mornings that my granny did not know someone whose name appeared. She would say, 'Mrs McCann's died and her only seventy-one. You know the McCanns that went to live up in St James? Bridie was her name. She married the one that does the acting whose cousin had the twins and one of them not half wise enough. McMillan her maiden was, a lovely girl. Her grandmother was one of the McDonalds came originally from Monaghan.' I heard variations of this a thousand times in the scullery as I prepared to leave for school in the mornings. It is one of the surest signs of growing older that you find yourself turning with relish to the death notices, as I did during the latter years of my imprisonment when Belfast papers were sent to me.

But as a child, play was not entirely made up of visits to the houses of the dead. Wherever a bit of shelter could be found, the younger boys would play 'marlies'. And in the streets, where the girls sang to their skipping games or made swings of ropes hooked around the tops of lampposts, we would play rally-O and tag. We also used to play at the back of the Royal Victoria Hospital at the corner of Grosvenor Road and the Falls. They used to store thousands of empty lemonade bottles there and we made off with as many as we could to collect the refunds, threepence a time. When small, when to buy bags of sweets at will was the height of your dreams, the lemonade bottles at the Royal was like having access to a Swiss bank account.

We played a lot of football. John, Danny, me and the others used to play in North Howard Street, a sort of industrial estate, on Sundays when it was quiet. By my early teens, I was going over to see Glasgow Celtic regularly. For youngsters under sixteen, a return ticket to Stranraer cost 12/6d. To get the money to pay for my fare, I used to go down to the Docks and buy under-age tickets for grown-ups, for which the men gave me a shilling or so. When we boarded the boat we put one adult ticket at the top of the block of tickets and had the whole lot punched.

To me, to watch Celtic was a dream come true, and the magic of it never really wore off. One time, however, we ran into some trouble. At Stranraer, as we were about to board the ferry home, a crowd of Rangers supporters came along, and for safety all the Celtic supporters bunched together. Among our crowd were a number of men from the New Lodge area who proceeded to break open some mailbags lying nearby. The police were called and on arrival arrested about forty people, me and John among them. I was one of several children arrested. We were put into a remand centre to wait until our parents came from Belfast to claim us. Not all the parents could afford to come so they chipped in and sent over Mr Donaghey, John's father. We returned home chastened, but also quite proud of ourselves for having at such a young age 'been inside'.

Quieter times were to be had up near Colin Glen where, when I was a bit older, I used to go camping with John and the rest. Colin Glen was a spot popular with people in the district, and only a little beyond the housing estates off the Glen Road. At weekends, with our big tent, tins of beans and other food, we walked the few miles to the Glen and found ourselves in the heart of the countryside. Occasionally, we went further afield; once on a camping holiday to Bray near Dublin. It was on this trip, when I was about fourteen years old, that I first heard the expression 'the Black North'. The van in which we were travelling broke down in a little village between Dundalk and Bray and we started to hitch a lift. The Garda, when they realized we were from the North, became suspicious and took us to the station where they searched our gear. A sergeant leaned over me and said, 'So you're from the Black North,' making it clear that he regarded all the inhabitants of Northern Ireland, regardless of religion, as dangerous undesirables.

Meanwhile, my career at school was proceeding along its pre-ordained lines. My teachers never expected me, or any of my classmates, to pass an exam, and never put us to the trouble of sitting one. After leaving Greenisland, I went to St Paul's Infants and then St Peter's primary school in Raglan Street. I went to secondary school (I did not take the Eleven Plus) at St Peter's, Whiterock. As in the other schools I had been to when living in the Docks and Greenisland, I was happy enough and continued to attend regularly. The teachers expected very little of us and this suited me. We were in school only because we had to be, and the teachers knew that as soon as we reached the age to leave, leave we would. No one ever asked, 'What do you want to be when you leave school?' Such a question would have been staggeringly unrealistic. It implied a choice we did not, and never would, have. Everyone knew exactly what they were going to do when they left school: they would look for work, manual or casual work, in one of the few firms in the district that had vacancies and hired Catholics.

At school, I liked the sports and still enjoyed history, which was taught in a way I cannot say was sympathetic to Republicanism, as is so often said about the teaching of history in Irish schools. The most that could be said was that it exhibited a faint sympathy towards constitutional nationalism, but it was not in the least radical. It awakened no interest in Republicanism in me, and for most of the time I was at school, Republicanism was considered a dormant or even, many believed, a spent force in Irish politics.

In my last year at St Peter's, I developed a strong interest in girls. My first serious girlfriend was Cathleen Keenan who used to work in one of the mills. She had long, blonde hair and was a couple of years older than me. I first got to know her while she was still at school, at St Louisa's. John Donaghey and I used to annoy the girls by snatching the berets off their heads. They were taught by nuns of the Sisters of Charity, who were known to be strict. The girls had to wear brown uniforms and were known locally as 'brown bombers', and they were scolded if they turned up at school without their berets. John had a satchel full of these, and so did I – one of them belonging to Cathleen. Cathleen's mother found out who had taken her daughter's cap and informed our headmaster, who we used to call Choppers. He chased me and John through the school and into a hospital but failed to catch us. Unfortunately, I had had to abandon my satchel to make my escape, and the next day Choppers called John and me into his office and ordered us to go to St Louisa's to take back the berets, inside which were labels with the girls' names and addresses. John and I had to go to Assembly while the girls were called up to have their berets returned. We had to apologize to each girl; very embarrassing.

That was how I came to be on speaking terms with Cathleen. After she left school and started work in the mill, we began to go out together. She was from around the district, and I knew her brother who was a boardmarker in a nearby bookie's. We used to go to youth clubs, run by the Church, to dance and to listen to local bands like Bus Stop which did their own versions of the hits of the time – the Beatles, Gerry and the Pacemakers and so on. The music was dreadful, but at the time, knowing nothing else, we thought it was fantastic. We would also look around for places where we could be more adult (the Church-run clubs were strictly supervised). There was one bar known for letting underage people buy drink. Or we would buy scrumpy, which was very cheap, and go to Riddle's Field near the hospital to drink it. Entries were popular, too; couples disappeared up them for a 'lumber' (kissing and cuddling). Baby-sitting, for which there was a huge demand because of the large families, provided other, pleasanter and more interesting opportunities to be together.

It was not easy taking a girl out at that age. The trouble was I never had much money. The expectations of easy riches raised by the commerce in the American Bar had proved over-optimistic; the lemonade bottles from the Royal belonged to a distant and more childish past. I and my friends, experiencing these strange new financial pressures, began to look around for a way to make a little money. We found it in the Pound Loney. At that time the Pound Loney, or Loney O, the area at the bottom of the Falls which was being knocked down for redevelopment (part of which was the Divis Flats complex – quickly to become a housing nightmare and now itself largely cleared away). The houses around English Street, Bow Street and Irwin Street were being demolished, and we discovered that the slates from the roofs – the best were called Bangor Blues – were a marketable commodity. We hired a handcart for five shillings a day, got a ladder and went up on the roofs to take our pick from the slates. These we sold to the Housing Executive for a shilling each.

The money from the Bangor Blues helped pay for my romance with Cathleen with whom I had started going out when I was about fourteen. By that time, my mother, Liz, Marion and two brothers (a baby, Martin, had been born after my father put in a brief appearance home) had left Cairns Street and moved to a maisonette in Turf Lodge, easing the pressure in my grandparents' house. I went out with Cathleen for a year or so and then we parted. I went out with some other girls every now and then, but did not have another serious girlfriend until Gina.

Gina Clarke lived with her father, whom she looked after, in Spinner Street, just around the corner from my grandparents' house, and she used to hang around with a gang of girls who were the sisters of my pals. I had known of her since she was twelve years old, but did not notice her until she was fourteen. One night, I was among a group of kids standing around a fire in the street. I found myself next to Gina. She was very pretty, and I started to talk to her. Her confidence, which I suppose must have come from running her father's house, made her seem older than she was. She went the same way home as me and we walked together. From then on, we saw each other regularly, and often walked home together. But we did not start going out with each other for a couple of years, not before I had left school and been away to England to find work.

Chapter Four

A MEMORY OF REPRESSION

My schooling came to its untroublesome end in the summer of 1969. At fourteen, I left St Peter's without a single qualification. This was nothing out of the ordinary. I knew of no one among my classmates who was staying on to take examinations. The thought of any form of higher education – college, polytechnic or university – was beyond my powers of comprehension. I was glad to be out of school, the classroom and playground, and to be entering the world of men and work. I was doing what everyone else in the district had always done and, as far as I could possibly imagine, would continue forever to do. I was going to look for work, in Belfast or perhaps in England. After a few years I would certainly marry, find a house, possibly on one of the new estates, where my family would be raised. And I would continue working long after my sons and daughters had grown up and started to work themselves. I would watch my children leave home and wait for my grandchildren to be presented to me. And I would continue working until physically incapable, hoping, by then, that my children would be earning enough to support their parents. That was what life was; the thought of anything different, of a life lived in any other way, was inconceivable. On the day I left school there seemed no reason my life should not shadow that of my granddad or any of the other men I knew on the Falls.

Work, of course, was the priority. In such a disadvantaged district, the search for work was compulsive. Jobs, where they could be found, how much they paid, were endlessly discussed. Families were large, so many mouths had to be fed, so much depended on bringing in a wage. For the younger ones, the pressure was less urgent but could still be felt. At first, I had hoped to go to the sea school at Gravesend in Kent. In those days, it was possible for a seaman to hand down his book to his son and I wanted my father to do this for me. However, he refused and so, disappointed and angry, I started to look for work around the Falls.

The opportunities were few. Unemployment in West Belfast was always high, even in relatively good times, and jobs for Catholics were hard to find. What work was available was as unskilled hands in the mills, as porters in the Royal, as casual labourers on the docks; a handful found employment in James Mackie's engineering works. I heard there was work at the Ulster Linen Company at the top of Roden Street off the Donegal Road, but one glance at the building told me that it would be impossible to work there. Union Jacks fluttered threateningly from the windows, and the walls were daubed with anti-Catholic obscenities. After a few days, I found a job with a birdseed manufacturer at the top of North Howard Street. My pay was 19/6d a week.

Although my thoughts during this period were largely concerned with everyday things – earning money, going out with girls, enjoying the crack – I was becoming aware that something important was taking place not just on the Falls and in Belfast, but all over Northern Ireland. During my last year or so at school, Catholics and progressive Protestants had organized the Northern Ireland Civil Rights Association, Peoples Democracy and other bodies to press for an end to discrimination against Catholics in housing and jobs, for an end to Gerrymandering, for the dismantling of the Special Powers Act, the disbanding of the B-Specials (the highly sectarian auxiliary police force), and for other reforms. The Unionist Government at Stormont, made up exclusively of Protestants, resisted the pressure for change and forced out the Prime Minister, Terence O'Neill, whom they considered too liberal. It is an indication of the bigotry among the Unionists that 'liberal' O'Neill was to say after his resignation:

> It is frightfully hard to explain to Protestants that if you give Roman Catholics a good job and a good house they will live like Protestants, because they will see neighbours with cars and television sets.
> They will refuse to have eighteen children, but if a Roman Catholic is jobless and lives in the most ghastly hovel, he will rear eighteen children on National Assistance. . .
> If you treat Roman Catholics with due consideration and kindness, they will live like Protestants.

The hardliners within the Government, having unburdened themselves of O'Neill, set their face against reform and used the Royal Ulster Constabulary (RUC) and B-Specials to break up meetings and demonstrations. But the demonstrations continued. As the civil rights movement gathered strength, political and sectarian tension increased. In Derry on 5 October 1968, RUC men wielding truncheons attacked a peaceful civil rights march, and drenched the marchers with water-cannons. The world's television and press witnessed the whole thing, and the pictures of RUC men battering helpless marchers had a powerful impact on those outside Northern Ireland who had previously had no idea of the nature of the state.

To Catholics on the Falls, however, it was nothing new. The RUC had always been seen by the people as a hostile force. It was predominantly, but not exclusively, Protestant; its Catholic members, if anything, were seen as even more vicious, like the blacks who serve in South Africa's racist police force. Our lives were littered with confrontations with RUC men, ranging from irritating forms of minor harassment to serious acts of violence. There was, for example, the famous Drango Kid, the motorcycle cop who would swoop into North Howard Street where we played football

31

on Sundays and steal our ball. A more serious incident, I recall, occurred one Saturday night when I was small. After a football match, the supporters of Linfield, the leading Protestant team, came through McDonnell Street and made their way towards Albert Street to catch the buses that would take them back to the Shankill (the Protestant equivalent of the Falls). Suddenly, the supporters burst into a charge and tore through McDonnell Street, smashing the windows of the houses as they went by, whooping and cheering like madmen. Local people gathered, and fighting broke out with the fans. When the police arrived, they rescued the Protestants and shepherded them towards their buses. They made no arrests. It was the first time I had seen the police act like this and I was unable to understand why they had not taken away the men who had caused the trouble.

Such was the antagonism felt towards the police that arguments in the street between neighbours, especially after the pubs closed on Friday and Saturday nights, turned into small-scale anti-police riots. These rows were between people who had worked hard all week and were letting off steam. The men struck aggressive postures and pushed and shoved; the women came out and screamed their dreadful curses. But such incidents rarely resulted in serious harm, and were quickly made up, quicker still if the police arrived. This would be the signal for the protagonists to join together and attack the RUC men.

Hostility to the RUC was fed not just by daily encounters of this sort but by a collective memory of past brutality, violence and repression. The RUC was just one of several forces used by governments past and present against the Nationalist community. The Black and Tans – the undisciplined and murderous force recruited to fight the IRA in the Civil War (1919–21) – the Auxiliaries, the B-Specials – all inspired fear and loathing among Catholics and, in communities as close as that of the Falls, contributed to the reputation of the police as little better than sectarian assassins.

As a child, I remember hearing grown-ups talking about crimes committed by the RUC, the Tans and the Specials from years before. They spoke of the murder squads that kidnapped and assassinated Republicans in the district during the 1920s; of confrontations during the 1930s when, on

32

one occasion, the police shot demonstrators in Cairns Street (where my grandparents lived). In Totten's barber's, where I used to get my hair cut, I used to see a pathetic soul slumped in a wheelchair, his big face blank, dribbling at the mouth, as permanent a fixture as the shop's mirrors. To a child, he was a frightening sight, and one day I asked my granddad and granny why he was like that. They explained that he was a relation of the barber's, and that years before, when just a baby, the B-Specials raided the house. After they had sledge-hammered the door in, the Specials pulled out the father and the sons and shot them dead. The baby they picked up out of the cot and smashed it against the wall, wrecking its brains. When I was in prison in England, I read an account of this incident in the 'It Happened This Week' column in the *Irish News*. But it was, as I was growing up, simply one of many such stories, told by the grown-ups with a mixture of resignation and bewilderment. Their effect was to create in me, subconsciously, a deep loathing and fear of the RUC who, in my mind, were not policemen but gun-toting bigots.

When I was ten years old, I saw for myself in the most dramatic way how the RUC treated the community. It was 1964, the year of a general election. Liam McMillan, a Sinn Féin candidate, was standing in West Belfast. The Republicans set up their election headquarters in a disused shop in Divis Street, and placed a Republican Tricolour in the window. Under the Flags and Emblems Act the Tricolour was illegal – as was the singing of Republican songs – and Ian Paisley, then a relatively unknown Loyalist agitator who was making his name attacking the policies of the 'liberal' Terence O'Neill, taunted the Government and the RUC for having gone soft on the 'Papishes'. If the police did not remove the Tricolour, Paisley announced, he would lead a march up to Divis and take the flag himself. The people of the district rallied and prepared to resist Paisley.

The Government, goaded by Paisley, ordered the RUC to take the flag, while Paisley held a rally in the city centre. Tension was running very high as the police approached Divis Street. After some tussles with members of the crowd, several RUC men smashed in the shop window with pickaxes and grabbed the flag. As they did so, all bedlam broke loose. The hundreds of people who had gathered in the streets around Divis started fighting with the RUC. Together with my pals, I climbed to the top of the Falls Library to get a grandstand view of the riot as it developed. The RUC, supported by armoured cars, baton-charged the people and turned the water-cannon on them. The people armed themselves with sticks and petrol bombs with which they set about the police vans. We watched, fascinated and excited, as the bottles, flaming rags stuffed into the necks, flew in high arcs over the police lines and crashed onto the armoured cars, one of which was destroyed. As the fighting continued, several trolley buses were attacked and burned. Meanwhile, the wounded were led up the Falls to the Royal to receive treatment. From the roof, I looked down into the road and saw a man named Dolan from our street being helped along: groggy and blood-soaked, he was in a dreadful state.

They say the Divis riots stimulated interest in Republicanism; but if it did, it was not to any significant degree. Before 1969 little was heard of Sinn Féin or the Irish Republican Army (IRA). If people in the district were sympathetic towards the cause of a united Ireland, it was in a way that was vague and almost nostalgic; concrete expressions of support were few. In spite of the riots, the Sinn Féin candidate in the 1964 election lost his deposit. On the other hand, most families had someone who had been at one time or another imprisoned, interned, shot or beaten. There was little enough Republicanism in my own family, but even we had my granny's brother, Geordie Hamill. In the 1920s, he was interned without trial with other Republicans on the *Argenta*, a prison ship moored off Carrickfergus.

The first time I really became aware of the history of the IRA was in 1966, when I went with my Aunt Anne and her boyfriend to Dublin for a few days. We visited Kilmainham Jail, where the British used to imprison Home Rulers, Nationalists and Republicans. But the notorious place it occupies in Irish history comes from the fact that it was in Kilmainham, in the Stonebreakers' Yard, that the British Army executed the leaders of the 1916 Easter Rising. The death of James Connolly, who for the last six years of his life had lived on the Falls Road organizing workers into trade unions before going to Dublin to take part in the Rising, stuck in my mind

34

as particularly cruel. Connolly had been so badly wounded during the fighting, and in such pain, that they had to strap him into a chair for the firing squad.

Shortly before we arrived in Dublin, the IRA had blown up Nelson's Pillar in Dublin's centre, and this event made a great impression on me. It came as part of the minor upsurge in Republican activity that followed the fiftieth anniversary of the Rising in 1966. I remember seeing the stump and being very excited; for a time it was the talk of Ireland. Nelson, perched on his high pillar, had loftily overlooked the General Post Office, the headquarters of the rebels in 1916, and many, including even the most moderate Nationalists, considered it an affront to the memory of the men and women who died during the Rising. A bomb removed Nelson from his commanding height and cut the pillar to a stump. Songs and ditties were made up almost straight away; I remember one that ended: 'Up went Nelson and his pillar too.'

But, in the years following the attack on Nelson's Pillar, there was little enough heard of the IRA. The people of the district were more interested in work, more concerned about unemployment and low wages than about Republicanism. My own working life was far from satisfactory. The attraction of working with birdseed for 19/6d a week started to wane, and, like millions of Irish men and women before me, I decided to go to England to look for better work.

I had first visited London in 1968 to see the League Cup Final, and I stayed for a couple of months. I lived with my Aunt Anne, who had by then married Frank Keenan, a Protestant from Belfast, and was bringing up her young family in North London. My second visit began early in July 1969, when I caught the boat to Liverpool and made my way to London where once again I stayed with Anne and Frank. I quickly found work with Essex Flour and Grain, whose warehouse was in Liverpool Road. At first, I was not aware of missing home too badly. London was a place of adventure and, besides, the wages were a big improvement. I got to know the city well during that time, so well that on my release from prison after fifteen years I was able to direct the car taking me to my aunt and uncle's house in North London. But being in London, being among people who looked on me as an outsider, did open my eyes to the extent of anti-Irish feeling that exists in England.

The island of Ireland today has a population of about five million. A century and a half ago, the population stood at over eight million. Then came the Great Famine. The potato crop, on which the Catholic peasantry depended, failed, and a million people starved to death or died on the 'coffin ships' on the way to America. From that day to this, Irish people in their millions have left their homes to seek work abroad. They started coming to England in large numbers during the famine years of the 1840s, refugees from a devastated land. They were Britain's first mass immigrants, and they crowded the poorer parts of London, Liverpool, Manchester, Birmingham and the other great industrial cities. In the same way as many black communities in Britain today, they were heavily policed. The more policemen there were in Irish areas, the more arrests were made. Irish people appeared before the courts out of all proportion to their numbers in society, giving them a reputation for violence and disorderliness. Already marked out as different by their poverty, religion (Catholic) and language (many did not speak English), they were resented by the native population; the more so because, unorganized, desperate for work, they undercut the unionized labour force and scabbed during strikes. The mass migration beginning in the 1840s reinforced an anti-Irish sentiment that has persisted to this day, and to which I was to fall victim.

It was while I was in London that the Falls was attacked and looted by Loyalist mobs and armed B-Specials. As the civil rights agitation had gathered momentum in the summer of 1969, the Stormont Government and the RUC encountered more and more difficulty in keeping the situation under control. In Derry, the people were in open revolt, and the Bogside was under virtual siege by the RUC. In Belfast, sectarian tension was rising. On 14 August, Loyalist crowds gathered on the Shankill Road; among them were B-Specials armed with rifles and sub-machine guns. That evening, they surged down the streets that connected the Shankill with the Falls, burning out Catholic houses in Norfolk Street, Dover Street and Percy Street. Later that night, the RUC brought in Shorland armoured cars fitted with heavy machine guns which they fired indiscriminately into the houses and flats around Divis. Two people were killed, including a nine-year-old boy. Hundreds of families, almost all of them Catholic, were burnt out or intimidated out of their homes. I read about the attack on the Falls in the newspapers and saw pictures of the devastation on the television, which I watched hardly able to believe that they were of the area I grew up in. They seemed to belong to a country at war.

Early in 1970, I returned to Belfast. I had been away seven months, and was homesick. I was also worried about my family and wanted to see for myself what had happened in the district. When I got back, I found the Falls changed out of all recognition. Down by Albert Street, Durham Street and Conway Street, almost all the mills stood charred and gutted; the houses that ran off the Falls towards the Shankill were empty, soot-stained and windowless; the walls around the windows and doors scorched by firebombs. The streets that ran off the Falls were barricaded and fortified, and vigilantes controlled access to them. Some of the barricades were ramshackle affairs; old bits of furniture and burnt-out cars and vans piled up precariously. Others were more solid. The barricade at the top of Leeson Street was a carefully constructed reinforced steel wall, held in place by scaffolding, in which there was a side door guarded by the vigilantes.

The attack on the Falls stimulated the growth of the IRA in a way that nothing had done for many years. The Falls in 1969 and 1970 was alive with rumours about the IRA. People were rushing to get involved. There were Republican newssheets and leaflets everywhere; there was a pirate radio station, Radio Free Belfast, operating from Cyprus Street; arms were being smuggled into the district. It was a war zone, and to me fascinating, exciting and terrible. I had a sense of being a witness to – or perhaps more, being at the centre of – something so important and dramatic that it would be remembered for ever.

But, as in all wars, ordinary things somehow edged into the dramatic to let daily life of a kind continue. Soon, it became hard to imagine that the streets had ever been without their protective barricades. My mother, by now, had moved with Liz, Marion, Patrick and Martin to the maisonette in Turf Lodge. I continued to live at the Cushnahan house in Cairns

Street, where I fell in again with John Donaghey and my other old friends. I was also becoming friendlier with Gina, and saw more of her. I started a job at one of the few mills that had not been destroyed, a flour mill at the back of Hamill Street in College Square, where I worked with a deaf and dumb lad. Together we had responsibility for keeping the 'coppers' filled. The coppers were the huge baths that held the flour and fed the shutes from which the women filled the bags. For this, I was paid £9 a week, a very good wage. One day, there was rioting on the Falls which I stopped to watch instead of going to work. When I showed up the next day they told me I was sacked.

I stayed in Belfast throughout the rest of 1970 and most of 1971. For much of this time, I was unable to find a job, but was able to make a little by going back to loot Bangor Blues from the Loney. One day, while we were busy stripping the roofs, an armoured car arrived. The police got out and told us to get down. We refused, a little fearful of what they might do to us. Reinforcements arrived and by then it was too late for us to do anything but wait until they came up to get us. Eventually, several policemen clambered up onto the roof and took us to the barracks where they lined us up against the wall and began to search us. I was wearing a blue bomber jacket with a pocket in the arm where my granny had put a little bottle of Holy Water. The police thought this was very funny and mocked me for it. Joe McKinney, who was with us, had a yoyo in his pocket and they made Joe play the yoyo, making fun of him all the time. Fortunately, their attention was distracted from us when another armoured car pulled up and a man, who it turned out had just been arrested with a rifle, was pulled out. The police instantly forgot about us and started in on their new prisoner, kicking and punching him as they dragged him to the barracks. No longer interested in us, they chased us away.

The political situation deteriorated throughout 1970 and 1971. Increasingly, the Falls was a 'no-go' area. The police did not dare come in and the Army, which had been deployed in Belfast after the attack on the Falls in August 1969, also, by and large, kept out. Meanwhile, the IRA, which had built up its numbers and weaponry, began attacks on Army patrols and police barracks. In August

1971, the Stormont Government reintroduced internment, the detention without trial of suspected Republicans. Just before dawn on 9 August the Army swooped and arrested several hundred men. They were taken to Crumlin Road Prison, and later, when construction was completed, to Long Kesh internment camp.

Northern Ireland exploded, and the level of violence surpassed even that of August 1969. In the weeks following the introduction of internment, there were hundreds of bombings, thousands of shootings. There were several riots a day. I remember one riot in the vicinity of St Peter's pro-cathedral at which Canon Murphy tried to intervene. Many people in the district thought that Canon Murphy was pro-British and out of touch with the feelings of his parishioners, and some of the rocks thrown in the soldiers' direction landed suspiciously near him. A couple were launched from my own hand.

In the weeks after internment, it was quite normal to see people on the street with rifles and sub-machine guns exchanging fire with soldiers. To us, these men were not terrorist gangsters. They were our neighbours, the brothers of our friends, the sons of respected people in the district. The Government used to say that the Catholic community was being terrorized by the IRA. But it was the police, the B-Specials (until they were disbanded) and then the Army that people saw as the aggressors. The RUC and B-Specials had come into the area and killed people, and had allowed Loyalist mobs from the Shankill to invade and burn it. The Army, after the initial welcome, was seen in the same light, especially after the curfew it imposed on the Falls in July 1970. Most people on the Falls wanted the IRA there to prevent anything like that happening again.

Many of my friends joined the IRA at around that time, and I understood why they did so. But not everyone rushed to take up arms. There were those, and I was among them, who, while they would not dream of picking up a telephone to inform on their neighbours who were in the IRA, still wanted no part of the organization. This did not prevent me from being picked up from time to time. During this period, almost every Catholic male in the district was taken in for questioning by the Army or police. I was in Castle Street in the city centre and with Gerry Fitzpatrick and Butsy Moore and another couple of kids. We went into a chip shop to get something to eat. When we came out we were confronted by policemen who arrested us and took us to Palace Barracks, then a notorious interrogation centre. While we were in the reception area, a man wearing a bus conductor's uniform was hauled in. His swollen face was covered in abrasions. After a few minutes, the police took him off to an interrogation cell from where we heard sounds of a man moaning and crying. We sat, nervous and fearing the worst, on rows of chairs while we waited to be called into the interrogation cells. From time to time, Harry Taylor, the notorious Special Branch interrogator, appeared and shouted abuse and threats. The windows were covered, and it was impossible to say whether it was day or night. Suddenly, we heard a great cheer from the police and soldiers and there were the noises of them beating someone. They lost interest in interrogating us, and we were separated, randomly it seemed to me, into two groups. One group was released, the other – my group – was sent off to Crumlin Road Prison for detention. However, when we had been picked up the police had confused the year of my birth and made me a year younger. I spent one night in Crumlin Road and the next day the governor came to me and said that as I was under age they were releasing me.

It turned out that the cheer we had heard had been the police celebrating the capture of two well-known Republicans, Martin Meehan and Tony Docherty. So pleased were the police and soldiers about having caught these two men, they had lost all interest in interrogating us kids. So, although we had had an uncomfortable and frightening experience, we avoided a serious beating. Shortly after my release, I was interviewed by a BBC television crew about Palace Barracks. Gerry, Butsy and I made statements to the Association of Legal Justice, which was collecting information about the ill-treatment of suspects held for interrogation by the RUC and Army, in which we made allegations of ill-treatment against Harry Taylor.

I returned home to find my mother extremely distressed, and she was now more determined than ever to see me return to England. There was nowhere I could go in Belfast to avoid the trouble around us. Both the Cushnahan house in Cairns Street and my mother's maisonette in Turf Lodge were in areas that saw daily confrontations between the people and the Army. One day, I was in my mother's house, near the Springfield Road, watching the football on television. Suddenly, I heard a great explosion, and I rushed out into the street and saw that Kelly's bar had been bombed. A number of people ran to the bar to pull people from the debris. As we were uncovering the wounded, Loyalist gunmen from Springmartin opened fire and we had to flee for cover back into Turf Lodge. I ran back into my mother's maisonette and from the balcony watched as two Ferret armoured cars, their engines making a high-pitched whine, raced up the road. Without any warning, the soldiers in the armoured cars opened fire with their machine guns, raking the houses and maisonettes. The bullets went through the thin outer walls.

My mother dug out more than thirty rounds from different parts of the house. She had been in the kitchen when the Army opened fire, and several of the bullets pierced the cooker by which she was standing. Some time later, the Northern Ireland Office paid compensation to the people whose houses had been hit. My mum received £39, about £1 for every bullet that struck the house. The day after the shooting, I read in the newspaper that snipers had shot at the Army from the flats and that the soldiers had returned fire. This was completely untrue. But it was not worth getting annoyed about; by then I learned what to expect from newspapers reporting Northern Ireland.

The bombing of Kelly's, the Protestant snipers and the Army shooting provoked a fierce riot in the area. It resulted in the Protestant families in New Barnsley being intimidated out of their houses which displaced Catholic families then moved into. My mother, whose maisonette had been shot up, was one of those who moved to New Barnsley.

At the beginning of November 1971 (soon after being arrested and taken to Palace Barracks), I set off once more for England. This was my third visit. In London this time I worked in a Bata shoe shop in Oxford Street and lived with Anne and Frank. I enjoyed life: the range of entertainment for a teenager was much wider in London; the shops had fashionable clothes (in which I was always interested); and there was new music to hear: I liked the New York

Dolls and Velvet Underground – bands almost unknown in Belfast.

I stayed in London for several months, until August 1972, and during this time the horror of what I had left behind in Belfast was brought home to me. Many of my friends and old classmates had joined the IRA. And they were killed. Jimmy Quigley was shot dead in Albert Street by the Army on 29 September. Danny McAreavey was killed a week later, and John Donaghey and Joe McKinney were blown up in a premature explosion on 10 October. These boys all died within a radius of a few hundred yards.

The news of these deaths made me sad rather than bitter. By 1972 violent death was common; it was a daily occurrence; it was part of life. I thought about my dead friends with the same kind of resignation and bewilderment that as a child I had experienced when listening to the grown-ups around me speaking of the Black and Tans and the B-Specials and the atrocities they had committed. It occurred to me that I was just one of the next generation in the long, sad history of Ireland, that I would, in the years to come, be repeating the stories of John Donaghey and Joe McKinney and that the children would listen, wide-eyed, not fully understanding that what they were hearing would happen again in their own lifetimes. I was glad to be out of it.

I also received a further piece of bad news from home. The Army had arrested my younger brother Patrick and a friend of his, a lad by the name of Carson, in possession of a shotgun. At that time it was common for the IRA to get youngsters to move arms around the district, and Patrick, who was only fourteen, had been given a shotgun and was taking it to a house in New Barnsley when he was caught. My mother was distraught and I was very worried, though not entirely surprised. Patrick was not a member of the Fianna (junior IRA), but by then it was nothing out of the ordinary for people, even youngsters, to be arrested in connection with 'the Troubles'.

Patrick went on trial and eventually received twelve months' youth custody for the offence. He was sent to a training school run by the Christian Brothers, a teaching order, where the regime was far from severe. The Brothers, though strict, could not control the boys, and Patrick, fed up more than anything else, decided to abscond. This he did simply by walking out the door. He first went home and then on to live in Dundalk in the Irish Republic where my mother went regularly to visit him and bring him clothes and food. As time passed, she began to look on her trips to Dundalk as a weekend holiday.

Much as I enjoyed living and working in England, I could not cut myself off from my home and my family. In summer 1972, I returned to Belfast to see my family. I did not stav long and returned to England within a few weeks. As on previous visits, I went to live with Anne and Frank and found a job with Robert Hart's construction company where I worked with Frank.

In December 1973, I caught the boat back to Belfast intending to spend Christmas with my relatives before returning to England. However, once there I realized how much I had missed the district. Belfast was familiar to me and, in spite of the violence, in an odd way it was reassuring. I was also becoming more interested in Gina and by the following spring we were going out together.

It was at this time that sectarian murders committed by Loyalist death squads reached their height. Men and women from the district would be shot down in the street by men in passing cars. Worse, some were kidnapped, taken away and tortured before being shot. One man from the district was found three days after he went missing, his head beaten to a pulp, his teeth ripped out with pliers. A Loyalist gang known as the 'Shankill Butchers' specialized in kidnapping Catholics from the city centre and torturing them to death. They claimed more than a dozen victims before they were caught.

The fear in the community at that time was worse than I had ever sensed it. My granny worried every time we went out. She would say to my granddad, 'Don't let them get you into a car, get hold of a lamppost, whatever, hang on to it, but don't let them take you away. Let them kill you there.' The streets running off the Falls towards the Shankill were notorious, Catholics could not safely walk up them. Cooper Street was completely out of bounds.

The assassinations continued, as did the shootings and bombings around the Falls. In the spring and summer of

1974 the victims included a policeman, shot in the face by a lone gunman as he sat in an unmarked car near Dunville Park; a Protestant man beaten to death with bricks in a derelict house in Leeson Street; and Brian Shaw, a former soldier, who some people said was an undercover agent. Shaw was kidnapped from the Glengeen Bar in the Divis Flats, taken to a disused house nearby, beaten and shot.

Another victim was a friend of mine, Martin Skillen. He was taking aim with an Armalite rifle at an Army patrol near Leeson Street but was seen and shot. A crowd of local women gathered around the body and kept the soldiers back. The rifle was spirited away before the soldiers could get it. Martin's was another name to add to those already in the stories.

After Martin's death my mother increased the pressure on me to go back to England; and, once I had persuaded Gina to accompany me, I left, intending, as usual, to return at Christmas. In fact, I did not see home again for fifteen years.

Chapter Five

IN ENGLAND, AUGUST–NOVEMBER 1975

A dream, a recurring dream, troubled me during my teenage years. I used to dream I was in an open coffin; my head, slightly raised, rested on soft, white satin pillows; my hands were crossed at my waist. The coffin was in the parlour of our house in Cairns Street, and around me my distraught family gathered. They prayed and sobbed and spoke with voices that ached. In the corner, sat Joe Walsh, the half-witted wake-goer, who howled and bit his hands. My granny moved silently and sadly among the mourners, refilling cups and offering sandwiches. My mother was red-eyed and drawn, and seeing her so sad made me feel intensely protective towards her. I decided to get out of the coffin to comfort her, to tell her everything was all right.

But when I went to get up, I found that the power of movement had been taken from me, and a feeling of panic swept over me. I tried again, but could not get up. The panic spread its cold hand over me. Without meaning to, I made a noise like a moan. The sound of my moan brought me immense relief for it meant, I realized at once, that I could still speak. I would explain to them, and soon be out of the coffin. I do not know whether my mouth moved in the normal way, but I heard my own words as I said, 'Get me up out of here.' No one responded. The panic returned. I said, louder, 'Get me out of this coffin!' Still no one stirred.

Suddenly, two men I did not recognize lifted the coffin lid and slammed it on top of me. The crashing of the lid was so violent that it jolted back into my body the power of movement. I began to beat the coffin lid, and to scream and shout. I was sweating with fear.

I do not know whether the coffin turned to glass, or whether part of me was able to watch the scene from outside and above, but I could see my Uncle Charlie and my granddad come to the coffin and lift it to their shoulders. This sensation of being moved was terrifying, although it was not at that precise moment, but a little later, that I fully understood what it meant: we were going to the cemetery, and I was to be buried.

In the street, there were people dressed in black; their faces were pale and drawn, and they bowed their heads and whispered prayers as we passed. My cries became more desperate. I tried to tear my way out of the coffin. With a choking terror I screamed for them to let me out, but on we went, on towards the cemetery. My mother and my granny and granddad walked beside the coffin, only inches away but deaf to my screams.

The terror of this dream was so strong and real that I would wake up, heart pounding, panting with fright. To be buried alive . . .

Gina and I left Belfast on the overnight boat for Heysham on 22 August 1974, just over a week after my twentieth birthday. Gina's father had let her have the money for her ticket, and my granddad had helped me out. With us were my sister Liz, and Joe Kane, a lad from the Falls who was planning to go to Manchester where he had a job. This was my fifth visit to England. Gina had been before when much younger to stay with relatives, a married sister and her husband, in Sholing, Southampton. Gina also had in Southampton a brother named John who worked on the Southampton–Le Havre ferry.

At Heysham, Special Branch officers routinely stopped

and searched the passengers. I had my birth certificate and baptism lines which I showed to the policemen. We also gave them the address to which we were travelling, and they allowed us to go on our way. We said goodbye to Joe, who took the train for Manchester, while Gina, Liz and I made for London, intending to stay in Holborn with my Aunt Theresa and Errol Smalley, her husband.

We got to Euston on Saturday morning and went straight to Theresa and Errol's. On arrival, we found my other sister, Marion, was already staying there with Janet, Theresa's daughter, as well as Errol's two sons from his first marriage. The house was packed and, since Anne and Frank had no room either, the following day we decided that Gina should go to Southampton and that I would follow her when she had somewhere sorted out for us to stay.

Gina went to the house of her sister Cathy, and Cathy's husband Malcolm Crosbie, also from Belfast. The Crosbys lived at Stainer Close, Sholing. I joined Gina a couple of days later. Soon after arriving, I went to the Labour Exchange to sign on, giving my name as Paul Michael Hill and my address as Stainer Close. Gina found a job in a stationery shop. I got a casual job without cards with the local authority as a street sweeper, but continued to sign on, what is known in Belfast as 'doing the double'.

One evening, Gina told me that as she was coming home on the bus she had seen Gerry Conlon, a friend, though not at that time a particularly close friend, from the Falls. Before leaving Belfast, I had heard that Gerry had gone to England, but did not know that he was in Southampton. The last I had seen of him had been a couple of weeks earlier when an Army foot patrol stopped us with my granddad on the Falls. The soldiers let my granddad go, but for a few hours they held Gerry and me for routine 'screening' after which we were released.

A week or so after arriving in Southampton, Gina and I went for a drink in the King's Arms, one of the bars favoured by Southampton's Irish. It was here, by chance, we ran into Gerry. From then on, Gerry and I would often meet for a drink. One Thursday night – I used to be paid on Thursdays – I went out for a session with him and ended up getting very drunk. I caught a taxi home and, drunk and stupid, I started an argument with the driver. The driver pulled over and I got out, or was told to get out (I was too far gone to remember). I was standing in a daze by the side of the road when a police car came along. After a brief exchange of words, ill-humoured on my part, the police took me to Shirley Road Station where I told them I was living in the Crosbie house. I watched as the desk sergeant entered these details into the station log. I was put into another car and brought to Stainer Close, where Gina and Cathy were not at all pleased to see me in such circumstances. Cathy was angry because I had brought the police to her house (Malcolm had had brushes with the law) and Gina was annoyed because I had drunk money I was supposed to be saving so that we could get married.

Gina blamed this, as she tended to blame any bad behaviour of mine, on Gerry, and resented my association with him. The truth was that in Southampton, where I knew no one, I was glad of Gerry's company. In Belfast, Gerry had been one of several lads I had knocked about with, but had not known that well. We had been to St Peter's together, though not in the same class. At home, Gerry was known as a bit of a rogue who was always looking for a way to get a few shillings, which he then handed over to the bookies. Gambling was his passion, and his life in Belfast, as far as I could make out, consisted almost entirely of wheedling money out of people so that he could dash to the bookies, back a horse and retire to a bar to watch the race with a pint.

When he had money he was generous, and his generosity was one of the things that made him so likeable, that and his crack. I remember him in Belfast coming into a bar one night wearing a huge leather coat, stolen of course, which, because he knew I had no money, he handed over to me. I put the coat on and wore it home where my mother took one look and fell into fits of hysterics. 'You look like an SS man,' she said. Gerry and I ended up selling the coat to someone in a bar one night when we were broke.

Gerry was useful to be with if you were without money, for he was a lucky person. Sometimes his luck even stretched to the horses. Once, I bumped into him outside a bookie's as I was on the way to pay the rent for my granny. Gerry was pacing restlessly up and down, looking frantic, and I asked him what was wrong. His problem was that he had two things that were driving him to distraction: no money and a dead cert, a horse that could not lose. I was not interested in gambling and had no desire to let Gerry have any money. But Gerry could be very persuasive, and when I foolishly told him that I had £3 to pay the rent he kept up a verbal barrage until he convinced me that his horse would storm home. Hardly realizing what I was doing, I handed over the money, at the same time trying to think of some excuse for my granny when she discovered the rent had not been paid. Gerry dashed inside to lay the bet. I need not have worried for he turned the £3 into £40.

Later, when Gerry and I left Southampton for London, we caught the tube from Waterloo to Mornington Crescent. We had less than £1 between us and no immediate prospects of improving our position. It was raining hard as we came out of Mornington Crescent station, I pulled my anorak hood over my head and made for shelter, skipping over a rush of water in the guttering to get to the pavement. Behind, I heard Gerry shout out, 'Look at this!' Floating in the gutter was an envelope that someone had dropped. Gerry picked it up and ripped it open. It turned out to be a wage packet containing about £25, which he shared with me.

Gerry always had his hands in something, was always gambling, always running about. Yet he was one of the kindest people I knew. If he had money he would share it with you; he bought drinks for people, was warm and liked a bit of warmth. He was good crack, and always liked a yarn.

Gina did not see Gerry like this. She thought he was leading me astray, and from time to time we would have words about it. There were other tensions in the Crosbie household: Cathy and Malcolm, who later separated, rowed often. Stainer Close was becoming uncomfortable. Gerry, who was keen to move to London, urged me to go with him. I decided to leave Southampton after an argument with Gina. Every time I went for a drink with Gerry, she saw the wedding day put further back. One night, Gina and I had a fierce row, and I hit her. I was immediately ashamed, and images flooded into my head of the times I had seen my father beat my mother. I thought of how I had detested the way so many of the men in the district had treated their women, and yet I was doing exactly the same. Ashamed, but too foolish to apologize, I left for London with Gerry the following day.

In London, I could have gone to stay with either Anne and Frank or Errol and Theresa, but I did not want to leave Gerry by himself. We spent one night at his Uncle Hugh's and the next day, at Hugh's suggestion, made for Hope House, a hostel for young Irishmen in Quex Road, Kilburn. Father Carolan and Father Ryan, who ran the hostel, let us have a room.

I got another job with Robert Hart's, converting houses into flats, working alongside my Uncle Frank who got Gerry a job on the same site. Our pay was £10 a day, good money by the standards of the time. It would go on having a good weekend and on a few drinks during the week. Every so often, I sent money home to my mother, and I repaid my granddad for my fare over. During the week, I would get up at 7am, shower and go to work. On the way home, Gerry and I would get a fish supper and stop to have a few drinks before returning to the hostel. The priests used to lock the front door at midnight, but we used to creep around the back and open the window of our room to get in. This was a popular way to enter the place, and when we were in bed asleep other lads used to come in, fumbling and stumbling in the darkness and crashing into the beds. This used to provoke some high words between Gerry and the late arrivals.

I used to spend Saturday mornings with Gerry, usually in Kilburn. On one occasion, as we were walking up Kilburn High Street, Gerry spotted someone he knew and stopped to speak to him. This turned out to be Paddy Armstrong, who came from the Divis Flats. I vaguely knew of Paddy, who was three years older than me, but had never spoken to him. I do not think I even exchanged a single word with him on that occasion. I got the impression he seemed a mild, inoffensive sort of person. When I got to know him better, while we were on remand together in Winchester and Brixton, my impressions were confirmed. Paddy was quiet, self-effacing and shy. At school, he was later to say, the other kids used to pick on him because he would not fight.

In the evenings, Gerry and I would sometimes see Paddy in the bars around Kilburn. Paddy lived nearby in a squat.

We also ran into some other Belfast people we vaguely knew or had heard of. Once or twice, I saw a girl who Gerry said Paddy was going out with. Her first name, which I was told and immediately forgot, was Carole. I did not hear her second name until during my interrogation at Guildford when the police decided she was one of my fellow bombers. She was Carole Richardson.

Apart from Gerry, I did not really have any friends in the hostel. Gerry was much more sociable and mixed with the people there, especially in the television room. I spent a great deal of time writing to Gina. We had quickly patched up our argument. The bond between us was very strong; we had no doubts that we would marry and raise a family together. I telephoned her almost every day; there was no phone in her sister's so by arrangement I called the number of a phonebox in Stainer Close. Every other day we wrote each other long letters of love pledged and extravagant expressions of our passion.

One night in Hope House, I woke up to find Gerry standing beside me. He had a plastic bag which he emptied onto the bed. It contained £500 or £600. He explained that he had seen in a phonebox or in a shop window a telephone number offering 'hand relief' or some such thing. He rang the number and got the address. That night he went to the flat and, after making sure it was empty, broke in and found the money. Gerry, generous as ever, shared the money out, and we went on a trip to Manchester for a few days to stay with one of his relatives.

Every Saturday, after spending some time in the bars with Gerry, I would go to Southampton to stay the weekend with Gina. On four consecutive Saturdays – from 28 September to 19 October – I went to Waterloo Station at about 3pm to catch the train. British Rail was making repairs to the line near Southampton and I used to see a notice saying that some trains would terminate at Eastleigh, just outside Southampton, and warning passengers that they may have to proceed to Southampton by bus. In fact, I never experienced any trouble because the work did not start until late in the evening and I always arrived at Southampton railway station before 6pm. I would then catch a bus to Butts Road (near Stainer Close) where Gina waited for me. Usually, she sat on a low wall near the bus stop. As the bus approached, I used to see her straining to make out the passengers – to see if I was among them. The expectancy with which she waited, and the pleasure she showed when she saw me, her spontaneity – all touched me deeply.

Gina was pregnant. Perhaps we should have been worried by this, being so young and having nowhere of our own to live. But we weren't. By the standards of modern England, we were young to be starting a family. But at home it was not unusual for youngsters to have children, for men and women to be grandparents in their early thirties. The thought of an abortion never crossed our minds.

The news of Gina's pregnancy made me feel still more protective towards her. She was a strong and capable person – she had run her father's house at an age when many girls are still playing with dolls. But sometimes she looked so helpless. In her moments of doubt she would turn to me to hear me say everything would be all right.

While I was working in London, she suddenly fell sick and had to go to hospital. She did not tell me this over the phone, but waited until I came to visit her one weekend to explain that she had miscarried. Both of us were saddened, and I was worried. I was concerned about Gina's health and whether she was looking after herself. I was struck – it was almost as if I had realized it for the first time – by how young she was.

On Saturday evenings in Southampton, Gina and I used to go to the pub. On three occasions we went to the Target, near Stainer Close, and once to the Eagle in Palmerston Road. The night we went to the Eagle, Southampton was crawling with American sailors; part of the Seventh Fleet had put into port.

These dates and times, the trains and the works on the line, became of crucial significance soon afterwards. The second Saturday I came down to Southampton fell on 5 October. That night in Guildford, at 8.50pm, the Horse and Groom pub was wrecked by an explosion; ten minutes later, a bomb went off in the Seven Stars. Both pubs were popular among the soldiers and WRACs stationed in the town. Five people were killed and more than fifty injured. That evening, I had arrived in Southampton on the train from Waterloo before

6pm and had taken the bus to Butts Road where Gina was waiting for me. We got to the house as Cathy was preparing the tea. Malcolm, who had been out drinking for most of the night, was still in bed. After our tea, Gina and I watched a little television before going to the pub – the Target – where we stayed until closing time, around 11pm. Then we walked back to Stainer Close and went to bed.

I found out about the Guildford bombs the following morning when I went to the shops and bought a copy of the *Sunday Mirror* which I read on the way back to the house. We discussed the bombings at breakfast. For us the shock was not as great as it probably was for English people. The explosions at the Horse and Groom and the Seven Stars were not the first in England but bombs were still relatively uncommon. In Belfast there were Guildfords almost every week.

The Guildford bombs were the first in a series carried out by an IRA active service unit that assembled in London during the summer and autumn of 1974 and was led by Brendan Dowd and Joe O'Connell. It went on to carry out many more attacks: it shot up, bombed or planted bombs at clubs, pubs (including the King's Arms, Woolwich), telephone exchanges, department stores, and hotels; the unit also attempted to assassinate Edward Heath, the former Conservative Prime Minister, by throwing a bomb into his London flat. The attacks continued until four members of the active service unit were captured after the siege at Balcombe Street in December 1975.

The Sunday following the Guildford bombings, I caught the train back to London at about 1pm, as I had the week before. The train was diverted through Guildford because of more works on the line. It did not stop and was the first time I had seen the town. I returned to Hope House in Kilburn and went, as usual, to work the next morning.

My last weekend visit to Southampton was on 19-20 October. By then, relations between Cathy and Malcolm were very strained, and the atmosphere in Stainer Close tense. Gina wanted to leave and she decided she would go to stay with another sister, Mary, who lived in Azov Street, Greenwich, with her brother-in-law, Louis Hammond. The next day, Sunday, she accompanied me to Waterloo. Gina

53

caught a train to Greenwich and I went back to my room in Hope House. There I found a note from Gerry to say that he had gone home to Belfast. I had only stayed in the hostel because of Gerry, so that day I moved out and went to Anne and Frank's in Brecknock Road. During the time Gina lived with the Hammonds, we saw each other when I visited her at weekends, or she came to Anne and Frank's.

During the week, we wrote to each other, and I telephoned her regularly at Azov Street from a phonebox near Anne and Frank's. I made one of these calls on Thursday, 7 November at between 9pm and 9.30pm. That night I had some difficulty in finding somewhere to phone from. I went to several phone-boxes; the first was on the corner of Brecknock Road and Camden Road. But there were several people, including a number of vagrants, around the box so I tried another outside the nearby post office. This was out of order, so I walked to Kentish Town tube station where I managed to get through. I spoke to Gina for about ten minutes and then walked home, arriving before 10pm. Anne and Frank were watching *News at Ten* on ITV with a neighbour, Yvonne Fox, with whom Anne was friendly.

Shortly after my phone call to Gina, at about 10.15pm, the IRA active service unit attacked the King's Arms in Woolwich, where soldiers from the nearby barracks used to drink, with a six or seven pound gelignite bomb which O'Connell threw through a window. Two men died in the explosion, one a soldier, the other a barman. A newsflash about the bomb came on just before *News at Ten* ended at 10.30pm. Mrs Fox had already left; Anne and Frank were horrified.

Late in November, Gina left Azov Street after a row and turned up at Anne and Frank's. I explained the situation to Frank and he said it was all right for Gina to stay with me in Brecknock Road, even though the flat was small and already overcrowded.

In the event, neither Gina nor I stayed long in Brecknock Road. On Saturday, 23 November, as Gina and I lay in bed in Frank and Anne's room, there was a knock on the door. Outside were two plainclothes policemen. They came into the flat and asked Anne and Frank if they had seen or knew the whereabouts of 'Benny Hill'. In Belfast, where almost everyone has a nickname, men with the surname of Hill were invariably called Benny, after the famous comedian. At St Peter's school, I had been known as Benny, but when I left the name was transferred to my younger brother Patrick. Both in the district and in the family 'Benny' was Patrick, and so when the police arrived Anne and Frank immediately and truthfully answered that they did not know where he was. Patrick, who had absconded from the training school some time before, was wanted by the police and on the run. The police then showed Anne and Frank a photograph of Patrick; they repeated that they had not seen him. Gina and I stayed in the bedroom. I had no intention of going out to volunteer any information. I did not want to become involved in any way with the police, nor did I want to be put in a position of being questioned about my own brother.

The police left, but Anne was annoyed. She rang Theresa who said the police had also been around. Anne, who wanted no trouble, suggested that Gina and I go back to Southampton. We packed our bags and caught the train that morning. We left because we really had no option. The flat had only two bedrooms, one for Anne and Frank, the other for their two sons, and we were always getting in the way. My aunt and uncle were, besides, very upright people and naturally alarmed at having had a visit from the police. It was clearly time for us to go. But as we travelled to Southampton, neither Gina nor I believed the police were looking for me. If we had, and wanted to avoid them, we would not have gone to stay at Aldermoor Avenue with Gina's brother John, a seaman, well-known in Southampton, who when young had been a fairly rough character and known to the police.

To Gina our life in England had so far not been all she had hoped. Our motive in leaving Belfast had been to escape 'the Troubles', to find work and stability so that we could marry. But a mixture of immaturity, inexperience and lack of money led us into a life that was disorganized and haphazard. When we left Anne and Frank's, Gina, who had missed a period, suspected she was again pregnant. In spite of this, and the turns our life in England was taking, we were optimistic about the future. We were young, and something would change to make things better.

In Southampton, we settled in with John Clarke's family,

and once again I started to look for work. On Thursday, 28 November, I got up and went to the shop with Tracey, John's daughter, to buy some cigarettes and a newspaper. Outside, I saw several parked cars with men sitting in them. One of these men watched me intently as I returned from the shop to the house. I commented to Gina that the street seemed full of strange cars. In the back of my mind there was the thought that the men were police, but it caused me no alarm. I sat down on the settee in the living room to read the paper while John's wife, Cathy, made breakfast. A minute later, there was a sharp rap at the door. Cathy opened it and a number of policemen burst in. I jumped up and they grabbed me by the arms. They asked me my name and I told them. They said I was being arrested for murder and bombing. I said, 'You're kidding.'

How do you describe the feeling when a policeman arrests you and accuses you of murder? Part of me thought, 'This is so ridiculous. We'll get this cleared up.' But another part of me was overwhelmed by the enormity of the accusations. I was frightened. The fear made me breathless; my brain seemed incapable of taking in what they were saying; my heart pounded; I was in a kind of private trance. The officers were moving in slow motion; their speech came to me as if it were echoes of something shouted along a cavern a mile below ground. My arrest was over in a matter of minutes. As they pulled me outside I had the same terrifying sensation that I had experienced in my dream at the moment my coffin was lifted. It is the feeling you get when you have been stripped of control over your own life, rendered helpless, and are being carried along by others. The terror comes from knowing that you are powerless, that nothing you say or do will save you.

Chapter Six

'PLACED IN THE CELLS'

It does not take long to lose a life. I was arrested on Thursday morning, 28 November 1974. By Friday evening I had confessed to eight murders. The police wrote out the statements and I put my name to them. With each signature I signed away my life.

The confessions were false. In our trial at the Old Bailey the following year I retracted them; but I could not claw back my life. The statements, the only evidence the prosecution offered against the four of us, condemned me, as those made by Gerry, Paddy and Carole condemned them. We insisted that we had made the admissions only after being brutalized, ill-treated and threatened, and that they consisted of a mixture of innocent background information, pure invention and details of the Guildford and Woolwich bombings supplied by the police themselves. The police, for their part, said we confessed freely and without intimidation, violence or undue pressure. They were believed and we were not.

For fifteen years we told anyone who would listen – lawyers, clergymen, politicians, journalists – the truth about

57

what went on while we were in police custody. In the early years, even the most sympathetic found it hard to credit our account. To believe us, they would have to accept that English policemen acted in a way more commonly associated with police forces under dictatorships. And there were those who, it was clear to me even as I spoke, were wondering to themselves, 'How can anyone confess to something he has not done?' There are people who are still asking the same question: you can tell them what it was like – you can describe the intimidation and fear – but, in the end, only those who have been through it really understand.

For fifteen years, the police maintained that the interrogations were conducted correctly and in accordance with the Judges' Rules – the guidelines laid down by the judiciary for interviews in criminal matters. Then suddenly, at the hearing in October 1989 in the Court of Appeal, the prosecution made a confession of its own. Roy Amlot, the barrister who appeared for the Crown, told the court that, as a result of recent investigations, new evidence had come to light to show that at the trial police officers – 'and not just junior officers' – had 'seriously misled the court' on several points, crucially on the timing and nature of the interrogations. Amlot said:

> . . . evidence of great significance has come to light. That evidence throws such doubt upon the honesty and integrity of a number of the Surrey officers investigating this case in 1974 that the Crown now feels unable to say that the convictions of any appellant was safe or satisfactory.

The judges – Lord Lane, the Lord Chief Justice, presided – went further than Amlot. In relation to Paddy Armstrong, the judges said, 'the so-called contemporaneous records of some of the interviews conducted by the Surrey police officers . . . and relied upon by those officers as they gave evidence were not contemporaneous at all. The officers . . . must have lied.' The notes were, they said, possibly the invention of 'some fertile Constabulary mind'.

The judges continued:

As to Hill, still further matters were to come to light . . . These took the shape of a series of manuscript notes relating to an interview with Hill . . . the contents of those notes were significant. They were never disclosed to the Director of Public Prosecutions. They were never disclosed to prosecution counsel before or at the trial . . . If they had been disclosed prior to the trial or at the trial, they would almost certainly have shown that Hill's fifth statement – one of the greatest importance – was taken in breach of the Judges' Rules and might very well have been ruled inadmissible if the true circumstances had been known. Moreover, the Surrey officers on oath, as it is conceded by the Crown, denied that there had been any such interview.

The detention sheets . . . support that discrepancy . . . There is before us . . . a schedule showing the discrepancies between the detention sheets and the record of interviews which were made by the Surrey investigating officers . . . [T]he detention records do in fact conflict with the officers' interviews, and there is no doubt that those are material discrepancies which, had they been known at the trial, might on their own, let alone in conjunction with these other matters, have made a grave difference to the outcome.

Language, legal language in particular, can perpetrate its own exclusive kind of injustice. Anyone who, out of vague curiosity, has stepped into the public gallery of a court to watch a criminal trial must be struck by how dull it all seems, how slow, how stilted. But there *is* a drama unfolding, people's lives *are* at stake. The drama is hidden by a fog of language; the anodyne words uttered by the barristers, judges and police defraud events and characters of the fear, anger, hate, rage, despair or love that made them what they truly were. I read Lord Lane's judgment and wonder at how lifeless it sounds, how cool are the phrases 'material discrepancies', 'in breach of the Judges' Rules', 'other matters'. These do nothing to describe what happened. But then I think of the words I have used, have been taught to use by my years of imprisonment. I learned to say, for example, that I 'retract' my confessions. No, that will not do: I do not 'retract' my confessions. I take them, screaming, and I rip them up and throw them in the face of the policemen who framed me and the judge who sentenced me. That is my 'retraction'.

The documents that describe my arrest and interrogation (in legal language they are known as 'statements of witnesses' or 'depositions') employ the same bland tones, the same empty words. One of the arresting officers was Detective Sergeant Anthony Paul Jermey. In his deposition, Jermey describes the events on the morning of my arrest in John Clarke's house in Aldermoor Avenue:

> I opened a door which led into the lounge, where I saw the accused Paul Hill sitting in an armchair. I said, 'What is your name?' He said, 'Paul Hill.' I said, 'Come with me.' He got up and we went into the hallway, where we saw D.I. Richardson. I said, 'This is Paul Hill.' I then said to Hill, 'You are being arrested on suspicion of causing explosions.' I cautioned him and he made no reply . . . I conveyed him to Guildford Police Station where he was placed in the cells. At 4.35pm the same day with Detective Superintendent Underwood, I again saw the accused Hill in the cells at Guildford Police Station. I reminded him he was still under caution, and introduced Mr Underwood to him. Mr Underwood said, 'I have reason to believe that you were concerned in the bombings of the pubs in Guildford.' He said, 'No, sir, not me.' Mr Underwood said, 'You know what pub bombings I'm talking about?' He said, 'Yes, sir, the soldiers' pubs.' . . . Mr Underwood said, 'We will see you tomorrow.' We then left the cell.

'Come with me.' How does that read? Flat on the page, it has nothing of the threat I heard, no trace of the menace with which it was uttered. Or the words, 'I conveyed him to Guildford Police Station where he was placed in the cells.' In essence this was true. I was taken by Jermey and other officers first to Shirley Road Police Station in Southampton, and then to Guildford. But Jermey's account makes it sound like an ordinary trip. My memory of it is different. On our way to Shirley Road, Jermey warned me not to try to run. 'You look like a fit bastard,' he said. In Shirley Road, they found in my pockets a book of matches from the King's Arms in Southampton. One of the officers spat at me, 'Is this the next target then?' He threw the matches at me. They took my watch. 'This is a bomber's watch,' they said. 'Were you going to use this for a timing device?' They searched me and found some religious medals and scapulars. 'The people of Guildford weren't so blessed,' one of them told me. Later, when I was alone in the cell, I heard Gina's voice, high and distraught, and I heard Mary, her sister, trying to calm her down. I had not realized Gina was in the police station. Was she under arrest? The sound of Gina in such distress, and the thought that the police had taken her in for interrogation, made me unsettled and upset.

A few hours later, as they were preparing to take me from Shirley Road to Guildford, Jermey came into my cell. He was accompanied by another officer, Detective Inspector Brian Richardson, who wore on his belt a holster from which he took a gun. Richardson produced some bullets and made great play of loading the gun in my presence. He made a point of showing me each bullet as he slipped it into the chamber. When he had finished he snapped the gun, pointed it at me and said, 'Try to run and you'll get some of this.' On the way to Guildford, we passed the Horse and Groom which was then being rebuilt. Richardson said in my ear, hatred on his breath, 'Are you proud of yourself, you bastard?'

When we arrived at Guildford Police Station I was taken from the car and into the foyer. There was a crowd of uniformed officers milling around the desk waiting to get a look at me. Jermey said, 'We got the bastard.' The desk sergeant replied, 'Oh, nice one Cyril!' And that, how does that sound? To me it was more sinister than Jermey's brutish and crude threats. The officers wore hard faces. They ran me along to the cells and pushed me inside. I was searched. All the time, they kept up their threats and insults. When they had finished the search, Jermey pushed my face into the wall.

He pointed to some graffiti: I think it said something like 'I love Chrissie'. 'I don't want to see any of that in here,' he shouted. They took my shoes with them when they left the cell.

This is what Jermey meant when he said I was conveyed to Guildford and placed in the cells.

Alone, waiting for something to happen, a knot of anxiety in my stomach, I began to tremble with fear.

After a short time, the door reopened, and I was taken to a small room where my hands were swabbed for explosives. When the officer had finished he went out and I was left alone. A policeman watched me from the door. A few minutes later, a woman police officer appeared. Gina was with her and my anxiety for her made me fight down the fear I felt. I did not want to upset Gina further by letting her see that I was afraid. She was upset, but we were able to talk and after a while she calmed down a little. She had been strip-searched, and the police had said terrible things to her. On arrival at Shirley Road, they had told her she was being 'booked for murder'. A WPC called her 'a fucking IRA bastard' and 'an IRA bitch'. They asked her if she was 'fucking proud' of herself. Detective Superintendent Ronald Underwood told her that our baby would be born in Holloway Prison. During a later interrogation, Detective Chief Superintendent Wally Simmons banged his fist on the table in front of Gina and shouted, after she had said that I had been in Southampton with her on the night of the Guildford bombings, 'You're a fucking liar. You know you're a fucking liar.' They wanted a statement. She made one, insisting that we were innocent. The detectives tore it up and threw it in the bin. It was not what they wanted to hear.

I told Gina that it would soon be straightened out, that as soon as the police realized their mistake we would go home. While we sat together we discussed the Guildford bombings and tried to remember what we had been doing on 5 October. A detective noted down our conversation, but this did not worry us. We were telling the truth, it was simply a matter of sorting out the dates. We remembered that we had read about the bombings in the papers on the Sunday morning at Cathy and Malcolm's, so the previous night I must have been with her in Southampton. I suddenly began to feel optimistic:

we had an alibi and we had witnesses. We agreed that I had never arrived in Southampton later than tea time, around 6pm. All that had to be done was sort out which Saturday it was and we could give a full account of our movements. As we sat there, the feeling of relief was growing stronger in me; we had a cast-iron alibi.

On three of the four Saturday evenings I spent with Gina in Southampton, we had gone to the Target. On the other night, when the American sailors were in town, we went to the Eagle. Was this the night of 5 October? Gina and I discussed it and decided it was. I said to the officers, scarcely able to conceal my excitement and relief, that on 5 October Gina and I had been in the Eagle and that we remembered because it was the night the sailors were in town.

We got the wrong night. It transpired that the sailors had been in port the following week. In the trial, this mistake cost me dear. But even then, before this detail had been checked, the police did not accept our story; even if we had got it right it would have made no difference to the subsequent course of events.

Gina and I were then separated and put into cells. The police version is that, following instructions from Simmons, I was not interrogated at all the first day, Thursday, nor on Friday, until two RUC officers who had flown over from Northern Ireland arrived to question me about incidents in Belfast. The time given for the first of the RUC interviews was 4.05pm. In other words, I was not interviewed until almost twenty-four hours after Jermey and Underwood came to my cell in Guildford and said, 'We will see you tomorrow', and more than thirty hours after my arrest. The police version is untrue, though it has been taken at face value by others, even by sympathetic writers like Robert Kee who says of this time, 'For nearly twenty-four hours Hill was left to ponder his predicament.'

In fact, even before the hearing in the Court of Appeal in October 1989, during which the Crown made available a schedule showing the discrepancies in the detention sheets and the interview times as set out by the interrogating officers, it was proved that the police story was not accurate. During my trial in Belfast, in June 1975, Jermey conceded under cross-examination that there were discrepancies in the records about the time of my arrest. And in his deposition, Detective Superintendent Peter Imbert, then of the newly-formed Bomb Squad, now the Commissioner of the Metropolitan Police, stated that he saw me with Detective Chief Superintendent Nevill on Sunday, 1 December at 6.38pm, making no mention of two earlier interviews on the Thursday and Friday. In the Belfast trial, however, he, too, agreed that he had seen me on two – unrecorded – occasions before the Sunday. Yet there is no trace of these meetings in the officers' records. Under normal circumstances, when a prisoner is taken from his cell for interview the time is recorded in the jailer's custody or detention sheets. (The jailer is the officer in the cells area who locks and unlocks the cells. Part of his task is to keep a record of the times his prisoners enter or leave the cells – the detention sheets.) Another record is made by the interrogating officers themselves, which again should show the times the prisoner was seen and questioned.

I maintained in my Belfast trial that, contrary to the police version of events, the two unrecorded Imbert interviews were part of a series of lengthy interrogations which lasted until the Friday evening, by which time, worn down by the constant questioning, ill-treatment, threats and worry about Gina, I made the first of my confessions. On oath, policeman after policeman contradicted me. The custody records apparently supported them, for they contained no entries to show that I had been removed from my cell for interview. However, in the Belfast trial, my barrister, Michael Lavery QC, cross-examined Underwood about these records.

LAVERY: But aren't records kept in police stations . . . for the purpose of knowing where a man was and who had custody at any given time?

UNDERWOOD: Yes.

LAVERY: And one ought to be able, by looking at the records, to see all the people who have spoken to the man during any given period?

UNDERWOOD:	Yes.
LAVERY:	And these records obviously do not show this?
UNDERWOOD:	That record is faulty.

Had the record not been faulty, had it been kept properly, it would have shown that there were other lengthy interviews between Thursday and Friday evening.

Interviews. Once again, legal language plays its games of deception. What associations does the word 'interview' hold for most people? Some exchange between two parties, a series of questions and answers, some search for information. For me the word is bound up with violence and threat. Now when I am asked by journalists for an 'interview' my mind goes back to the days and nights I spent in Guildford undergoing police 'interviews'.

Guildford Police Station had not been open long in 1974. In the holding area the cells had modern reinforced steel doors with a long flap through which food was passed to prisoners. Apart from a toilet and a raised area of concrete, covered by boards, that served as a bed, the cell was empty. High up, there was a window of small squares of thick bubble glass which allowed in some light but was impossible to see out of. In court, one police witness was to describe the cell as 'luxurious'. As I paced up and down, policemen would kick the door and shout abuse. The flap fell open. The muzzle of a revolver was poked through and pointed at me. A voice said, 'That is all for you, you bastard.' I froze; the gun was withdrawn.

I had been in custody – very briefly – before, in Belfast. But that was different. There you knew it was just harassment, that after a bit of roughing up they would kick you out onto the street and you could go home. In Guildford, I knew that this was trouble of a different order. No one was listening to me. The more I denied their accusations, the angrier they became. Their hatred was so intense. It seemed to me that everyone in the station was coming down to see their celebrated prisoner. Every few minutes, they kicked the door. I tried to ignore them, but there was nowhere in the cell that could not be seen from the flap, nowhere for me to hide. It was hard to collect my thoughts under this barrage, and I am sure that that was partly their intention. That and to terrify me.

Between the early afternoon of Thursday and about 4pm on Friday, I was taken out of the cell for lengthy interviews. I was so frightened, my mind in such confusion, that I am unable to distinguish one interview from another, and cannot remember how many there were. On each occasion, detectives took me from the cell to a stairway, up to what looked to me like an incident room or nerve centre on the second floor. In the trial, the police denied that I was ever brought to this room, yet I can describe everything in it. It was at the front of the building and was right above the station's main entrance. Its windows gave onto the open area at the front of the station. On the walls were photofits of the suspects, and plans and diagrams of the Horse and Groom and the Seven Stars showing the positions in which the bodies had been found.

The interviews followed more or less the same pattern. Jermey, Underwood, Detective Inspector Timothy Blake and others would take me into the room where I would be placed on a chair. There were usually at least three or four officers in the room at any one time (their numbers varied – some would come in, others would go out). They would pace up and down, shouting abuse at me, shouting, 'You murdering bastard!' They would be outside my field of vision, behind me, to the side of me. Sometimes they would unexpectedly shout in my ear. After they had done this once or twice the hair on my neck would bristle in anticipation. If I tried to turn my head to look at them, they would shout at me. They would put their faces close to mine until I felt the threats on their hot breath. Jermey read out parts of the love letters I had sent to Gina, which they had uncovered during the search of our things in Aldermoor Avenue, and sniggered over them. Blake knocked me off the chair and sat on top of me, his knees on my shoulders. He grabbed a handful of my hair, which was quite long, and violently shook my head. They repeated time after time the name of Caroline Slater, one of the young victims of the Guildford bombs. They circled me, prowled around me. I never knew what they were going to do to me next. During one of these interviews I was handcuffed; the chains made me feel vulnerable, exposed and humiliated. Jermey and Underwood said Gina was in custody, and that they would charge her with the bombings. I knew from newspaper reports that the police had been looking for two women in connection with Guildford, and I took their threats seriously.

I did not cry at this stage, though I was on the verge of tears. I shook, even during those moments they quietened down. I shook and waited for the next assault, always fearing it was going to get worse, always fearing that I would make them angry, so angry they would overstep the mark. I did not want them to lose their temper. Like a child faced with a violent and unpredictable parent, I said as little as possible, fearing that any word of mine would set them off. All the time, the main thought in my head was what was happening to Gina? Were they doing the same to her as they were to me? She was pregnant. The thought that they were abusing her almost made me ill.

Of course, they were not about to lose control. It was their method, it was their way. They wanted to frighten me, to make me so frightened that I would agree to what they wanted. I do not know how long these sessions lasted, hours certainly, and I cannot be sure how many there were. When they had finished they would take me back down to the cell. But there was no rest there for me. Through the flap they continued to shout their threats. At one point, on the night of Thursday–Friday, I do not remember when exactly, several officers entered the cell and told me to take off my clothes. They gave me a thin towel to cover myself. My clothes were taken away, they said for forensic examination. Later, they told me that they had found traces of explosives on my hands and clothes. I said it was impossible and that they were lying. They gave me my clothes back in a plastic bag the following morning.

In one interview, Underwood said to me, 'Remember Kenneth Lennon? You know what happened to him.' Kenneth Lennon had spied on the IRA after, it was alleged, being blackmailed by the police. Lennon told his story to the National Council for Civil Liberties, and then disappeared. He was found shot dead in a lane in Surrey, and there was at the time a great deal of speculation that the security services had killed him. Underwood said, 'You don't want to end up like him?' Of course, in retrospect, it would have been impossible for the police to take me out and kill me in a Surrey Lane. But in the police station at that time, with men pointing guns at me and threatening me, with my mind so confused, I began to suspect they were capable of anything.

An officer brought a black briefcase into the interrogation room from which he took out a selection of photographs. 'Look at what you and your friends did, you murdering bastard! Look!' An officer snatched up a picture and held it in front of me. Underwood called out the names of the victims. The photographs were of naked bodies, torn and horribly mutilated, lying on cold mortuary slabs. There was a girl who had no leg, just a stump; there was a man with a wound in his stomach – a huge fleshy exploded mushroom. One of the girls was so young; she was Caroline Slater, eighteen years old. I thought, 'My God! Just about Gina's age'. I was dizzy and wanted to be sick. They said I had murdered her. I turned away. Blake hit me a blow on the back of my head and knocked me onto the floor.

I do not know, I cannot be sure, but I think that during the night, by the end of what was perhaps the fourth interview, they were less confident about whether they had got the right man. My denials had not been calm or measured but they had been consistent. I began to sense that they half believed me.

Back in the cell, I flushed the toilet and scooped water from the basin. The cell was stuffy, I was sweating with the heat and it was the only way to get water. I was given nothing to eat on the Thursday. During the interrogations in the small hours of Friday morning I had been without food for more than thirty-six hours. The first food I got was from Underwood. He entered the cell with Imbert some time on the Friday and threw down a packet of potato crisps.

Once, after being returned to my cell, I tried to sleep. There was no mattress in the cell, but it was not the hardness of the boards that kept me awake. The police in the holding area kept up their noise, banging and kicking on the door to disturb me.

By Friday morning, I was exhausted and, although I would have found it impossible to have eaten, weak from hunger.

Mentally, too, I had no reserves. I had not been given time to think, to reflect, to go through my position and rationalize it. Had I been able to think logically perhaps I would have been able to continue resisting. But logic is an early victim of isolation and abuse, and normal thought processes are interrupted by fear and paranoia.

Gina was constantly in my thoughts. The police had said that she was one of the girls who had planted the bombs. They told me she would be charged. I could see her face; I imagined her bewildered and crying. What could I do to protect her? One thin hope was that perhaps they were beginning to believe me. I began to convince myself that I had detected signs of their doubt.

The dashing of this hope with the arrival of the RUC men brought me down even further. By the time the police say the interviews started, at around 4pm on Friday, they were for me finished. It was then that they stopped being interviews – as long as I was capable of maintaining my innocence they were 'interviews' of sorts, in spite of everything – and became something fantastic: a nightmare in which I mechanically repeated and accepted allegations of multiple murder. When Detective Chief Inspector Albert Cunningham and Detective Constable John McCaul, the two RUC officers who had flown over from Belfast, arrived to interrogate me, the Surrey police had completed their preparatory work. I was wrecked. I had been softened up; they had made me ready for them.

Cunningham and McCaul entered my cell with Jermey and Simmons. I had always thought of the RUC as a corrupt, bigoted and violent force. Conversely, I had always been led to believe that English policemen were somehow different – that they were honourable, honest, interested in justice; for that reason, their behaviour at Guildford was all the more shocking and frightening. I expected worse to come from the RUC men. Cunningham put a series of allegations to me: that I had shot the policeman who had been sitting in his car near Dunville Park; that I had murdered the Protestant man found dead in the house in Leeson Street; that I had been involved in the kidnapping and murder of Brian Shaw, the former British soldier whose body was found in Arundel Street. Cunningham and McCaul produced from a briefcase a gun wrapped in a polythene bag, which they said was the gun that had been used to kill Shaw. I told them I knew nothing about Shaw's death and I denied the other offences. They did not believe me.

Jermey handcuffed me and took me to an interview room upstairs. Cunningham and McCaul continued to press me on the allegations they had made earlier. Over the course of the interview, they began to show increasing enthusiasm about the Shaw murder, and the other charges were mentioned less frequently. Cunningham smoked a pipe and he leant across and blew the smoke into my face. They produced a copy of the statement I had made in 1971 to the Association of Legal Justice complaining about the behaviour of Harry Taylor, the Special Branch interrogator. Cunningham told me he was a personal friend of Taylor, and did not like people saying the kind of things I had said about him.

In their evidence in the Belfast trial, the RUC officers maintained that I was calm and composed; Cunningham was to go as far as to say that I was 'confident'. I do not think that anyone, even the most hardened of suspects, would be 'confident' in such circumstances. I certainly was not. I was wrecked, frightened; I knew what I would get if I did not agree. I wanted to get away from them, I wanted to get down to the cell and keep them away from me. They put allegations about Shaw to me: I told them what they were saying was lies. But they would not listen. They kept on and on and at last I agreed – anything to finish it, anything to get it over with. I was in no condition to dictate a statement, so they helped me. They put allegations and details to me, and I agreed to them. On two or three occasions, I tried to stop, but they would not listen. Once, Cunningham took off his coat and rolled up his sleeves; he blew pipe smoke into my face. I was hardly aware of what I was doing; by that stage my resistance had gone. All I wanted was to end the questioning, to make them go away.

As I signed, I broke down and wept. Until then, although I had been close to it, I had held myself back from crying. It was as if I had been too frightened to let tears fall. But once I had signed, once they had broken me, the fear left me and all my inhibitions went. I cried and cried. I had admitted to the Shaw murder; but I would, if they had pressed me, have admitted to the other two offences as well. As far as I know, the identity of the person who shot the policeman near Dunville Park was never discovered, but I later found out that the man killed in Leeson Street was a wino who had gone there with other vagrants to drink. An argument broke out and he was battered to death with a brick; it was completely unconnected to the IRA. These incidents, like the Shaw murder, all took place in the Lower Falls and had not been solved. There was nothing to connect me to them except that they occurred near where I lived. I can imagine the RUC men, having been informed of my arrest in England, searching through their files of unsolved cases and saying, 'These look promising. Yes, these'll do.'

I had expected that after signing for Shaw the interrogations would come to an end. I had thought, 'They just want you for something, it doesn't matter what.' I had, I naively believed, given them what they wanted. I expected to be left alone. But then Jermey, Simmons and another officer entered. In his deposition Simmons describes how he began the interview:

SIMMONS:	I now wish to speak to you regarding the pub bombings here in Guildford.
HILL:	I don't know anything.
SIMMONS:	I think you can help us on this matter.
HILL:	I can't.
SIMMONS:	Two bombs were placed in two public houses in this town. I think you know something about this matter. That is why you are here.
HILL:	All right. I'll tell you what I know.
SIMMONS:	Start from the beginning.

Every time I read these words I feel a rush of anger. They are so improbable. My anger comes not just from the way the police gave their accounts of the interviews but from the fact that they were believed for so long. I felt like screaming at people, 'For God's sake, how can you believe it was like that! Do you think that the police would keep a suspect in custody for thirty hours before questioning him? When time could be of the essence in preventing the escape of others or in pre-empting further offences?' And if I had been, as they claimed, an experienced IRA man would I, after just two simple questions, have agreed to confess? If I had been the IRA man they say I was, and responsible for so many murders, is that how they would have spoken to me? How did people believe something so blatantly false as 'All right. I'll tell you what I know'?

With the Shaw confession I had crossed a threshold. When Simmons and Jermey began the next round of abuse, I put up a token resistance. They said, 'We know you're in the IRA now, you've confessed to the murder of a soldier.' It made no difference to me now and so I said what they wanted to hear. I told them about arriving in England, about going to Theresa and Errol's, about Southampton. They already had Gerry and Paddy's names from my letters to Gina, and they insisted these were my fellow bombers. I agreed. They wanted other names. I said Father Carolan who ran the hostel at Quex Road was involved. I named Hugh Maguire, Gerry's uncle with whom we had stayed one night after leaving Southampton. They wanted more so I invented names for them, a 'Dermott' who never existed, a 'Marion', equally unreal, an 'Anne', a 'Wilson', a 'Paul'.

Simmons says he asked for 'Paul's' surname. According to his deposition, I answered, 'I don't know. Shall I go on?' To which he claims to have replied, 'Yes, please.'

Yes, *please*? Why did anyone believe this?

I knew nothing of the Guildford bombings except what I had read in the papers so the police had to help me with the details. As with the Shaw confessions, they suggested things and I agreed. The statement was drawn up in this way and I signed it.

When the interview ended I was brought back to my cell, once again hoping that they would now be satisfied. I was still terribly confused, but I had moments of lucidity. I remember thinking that when the police checked out the details of my story they would realize it was utterly fantastic. Father Carolan and Hugh Maguire were known to be hostile to the IRA. Gerry and Paddy had no part in Guildford. Sanity, I thought, somehow would prevail.

Instead, the madness continued. At one point, Jermey entered the cell. He had some news for me, he said. Parliament had passed a new law, the Prevention of Terrorism Act, which, among other things, enabled the police to hold suspects for up to seven days. I had the honour of being the first person detained under the Act. The effect of this news, as I am sure it had been calculated, was to depress me still further. I had been in custody some forty-odd hours (at a guess – my watch had been taken away from me), and already it seemed like an eternity. In the back of my mind I had been thinking that soon it would come to an end; that they would have to let me speak to a solicitor, or charge me, or release me. But the thought of seven days in custody threw me into despair. I thought at first it could not be right, that he was lying, that it was just another of their tricks. But Jermey was smiling and confident, and I believed him.

I was charged with the murder of Caroline Slater on Sunday evening, 1 December and made a brief appearance at Guildford Magistrates' Court the next day. On the way in and out, a blanket was draped over my head. I was aware of the crowd outside the court, and I imagined what the scene must have looked like. On television, I had seen blanket-covered rapists and child murderers being led into court while people outside howled for vengeance. Now I was in the same position. It was the most humiliating experience of my life, and I felt deeply ashamed.

Jermey's news about the Prevention of Terrorism Act had not prepared me for the court hearing. I had expected to be remanded by the magistrates to prison, but was told that the Act enabled the police to take me back into custody. People are now used to the provisions that allow for extended detention, but to me then it came as a terrible shock. I felt as if I had been out of the real world for an eternity, and that profound changes that I could not comprehend had been made while I was away. The thought crossed my mind that Britain had become a police state. It seemed they could do anything they liked with me.

The madness went on. The police arrested Anne and Frank, and claimed they had misled the police when they had arrived at their flat looking for 'Benny Hill'. The police said they had been after me. Anne and Frank tried to explain that 'Benny' was Patrick and that the photograph was of Patrick. They were told they were 'lying Irish bastards' who were going to get what they deserved.

They arrested Paddy and Gerry, Hugh Maguire, his wife Kitty, and Father Carolan. With each arrest the list of suspects lengthened. Paddy's friends were taken in. The police began looking for the Dermott, Marion and Paul I had mentioned in my first statement. Anyone with these Christian names was already in serious trouble. They found a 'Paul', Paul Colman who was unlucky enough to be Irish and a friend of Paddy Armstrong's.

When they could not find people with these names they decided I had tried to cover for them. So they began to put to me the names they wanted to hear. They suggested a woman called Lindberg had been involved. I agreed. At the trial, the prosecution claimed that I had supplied false names in a cunning attempt to mislead the police. It is true I was inventing names to placate them, but I would never have thought of Lindberg; that just was not a name that would have crossed my mind. The names I gave were Irish, the sort of names I was familiar with. During a subsequent interrogation, I am supposed to have told Blake that the 'Marion' was Carole Richardson. But it was the other way around. The material brought to light in 1989 proved that, contrary to what the police said at the trial, I had not mentioned Carole until Blake suggested her name to me.

I had also referred to an older woman as being one of the bombing team at Guildford. After Gerry was arrested the police decided the older woman was his Aunt Annie. Annie Maguire, her husband Patrick and their children, including Francis who was four years old, were taken in. Gerry's father, Giuseppe, who had come over from Belfast to help his son, was also arrested. He was, everyone knew, a mild and honourable man, and in poor health. He was to die in prison.

There were more interviews, more names, more confessions. During one interview, Simmons burst into the room. I thought he was deranged. He screamed at me, 'Who is Mrs Davey? Who the fuck is Mrs Davey, she's got you a fucking mouthpiece.' I was so frightened by his rage that I thought to myself, 'Why did they have to go and tell a solicitor, it's just made them more angry.' Simmons told me that there was no way I was going to see a solicitor.

The madness went on. I admitted to bombing the King's Arms in Woolwich. I was confronted with Gerry and Paddy. Yes, they were the ones, they were all involved. Gerry and Paddy started making statements. Because they knew nothing of the details surrounding the bombings they made things up to placate the interrogating officers. The accounts I had given conflicted with what Gerry said; what Gerry said was at odds with what Paddy told them. Carole gave a different version again. It seems that it did not occur to any of these experienced investigators to pause and ask themselves if they had the right people. Instead, after the different interrogating teams compared notes and saw the discrepancies they determined to have them reconciled. They would burst into the interview room and would scream, 'What you've said isn't what Conlon's saying. Start again and this time it better tally with what Conlon has told us.'

So it would start over again. What colour was the car? Who was Marion? Who went to which pub? Who made the bombs? Where were they made? From time to time a detective would appear at the door and there would be whispered conversations. Then the interrogating officers would say to me, 'Armstrong says it was like this' or 'Conlon says it was like that.' And I would agree. Anything to stop the madness.

With the confessions signed, there remained only one thing for the police to do. Gina was still insisting that I had been with her in Southampton on the night of the Guildford bombings and that I had arrived before tea time. Gina had been released from police custody but was arrested again on Tuesday. She remained in custody overnight but refused to alter her story. The police were determined to break the alibi. Blake came into my cell and told me that unless Gina changed her version of events she would be charged. But that is not how Blake recounted this episode. According to Blake's deposition, he entered my cell that morning and said,

'Good morning, Paul. How are you this morning?'
Hill replied, 'Fine, sir. Have you got Gina here?' I

said, 'Why are you asking that?' Hill replied, 'Can I see her?'

I replied, 'If you are going to say anything else about the job then remember you are still under caution.' I then cautioned him and he replied, 'Look, I want to see Gina. She has nothing to do with the bombings, but I told her to give me an alibi. If I don't tell her to tell the truth she will lie to you and then she'll be in trouble and I don't want that.' I replied, 'I'll see what I can do.'

An absolute invention.

Later that evening, I was taken to see Gina who once again was in the station. She was crying and near hysterical. I said, 'I've signed the statements. Don't be worrying.'

Gina was shocked and said, 'But you weren't there.'

'Just tell them I was there later.'

Gina began to cry and insisted, 'But you weren't there later.'

'Just tell them I was. Say I told you I broke into a shop or something and that's why I was late.'

I was taken away while Gina made another statement in which she said I had not arrived in Southampton until 'about 10.15pm'. She added that the next day, on our way to the Southampton railway station, 'Paul told me that there had been engineering works on the lines and that he would have to change [at] St Denys and get a bus to Eastleigh and get on the train at Eastleigh again.' My alibi, which had already been dented by our earlier confusion over the night the American sailors were in town, now lay in tatters.

They had identified Gina as a weak spot and had continually played on my anxiety about her. They had assured me she would be charged with the bombings. They said that I had got her involved, that I was responsible for ruining her life. She would spend the best part of her life in prison because of me. 'She is sticking to you like shit to a blanket,' was how they put it. I told Gina to change her story not because she was lying, but because to insist on telling the truth was dangerous. I wanted to save her; I thought, perhaps in the macho way of working-class Belfast, that I was being manly in getting

76

her out of trouble. Where I come from men are expected to look after their women, whatever the consequences.

During one interrogation, Simmons burst in, grabbed me by the hair and dragged me along the corridor which was lined with uniformed officers. As he dragged me along he gave me rabbit punches in the back of the head. Some of the officers in the corridor joined in. I was pushed through two swinging fire doors and onto the stairwell. I was pushed down the stairs. Simmons pulled me up by the hair and dragged me to the door of another interview room. The fear was so intense I could hardly feel my legs and was unable to stand. I had no idea what this was leading to or where it would end. The door opened and they brought me inside. They had to support me under the arms. I saw a woman. They said, 'Is this the woman?' I shook my head and they shouted at me, 'Is this the fucking woman?' I said, 'Yes.' It turned out to be Annie Maguire, Gerry's aunt. I had never seen her before. Then they took me out.

I spent seven days in custody. I signed six statements, and confessed to eight murders. On Wednesday, Gerry and I were taken to Guildford Magistrates' Court. We could see crowds of people and journalists from the police car. An old woman was waving a Union Jack, people were shouting hysterically, 'Hang the murderers!' The police draped blankets over our heads, and led us by our handcuffs into the court. We were stumbling like blind men, but the blind have people around them they can trust.

The magistrates remanded Gerry and me to prison; it came as a relief when the gates of HMP Winchester closed behind us.

Chapter Seven

'ONE ON'

On arrival in prison, whether for the first or for the hundredth time, prisoners go to the area called reception. Old hands know the procedure and they wait patiently. At last, the screws call their names. The old hands repeat their antecedents and are then stripped and given a bath. They are escorted from reception to the wing; on the way, they will see prisoners slopping out or scraping muck from the metal dinner trays into huge, heavily encrusted bins. The smell will be of piss and disinfectant; faintly of decaying food. An old hand will follow his escort calmly and mechanically. At the gate of the wing, the escort will hand his prisoner over to the wing prison officers who will unlock the gate and motion the man through. As they do so, the screws will shout, 'One on!' A new prisoner has come to the wing.

Old hands accept this as normal, and over the years, after more than fifty 'ghostings' (sudden transfers between prisons), I came to know the routine better than most. But my first time, after my appearance in Guildford Magistrates' Court, I was new to it (the procedure in Crumlin Prison in

Belfast, where I had spent one night in 1971, was nothing like this) and I kept looking nervously around to try to make sense of this awful place with its smells and squalor. I thought, 'This can't be what it's like for ever, not every day, day-in, day-out.' The thought panicked me but I tried to carry myself with confidence; a confidence I did not in reality possess.

In reception, the screws had given Gerry and me special uniforms known as 'patches'. Patches are usually reserved for prisoners who have attempted to escape or who have escaped and have been recaptured. But in Winchester, a local jail without high security facilities, it was the norm to put in patches Category 'A' men (prisoners whose escape, as the Home Office puts it, would be harmful to the public). The escapees' uniform, made from a heavy, brown denim cloth, takes its name from the large 'patch' of bright yellow material sewn onto the back of the jacket. There is also a broad stripe in the same colour that runs from shoulder to ankle. They gave us a blue-striped shirt each (mine was many sizes too big), a vest and underpants that would have fitted Queen Victoria. The shoes were plastic and had elastic sides. Each shoe had a hole punched through it so that pairs could be tied together. They were, I noted with amusement, made by Bata – the firm I had worked for in Oxford Street; but I had never seen shoes like these on our shelves. To complete the kit was a pair of slippers – which smelled as if someone had vomited in them – and a pair of grey woollen socks circled at the top by a yellow band.

It was odd wearing prison clothing for the first time. Everything fitted so badly; strange smells oozed from the fabric. And then there were the yellow patches; I thought of Jewish prisoners in Nazi Germany. The prison had identified us, picked us out – Gerry and me – and set us apart from the general population, who mostly wore their own clothes (as remands) or ordinary uniforms. As we walked through the prison to get to the wing, I felt self-conscious, as if Gerry and I were a different and especially loathsome kind of prisoner.

We were taken to the basement, which had been converted into a special security unit – known as C1 – and placed in separate cells. My cell was dank, cold and infested with mice. The window was high, but when I got up to it I saw that it was at ground level. The walls were freezing to the touch and possessed something that made me want to shiver when I put my palm against them; it was something like that quality that belongs to caves; it tells you that sun does not reach here. It was so cold; what heating there was came from a ventilation shaft in the wall and was useless. As the winter hardened, broad, glistening bands, like slimy trails left by giant snails, appeared on the walls which, as it became wetter, gathered volume and speed until they turned into rivulets. The high ceiling made the space seem vast and colder still. All down through the years, as I was moved from prison to prison and got to know many different kinds of cells, I grew to prefer the smaller variety with their lower ceilings; in these I could feel almost cosy.

In the cell there was a bed with a horse-hair mattress, stained and lumpy and leaking its coarse insides. There was a chair and a small table, a plastic water jug and a pisspot. The utensils – mug, plate, bowl, knife, fork, spoon – were all of plastic and took some getting used to; the knives in particular, for they cut nothing. However, as I was soon to discover, that rarely mattered. Prison food is cooked and stewed until it is a pulpy, tasteless, formless and nutritionless mess. Occasionally, very occasionally, they served up something sinewy, like chicken, but so tough that the plastic knives could not handle it and would snap as if their patience had given out.

Prisoners used to speculate endlessly about the tea: *what* did they put in the tea? Some said bromide, but I do not know. On the surface there used to be something resembling a fine slick of oil. I used to hold my mug up to the light and look at the oily purples, mauves and blues. I would trace my finger through the grease after emptying the mug; it reminded me of an unwashed pot in which a chicken had been broiled. From then on, I drank only water with my meals – a habit that was to endure for fifteen years.

During my first few days in Winchester, I ate everything I could. The time in police custody, during which I had been given very little, made me temporarily indifferent to the taste and quality of prison food. By the time I had satisfied my hunger and was beginning to take notice of what I was eating, Gina had started to come on visits, and she brought me food almost every day. I was also able to supplement the prison diet with 'canteen' – goods purchased from the prison canteen with money left in by family and friends. Remand prisoners in those days had access to untold riches in this respect. A couple of years ago, however, the Home Office stopped the practice with blithe assurances about the quality of prison food. Whoever made that decision had clearly never spent a day in prison sampling the delights on offer.

As a new prisoner, I knew nothing of the rules and I knew nothing of how to conduct myself. Now I think back on the things I did, I shiver at my naivety. As Cat. 'A's we were not allowed out of the special security unit to collect our food. Instead, the trays were brought to us by orderlies from the kitchens two wings away. What happened to the food on its journey? In Bristol prison, after being sentenced, I had trays of food brought to me in the same manner. By then I was more on guard, alert to the ways of prison; when I inspected the food, I saw that it was sauced with spittle and yellow phlegm. By then, too, I had learned that it was not uncommon for screws to urinate in prisoners' tea. What had I eaten and drunk in Winchester in those first few days when I had bolted down everything?

The screws in Winchester were not, by and large, violent towards us. But they were far from friendly. On arrival we tried to tell them we were innocent, but they laughed at us. After that, I did not waste my breath. Their reaction had made me feel pathetic, that I had whined. They had heard it all before and did not want to hear it from us.

But if their manner was rough, nevertheless I was assaulted only once during my time there (about three and a half months), after an argument over a radio. They had, one night, shouted into my cell to turn the radio down. I turned it down. They came back a little later and told me to turn it down more. It was not that loud so I ignored them. They came in, hit me in the face and turned down the radio. But on the whole the atmosphere was not violent. In my travels around the country's prison system I was to return, years later, to Winchester. By then, I had had many problems with the authorities in different jails, but in Winchester I rarely encountered trouble. The last time I was there was in July 1988 and I met an AG (Assistant Governor) who had been a Chief (Chief Prison Officer) when I had first arrived in December 1974. Back then, I had had an argument with him during which he had shouted, 'You might be innocent Hill but you can't fight the prison system. Better men than you have taken on the system and lost!' I replied, 'I'm not fighting the prison system. I'm fucking basically asking for my rights.' After we had exchanged these words the Chief went off and spoke to the screws on the wing and sorted out the problem.

On another occasion, I was returned to Winchester to do fifty-six days in the strip cell. Strip cells are hard places and so Winchester was no holiday camp, but if you did not go out of your way to look for trouble they did not give it to you. For me and Gerry, newcomers to the world of prison and its strange rules and demands, it was probably as good a place as any to start.

We had arrived in the afternoon, and by the time we had been processed in reception and got to our cells it was early evening. The screws explained something of the regime, what the different utensils were for, how and when to slop out and so on. I made my bed and got into it. It was early, but I was very tired. I felt uncomfortable and cold as I lay there gazing at the high ceiling. The screws turned out the light in the cell, I think at 9pm, and a red light came on. This was almost as bright as the ordinary light. At first I thought there had been a mistake, that the screws had flicked the wrong switch, but soon I realized that they had not. It was so bright. I thought, 'Is this what I am going to have to put up with every night?'

That night was the first chance I had to go over in my mind what had happened to me. 'As soon as I can get to a lawyer,' I thought to myself, 'this can all be cleared up.' Part of my thinking during the interrogations had been that if I confessed, everything could be explained later, in a calm atmosphere. I had confessed to escape the police, trusting that later, with the support of a lawyer who would understand, everything would be put right. The more I went over things in my mind the more convinced I became that it could not possibly stand up in court: no lawyer, no judge, no jury, *no one* in their right mind would believe it. I took comfort from the fact that this was happening in England, away from the bigotry and sectarianism of Northern Ireland. I did not trust Northern Irish courts (which, had recently dispensed with juries), and I had a high opinion of British standards of justice.

Based on what? The sudden thought was too uncomfortable and I did not let it take hold. What I failed to grasp was that the racism which runs through British society, and counts among its victims Irish as well as black people, would reach into and touch the courts. I failed to understand that there were interests and reputations at stake, that these needed us to be convicted.

I started to worry about Gina. At one point during the interrogations in Guildford, I had pleaded with her to go home, meaning *home* – Belfast – so that she would be out of harm's way. And when I realized that she had not gone, that the police had her in the station, I signed to try to get her out of trouble. But when I began to think about it rationally I realized that the police could do whatever they wanted with her, that my signature would not be enough to save her. They could still charge her. Where was she? In prison? The thought was too terrible to pursue and I shut it out of my mind.

Thoughts of Gina led on to my mother; I knew she would be hysterical. The more I thought about Gina and my family the more worried I became. I discovered then, on my first night in prison, that you can think so much about things that you can be physically hurt: a pain took hold of my stomach and squeezed the worries out of my mind. In later years, when worries threatened to suffocate me, I would get up and run on the spot or do step-ups. Or I would do yoga, which I had taken up, as did many prisoners, in an effort to find a way out of the tension: I would concentrate on a spot on the wall until every sound and sight of man in this world was gone. Or, in smaller cells, I would press my back against one wall and my feet against the other, and concentrate on not falling. There was no room in my mind for anything else: all I could think about was not falling, so much so that Gina and my mother's insistent pleas to be let in were lost on me.

Although I was not very religious, I did say prayers. I said an Our Father, three Hail Marys and an Act of Contrition. I do not know why I did this. It was something that I had done as a child; my granny would come to my bedside and we would say the prayers together. It was comforting to repeat them, a reminder of childhood and the loving and protective adults who surrounded me and who, with the simple wave of a hand, could chase away even the most frightening monsters and bogeymen. But after a while, the images of my family created by my prayers changed before me: I did not see my granny as she was beside my bed, but as an old woman listening to someone tell her what had happened to me. Her face became sad; the thoughts were too painful.

Sleep came to relieve me.

My first night in prison went quickly. I was exhausted. Even the red light could not keep me awake. I fell into a deep, dreamless sleep.

The next morning was odd. The night had been so restful that I woke up, for the first time in a week, without feelings of fear or foreboding. At first I did not know where I was. But then the memory of the police stations, the interrogations and the confessions rushed up and hit me like a fist.

I can understand people who crack in prison. They simply cannot go on, and so they knot a sheet and hang themselves from the window; it is a slow death, by strangulation. Sometimes, when they go to cut the body down, they find the dead man's toes a fraction off the ground. There are people who cannot understand what drives people to take their own lives, to submit to death in this gurgling, choking way when all they have to do is stretch out a foot to save themselves. But I can. Although during even the bleakest days I spent in prison I never considered harming myself, I could understand why there were people who did. On waking that first morning, Thursday, I felt almost overwhelmed by depression.

But I got up and tried to collect my thoughts, to think rationally. The more I thought the more I experienced feelings of hope.

At first, Gerry and I were the security unit's only inmates. We slopped out and had breakfast. Later, we were taken separately to be photographed. The screws keep one set of photographs with the prisoner's main file; the other, for Category 'A' prisoners, is put into a black, passport-sized book known as the 'A' Book (inside, a Category 'A' prisoner is often referred to as 'being on the book'; decategorization from 'A' to a lower status, 'B' to 'F', is called 'being taken off the book'). The book follows the 'A' man everywhere. Whenever the prisoner leaves the wing – for a visit, to chapel, to court – a summary is entered into the book as well as the time of departure and return.

Later that day, Gerry and I were exercised together for about half an hour. It was the first proper chance we had to talk things over and discuss what had happened. Gerry looked pale and drawn and very rough, and I suppose I must have looked the same. It came as no surprise to learn that in Guildford he had received the same treatment I had. He confirmed that he had signed statements, but instead of depressing me still more this gave me hope. I did not see the statements as evidence of guilt; the more of these fantastic stories the police collected, the more incredible the whole thing would be. We compared what each of us had said, and it quickly became apparent that our statements conflicted on nearly every point: we had described the same events, in which we were supposed to have participated, in entirely different ways.

Apart from trying to sort out our case, we also had to become used to the prison. Gerry and I tried to get our bearings and we pointed out the different buildings and tried to guess what they were. Our special security unit was separate from the main prison so there was no one we could ask about these things. The other prisoners knew who we were and they watched us from their cell windows. As we walked around the exercise yard in our yellow patches under their gaze, I felt more conspicuous than ever. Some of the prisoners shouted abuse at us, shouting 'You murdering Irish bastards!'

On the Friday we got company. Giuseppe, Gerry's father, arrived with Paddy Armstrong and three other 'conspirators': Paul Colman, Sean McGuinness and Brian Anderson. I also learned that Carole Richardson and Annie Maguire had been charged with Guildford. Paddy looked terrible. He was dishevelled, in bits, with a dirty growth of beard. His long, fine hair hung lank and greasy.

To begin with, there was some bad feeling about the fact that we had named names. Paul, Brian and Sean blamed Paddy for having named them; I had named Gerry and Paddy; they had named me. We could all blame each other and there was part of us that did. People, especially when they are under stress, tend to blame those nearest to hand. But, when tempers cooled, we stopped blaming each other: the simple fact was that we had collapsed in front of policemen who had brutalized us. Was that our fault? Or theirs?

The Guildford Four were originally the Guildford Eight: Gerry, myself, Paddy, Carole, Annie Maguire, Paul Colman, Brian Anderson and Sean McGuinness. I had seen Paul Colman in the pubs around Kilburn but had never spoken to him. I had never even seen or spoken to Brian or Sean. These lads had been arrested at addresses in Cricklewood and Kilburn (Rondu Road and Algernon Road), and had been friends of Paddy's. After their arrests Christopher Rowe, the Assistant Chief Constable of Surrey, told the *Daily Mail* that the police had broken up 'a tightly knit group of terrorists'. There was nothing at all to link them to any offence: no explosives, no guns, no forensic evidence, no identification evidence. They had been arrested and charged simply because they were Irish and were linked to Paddy, and through Paddy to Gerry and me. Crucially, they had made no statements. By the time they had been arrested, the police probably believed they had enough evidence to convict everyone. Paul, Brian and Sean did not have to be squeezed for confessions and, perhaps because they had reserves we did not possess, they were able to hold out.

Another set of arrests had centred around Annie Maguire and her family who also lived in North London. Annie, her husband Patrick, her sons Vincent and Patrick (who were in their early teens), Gerry's father Giuseppe (who had come over to England from Belfast to help his son), Sean Smyth (Annie's brother) and Patrick O'Neill (a neighbour of the Maguires) were taken in and at various stages charged with possession of explosives, even though no explosives had been found. They became known as the Maguire Seven and the charges were based on the results of the now discredited Thin Layer Chromatography (TLC) test for the presence of explosives. Sean Mullin, another inhabitant of the house in Rondu Road, who I also did not know, was charged with possession of explosives, again without any explosives being found.

It seemed to us the police had gone completely mad. They had charged people who, even in their wildest flights of fantasy, they could never have believed were in the IRA.

Giuseppe was a very sick man, suffering from tuberculosis and pulmonary fibrosis. Annie Maguire had five children and had no time for Republicanism. In Durham prison, after she was sentenced, she kept a large portrait of the Queen on her wall, and, in later years, she rejected the help of politicians she considered too 'left wing'. Carole Richardson was English and had tried to join the WRACs. Paddy was nervous all the time; it was hard to imagine him crossing the road by himself never mind planting a bomb. When he and Carole had gone hitch-hiking around the south of England the previous summer, they had got into an argument with a man in a phonebox and called the police – they *called the police* when they were supposed to be part of a 'tightly knit group of terrorists'. All Gerry cared about was backing horses and finding the money to go on backing them. A routine police check at Holyhead after he left the hostel in Quex Road to return home came up with 'no trace, not wanted'.

Everything about us contradicted the police claim that we belonged to the IRA. Just how much we fell short of matching the profile of IRA men in England comes from looking at the members of the active service unit. After the arrests of Joe O'Connell, Harry Duggan, Eddie Butler and Hugh Doherty at Balcombe Street in December 1975, the police discovered that the men had been leading lives of total clandestinity: they rented flats under false names; hired cars using stolen papers; and had large sums of money sent to them at regular intervals. Harry Duggan had even faked his own death to facilitate his disappearance from Ireland.

By contrast, we all lived under our own names and kept in regular contact with our families at home. We had no false papers. Even if we had had the money to hire a car, we did not know how to drive (in spite of having confessed to driving to Guildford to plant the bombs). We were always broke or on the point of it. Paddy never had a penny; Gerry was occasionally flush after a win on the horses but was usually penniless; and I had only what I earned on the sites and drew from the Labour Exchange, and that I spent, much to Gina's dislike, on having a good time at the weekends.

The more we talked, the more laughable we considered the case against us. Our confessions were riddled with inconsistencies. In the trial, Sir Michael Havers, who appeared for the

Crown, made the novel claim that we had undergone IRA anti-interrogation training and that the contradictions were part of a cunning plot to mislead the police. But if we had undergone counter-interrogation training, why bother to confess at all when silence, in the absence of any other evidence, would have resulted in freedom?

But the truth was that we could not have made consistent statements because we knew nothing about the bombings. Under interrogation, Gerry and Paddy, like myself, had followed the line of least resistance, agreeing to whatever the police put to them, altering earlier confessions to fit whatever new 'information' the police had come up with from another interrogation. But no amount of alterations could have made the confessions consistent. Later, the defence were to count more than 150 discrepancies in our statements. I had, for example, said we had driven to Guildford in a yellow Granada. Gerry said it was a dark, four-door saloon; Carole a light-coloured Ford Anglia; Paddy a grey Capri. Who drove? Who made the bombs? Who planted them? How many people were in the bombing teams? We had all given different and irreconcilable answers. Carole had admitted to bombing both the Seven Stars and the Horse and Groom – physically impossible, since it would have required being in two places at once. On every detail there was disagreement.

During my time in Guildford Police Station, the police had driven me around various parts of London in order to identify bomb factories. Of course, no bomb factories were uncovered. In Brixton, during one trip, I pointed out at random a block of flats. The police raided it and found nothing. Another block of flats I identified turned out to be the accommodation of prison officers from Brixton. The police claimed later that I had pointed out the house in Rondu Road, North London, where Paddy, Brian and Sean had lived. This is completely untrue. I had never been to Rondu Road. I did not know of its existence and could not have shown it to the police. It seems probable that the police were led to Rondu Road by watching Paddy who came to their attention after they had found his name in my letters to Gina. They alleged that I had pointed out Rondu Road to try to prove a link between me and the inhabitants of the house.

On our weekly remands to the magistrates' court, which were conducted amid strict security, we appeared together in the dock. Of the fourteen people charged – eight for Guildford, including Annie Maguire, and six others connected with Annie's explosives charge – I knew only Gerry. I had spoken to Paddy briefly once or twice, to Carole possibly once; I had never seen Annie before I was brought into her interrogation room in Guildford. How could we be a closely knit terrorist cell? As we stood in the dock Paddy used to shake from fear.

The weekly remands were breaks in an otherwise dull prison routine. We were allowed to shower once every seven days, and our laundry – towels, sheets, underwear – was changed every two to three weeks. Apart from slop out, they unlocked us for an hour's exercise a day (weather permitting) and, Monday to Saturday, for a fifteen-minute visit. To pass the days, I read or listened to the radio. I was fortunate in that Gina was living nearby, with her sister in Southampton, and came every day to the prison to visit me. We were separated by a glass partition, and the visits, though welcome, were often awkward affairs, made more uneasy by the four prison officers, the dog-handler and his animal who surrounded us and listened to our every word.

On the way to the visiting area, I had to pass through two wings. Prisons are noisy places: doors slamming; keys jangling; iron gates hitting their jambs; men calling one to another in swearing, violent voices. But when I came through the wing all sound was crushed. The prisoners glared at me and muttered threats. I tried, and I think I succeeded, in keeping up a brave front, but inside I was terrified. On the first visit, the screw had said, 'Whatever you do, stick close by me.' I wondered why he was telling me this. As we approached the visiting area, he handed me over to another screw, saying, 'Keep an eye on this one – they're liable to attack him.' It did not set me up for the visit. I would have to go in and pretend to Gina that everything was fine, no problem.

Still, it was at least some contact with the outside world. Paddy did not get visits. He saw Carole only on our weekly remands for a few moments. (Carole was being held with Annie Maguire in Brixton, a prison for men, in 'D' Wing, the top landing of which had been cleared out for the two women.) Paddy's family, from Divis Flats in Belfast, had no money and could not come over to see him.

The time passed slowly. During our exercise periods, we would go over and over the evidence. New discrepancies would surface, each one we thought sufficient in itself to damn the whole case against us. Outside, the active service unit continued its campaign of bombings and shootings in London. Surely, we felt, the police would have to admit they had the wrong people.

Our hopes received a boost early in February when the charges against Brian Anderson, Paul Colman and Sean McGuinness were suddenly dropped. Three weeks later, on 24 February, Annie Maguire was also cleared of murder and was released, although she was immediately rearrested and charged with possession of explosives. Sean Mullin, who had also been charged with possession of explosives, had the charges against him dismissed. It seemed the case was collapsing.

Meanwhile, through our lawyers, we were learning something of the complexities of the legal system. My lawyer was David Melton, who was not actually a qualified solicitor but a solicitor's clerk. Melton had been contacted after Errol and Theresa went to the National Council for Civil Liberties following my arrest and asked for the name of a law firm in Southampton. I had first seen David Melton in Guildford Police Station after I had made my first admissions. He had seemed more frightened than me, very much overawed by what was going on around us. He kept his head down and gave me a legal aid form to sign before hurrying away. I saw him again, for less than a minute, during my appearance in the magistrates' court on Monday, 2 December. He told me he would see me when I was remanded to prison which, I reflected bitterly, was not going to be of much help as I had just been remanded back into police custody. He had been told, I assume, that he would not be allowed to be present during the interrogations.

I was anxious for Melton to explain how the whole thing worked. How long can they keep us? When would we be put on trial?

'First,' he explained, 'the police must complete their

inquiries. When they have gathered their evidence they will make a report to the Director of Public Prosecutions – a lawyer who is also a civil servant – and he will decide whether there is sufficient evidence to warrant continuing with the case. If he says yes, the police and the Director's office will select from the material gathered by the investigating officers what they wish to put before a court. This material will be served on the defence in the form of "statements of witnesses".'

'Then do we get a trial?'

'Not immediately or even necessarily. The prosecution, you'll also hear it called the Crown, is required to put its evidence before magistrates at a committal hearing. This will consist of its "statements of witnesses", sometimes called "depositions", and other evidence it will rely on to prove its case in the trial: forensic evidence and so forth. It is then, in theory, up to the magistrates to decide whether there is a case to answer; that is, whether the prosecution have shown that they have a case against you.

'If the magistrates decide that there is a case to answer, the accused are then sent, or committed, for trial. In the trial, the Crown – prosecution, if you like – will be represented by at least two barristers, or counsel, a senior counsel and one or more juniors. In serious cases like this, you, too, will be represented by two barristers – paid for, of course, from the Legal Aid Fund.

'Anyway, first steps first. We have to see what they have in the witnesses' statements.'

What I did not realize was that the Crown does not hand over all the statements of witnesses. Those it does not consider helpful to its case it retains in a bundle (known as 'non-material statements'). It was to emerge, many years later, that the Crown withheld crucial evidence that supported our case. But in 1975 we were not to know that.

I do not think any of us were greatly impressed by our legal representatives. I was not convinced Melton believed in my innocence. Like most people, he probably found it hard to accept that the police had behaved in the way we were claiming they had. Like me, Gerry did not have a fully qualified solicitor but a clerk, David Walsh. Paddy had as his solicitor Alastair Logan, who was to follow the case through to the end. But in 1974 Logan was not the experienced criminal lawyer he now is. His involvement in the case came about simply because he was the duty solicitor at Guildford when Paddy was brought in. At best, we were represented by people with little experience of this kind of case.

During the early visits, Melton and I went over the details of my background: where I had grown up, my reasons for being in England, what I had done since I had arrived. We also talked about my alibis for Guildford and Woolwich. Although Gina had been up to see me in Winchester, we had not discussed the alibis because the prison authorities told us the visit would be stopped immediately if we mentioned the case. This added a surreal element to our visits: it was as if we had to pretend that the case did not exist – yet here I was in prison facing charges of multiple murder.

Gina had, of course, spoken to Melton about the alibis, and I did my best to give him as many details as I could; but inevitably I made mistakes. The events I was trying to recall had occurred in October and November – several weeks earlier – and I had no way of checking whether what I remembered was accurate. I was convinced that on 5 October, as I was leaving Southampton railway station, I had seen a man and a boy wearing blue and claret football scarves and bobble hats. I was certain there must have been a football match in or around Southampton. Melton got a fixture list and we went through it together, but there was no match played in Southampton that day. Similarly, on the night of the King's Arms bombing in Woolwich, 7 November, I was sure I had watched a boxing match on television. However, the television schedules showed that no boxing match had been screened. Yet I was so certain, and I would get angry if contradicted. Prison takes a heavy toll on memory and the sense of proportion.

I emphasized to Melton that I had led a normal, if unsettled, life in England. I had not assumed an alias; I had not tried to avoid the police. I told him about the argument with the taxi driver in Southampton and being taken to Shirley Road Police Station where the desk sergeant had entered my name and address in the station log, and then going in a police car to Cathy and Malcolm's at Stainer Close. I told him that while I was staying at Anne and Frank's I had been seen by a doctor and that I had given him my correct name and details. I wrote home to my family with details of where I was staying. I worked almost every day I was in England, and I signed on in my own name at each site. If I had wanted to avoid the police the very least I would have done would have been to steer clear of the Labour Exchange. Yet I signed on there in my real name.

Around the beginning of March, there was great excitement when we received the prosecution statements. At last we could piece together exactly what the police were saying about us. As we had suspected, their case rested entirely on the confessions made by myself, Gerry, Paddy and Carole. Carole had been on several identification parades and no one had picked her out, and there was no other identification evidence. There was no forensic evidence to link us to the offences and, contrary to what the police had told me in Guildford, no traces of explosive substances on any of our clothing or hands. The police had nothing to corroborate our confessions. I thought, 'People just do not get convicted on this kind of evidence.'

But I was being naive, and making the mistake of thinking that the trial would be conducted fairly. The press had been quick off the mark and was busy doing its bit to whip up feeling against us. Throughout our years in prison, newspapers ran stories against us. One had it that I had been visited in Winchester by Eddie Gallagher, a leading IRA man who had, just before the article appeared, been captured in the Republic after kidnapping a Dutch businessman near Limerick. The story was a complete fabrication. As a Category 'A' prisoner, any visitor of mine needed special permission from the Home Office which was granted only after Special Branch officers had interviewed and approved the proposed visitor. In addition, my Cat. 'A' book would have shown that during the whole time I was in Winchester I did not have a single male visitor. In spite of this, the Home Office announced, in reply to the article, that it would be tightening security in the prison.

The press, it was already clear, would not be doing much to see that justice was dispensed fairly. As it was to turn out, during the trial reporters repeated without any kind of scrutiny every titbit thrown to them by the police. These included different police accounts of how I had become a suspect. *The Times* published an article saying that a Surrey detective, Detective Inspector Brian Richardson, had gone to Belfast where he met an informer in a bar. Richardson, *The Times* said, handed over £350 in used one pound notes in return for my name. Richardson did not, in fact, go to Belfast, never met an informer, never passed over the fictitious £350. But *The Times* never bothered to correct its story. Other newspapers, including the *Daily Telegraph*, ran a story claiming that an officer in military intelligence had recognized me from a photofit that was circulated after the Guildford bombings. They neglected to say that the photofit was that of a female victim and had had to be withdrawn once the mistake had been spotted.

The issue of how I came to be a suspect has never satisfactorily been explained. As late as 1987, Douglas Hurd, then Home Secretary, claimed that Army intelligence knew as early as August 1974 that I had travelled to England to carry out bombings. Yet I was living openly between arriving in England that summer and my arrest at the end of November. If it was known that I was a bomber, why was I not put under surveillance?

All of these allegations, so credulously repeated by the media, confused the issue and misled many people, even those sympathetic to our case. The references to Army intelligence and informers encouraged people to think that there was no smoke without fire. The most obvious lies and implausible stories spewed out by the disinformation machine were slavishly followed by court correspondents who never bothered to check their facts.

The simple truth is that, following the Guildford bombings, scores of Irish people were arrested as suspects. They were picked up, held and questioned while the police made investigations into their background and associations. One of these suspects was my sister Elizabeth who had come over to England with Gina, myself and Joe Kane. She was arrested on a march in Coventry on 21 November. Two days later, the police came to Anne and Frank's, and Theresa and Errol's in search of 'Benny' Hill.

It is highly likely that these two events were connected. After Elizabeth was arrested (she was released without charge), the police would have discovered that her brother Patrick ('Benny') was wanted after having absconded from training school in Belfast. Accordingly, they went to Anne and Frank's and to the addresses of other relatives in England to look for Patrick. But they would also have been aware that Elizabeth had entered England in August with me – a Special Branch record exists to show we were, as part of a routine security check, stopped at Heysham, searched and questioned before being allowed to go on our way. After Liz's arrest, the police were alerted to my presence. They would also glean from their files that in 1971 I had been arrested in Belfast and interrogated in Palace Barracks. I, therefore, become a suspect. This is an entirely logical and straightforward explanation of how I came to be arrested, but one that lacks the sinister connotations and intriguing associations with military intelligence and informers: it lacked the ingredients of what reporters like to call 'a good tale', and was rejected for more fanciful speculations in which my past could be presented as murky. Such was the density of these smoke screens that even our supporters were blinded. Grant McKee and Ros Franey wrote in *Time Bomb*, their book on the case published in 1988, 'Paul Hill – his motivation and the truth surrounding his exploits – remains a mystery.'

But the worst miscalculation we made in thinking that the charges against us would not stand up was that to refute the allegations of the Crown we would have to make allegations of our own against the police. This did not mean attacking one or two junior policemen. Allegations of assault, improper conduct and fabrication of evidence would have to be made against several officers: and the clear implication would have to be that senior officers connived in the wrong-doing. As Sir Michael Havers for the Crown was to put it in the trial, if what we were saying was true, then 'a really gigantic conspiracy', involving senior officers from Surrey and the Metropolitan Police Bomb Squad, must have taken place.

The enormity of the challenge of proving this 'really gigantic conspiracy' was not lost on our solicitors, and it contributed, no doubt, to the lack of conviction they exhibited when going over the case with us. Who was going to believe us against the police? Yet, strangely, I do not remember, during the early stages of our remand at least, being at all deterred by the odds against us, so convinced was I that the truth would come out.

The committal proceedings were undramatic. They began on St Patrick's Day, 17 March 1975, and took place in Guildford. There was very heavy security, which caused me to laugh: there were policemen with sniper rifles and guns; sniffer dogs checked people going in and out of the building. *And all for us?* Paddy was trembling so much he could barely stand up. Our lawyers had already made it clear that we would be sent for trial, so there was nothing to be gained in challenging the police evidence. This, I later discovered, is standard practice. Magistrates, who are at this stage meant to scrutinize and question the evidence to decide whether there is a case to answer, show extreme reluctance to dismiss cases and do little more than rubber stamp the process. The police evidence was read out by Michael Hill, who was to be the junior Crown counsel in our trial (with Sir Michael Havers leading). It was hard to sit and listen to the lies being read out, and once or twice there were interruptions from the dock. Gerry in particular had some things to say about his so-called confessions and the way in which they had been extracted.

After committal, we were taken to Brixton prison and Carole was moved to Risley Remand Centre. For us, Brixton was a big improvement on Winchester. We were in a special security unit – 'A' Segregation, known more commonly as 'A' Seg. It was clean, bright and for the first time since our arrest we were able to associate together for a couple of hours a day, as well as take exercise in the yard.

At first, the other prisoners were a bit stand-offish, but they soon came to accept us and accept that we were innocent. It was Gerry's father, Giuseppe, who persuaded the other prisoners that we were falsely charged. He did this not by lecturing them; it was just the way he was. He was a kind and gentle man, a likeable person who mixed easily. He was also terribly ill. The other prisoners were mostly armed robbers from London, career criminals who took big risks for big rewards, and they had the sense to see that Giuseppe was not the kind of person who would be involved in anything illegal. It quickly became established that we were innocent.

I began to make friends among the prisoners. One man

who made an impression on me was an East European who was in for murder. On his arm he had a faded blue tattoo of a number. It turned out that he was a former concentration camp inmate. He rarely talked about his time in the camps, but when he did I used to think that it was sad that after being through so much that he had ended up here. 'Wherever you are,' I thought, 'someone has been through something worse.'

Many people in England have Irish connections. They talk like Cockneys, Geordies or Brummies but they have Irish names and parents or grandparents who speak with brogues. In prison, these men were usually friendly towards us. I got on well with a lad called Pat from Canvey Island. Years later, in Canterbury, I met his brother Sean, who was a very rebellious prisoner. One evening in Canterbury, Sean appeared at the observation slit in my door and passed through some tobacco, but a screw came along and chased him before I could properly thank him. That night I could hear the urgent voices of prisoners passing news to each other from window to window. Someone, they were saying, had been dragged down to the block and the screws were coming to take him to the strip cell. Prisoners banged their doors in protest, and that night a sad, impotent clamour echoed through the wing.

The next day a cleaner came to my door to tell me that Sean was dead. He had apparently hanged himself in the block. I could hardly take it in: only hours before he had come to my door to give me tobacco. It is a shock to be reminded that a life can go so quickly.

In the event, I was not to remain in Brixton long. As the weeks passed, I had become more sceptical about our chances of receiving a fair trial. I could read between the lines of what Melton was telling me. I was becoming aware of what our defence implied: that senior officers were involved in a huge conspiracy to pervert the course of justice. But my views would alternate: there were times when I somehow felt that no matter how much they loaded the dice against us, we would still have to win. But even then, after more than four months in prison, I was unprepared for the lengths to which they would go.

Chapter Eight

'I NEVER MET IT SO EASY'

A tunnel runs below Crumlin Road Prison to the courthouse across the road. It is a dungeon tunnel, a fat and rank prison intestine. It carries the thick, cast-iron hot-water pipes of the prison's heating system, and the humidity is appalling. But the rats do not mind: they can be seen, evilly hump-backed, scurrying out of the way before the tunnel's human traffic; for it is through the tunnel that screws lead handcuffed prisoners from the jail to the court. To appear at their most presentable, the men shower and shave and put on their best clothes; by the time they emerge from the tunnel, jackets and sweaters feel oppressively heavy, and shirts are sticky with sweat that is turning cold. In this tunnel I realized someone was playing a trick on me.

I had been in Brixton for about a month when several screws appeared and told me to pack my kit. They took me down to reception and handed me over to police custody. I was flown in a Royal Air Force plane to Belfast and brought to Crumlin Road Prison where Detective Chief Inspector Albert Cunningham and Detective Constable John McCaul, my RUC interrogators at Guildford, arrived to see me. The meeting, on 15 April, was brief – they were there to charge me with the murder of Brian Shaw, the former soldier whose body was found in Arundel Street on 20 July, 1974. The charges were put to me and to each of them I replied 'not guilty'.

It was in the tunnel, on my way to the court to stand trial for the Shaw murder, that the full extent of the Crown's cynicism dawned on me. It was a clever move. Their aim was to brand me an IRA man before I went on trial for Guildford and Woolwich, and it worked better than they could have imagined. Not only did the press in England point out that I had been charged, further prejudicing the already meagre chances of a fair trial, but subsequently, during the long campaign to clear our names, the Shaw conviction was used repeatedly to blacken me. People who believed we did not bomb Guildford and Woolwich nevertheless used to wonder about my conviction for Shaw. In his influential book, *Trial and Error*, published in 1986, Robert Kee goes as far as to say, 'Hill today admits that he had something to do with Shaw's kidnapping.' But this is untrue. Kee never spoke to me, and I always denied the Shaw murder with as much vehemence as I did Guildford and Woolwich. What Kee and others failed to recognize was that the evidence which convicted the four of us on the bombing charges was exactly the same as the evidence against me on Shaw: an uncorroborated confession extracted in Guildford Police Station. The Guildford confessions have now been shown to be utterly false; the Shaw confession, equally false, was taken in the same way, at the same time, in the same circumstances. But it is testimony to the success of the authorities' tactic that so many of our supporters were prepared to believe for so long that I had been involved in Shaw's death.

Brian Shaw had served in the Royal Green Jackets and had been on several tours of duty in Northern Ireland. In May 1974, he bought himself out of the Army and decided to settle in Belfast where he married a local girl. Soon after the wedding, he bumped into another ex-service man, Hector Young, a Catholic, who at that time was living on the Antrim Road. Young, who appeared to have no family, was not known in West Belfast. He worked as a tarmac layer, a job usually associated in Belfast with tinkers.

Shaw and Young went for a drink in Mooney's and then on to the Unicorn. Both bars were in the city centre and would have been safe for Shaw, as an English ex-serviceman. Shaw, according to what Young later told the police, wanted to go to a bar on the Falls and they took a taxi the short distance from the Unicorn to the Divis Flats, where they went to the Glengeen Bar. This was a very odd choice, for the Glengeen, unlike Mooney's and the Unicorn, was not safe for Shaw. The Divis Flats was strongly pro-Republican and the people suspicious of any strangers, much more so if one of them was English. After they had had a few drinks, someone overheard Shaw's English accent and remarked on it. A little later, a number of men came into the bar and took Shaw out. Young told the police he saw him being led from the bar but did not know the people who took him and did not know what they were going to do with him. Young went on his way but Shaw was brought to a derelict house in nearby Arundel Street, where he was questioned, beaten and then shot. An Army foot patrol later discovered his body.

The IRA claimed Shaw had been found with an automatic pistol of the kind issued to undercover agents during that period, as well as incriminating documents, and that they had shot him as a spy. The authorities, following their usual practice, denied the IRA's claim. Some days later, Young was abducted from a city centre bar by a group of men and taken away to be searched and questioned. Apparently, nothing incriminating was found, but a hood was placed over his head and he was put into a car. At this stage, Young must have thought that he was about to be assassinated. However, strangely, the car came to a sudden halt at the bottom of Broadway where there was a permanent Army checkpoint. Young was thrown from the car and taken into custody and immediately confessed to complicity in Shaw's murder. The car, meanwhile, had sped off.

The prosecution case was that Young had been picked up by the IRA. However, the circumstances of his abduction seem at odds with this theory. It would have been unusual for the IRA to attempt to pick him up in a bar in the city centre, which was always heavily patrolled. But, most tellingly, the IRA would never have dumped him at a heavily fortified Army checkpoint where they would have risked being shot. The affair was odd and has never been satisfactorily explained. One rumour was that Young had been kidnapped by one of the many murky Army under-cover units at work during that time – possibly the Military Reaction Force.

Shaw's murder was discussed in the district for a day or so after news of it got around; and then it was forgotten. It was just one more killing at a time when people lived day-in, day-out with violent death. By the end of July 1974, Young had been charged with the murder and remanded to Crumlin Road Prison; the charge was based on his admission that he had brought Shaw to the Glengeen Bar.

It has been said, by the *Observer* among others, that I was 'in trouble' over Shaw by the time I came to England in August 1974. This again is completely untrue. Had I been wanted by the police or the Army they could have arrested me at any time before I left Belfast, where I was living in Cairns Street with my grandparents. Or they could have arrested me at Heysham where I was stopped for the routine check by Special Branch officers. Or they could have found me in Southampton, where I signed on at the Labour Exchange, or at my Aunt Anne's or my Aunt Theresa's. There was nothing to link me to the Shaw case and I was not wanted in connection with it. Shaw's murder was something taken from the files along with a number of other unsolved serious offences and put to me after I became a 'general suspect' late in November 1974. The police hoped to make one of these stick; it turned out to be Shaw. It could just as easily have been one of the others. All they needed was a statement.

The statement I signed came after I had been softened up for nearly thirty hours by Surrey detectives. I admitted to being one of the men who had taken Shaw from the Glengeen bar. I was so dispirited that I did not even bother to read through what Cunningham and McCaul had written.

Once flown to Belfast, I was taken to Crumlin Road jail. Crumlin Road was very different to Winchester and Brixton. In 'A' Wing, Republican prisoners enjoyed what was called 'Special Category Status', effectively political status, which the British Government had conceded after a hunger strike in 1972. The Republicans, who kept themselves apart from the ODCs (ordinary decent criminals, as the authorities called them), controlled everything within 'A' Wing. The IRA had its own command structure and organized classes in politics, history, Gaelic and remedial education. The cell doors were left unlocked for most of the day, and prisoners could associate in each other's cells, on the landing or in the exercise yard. At least once a week, the IRA held parades in 'A' Wing yard and drilled its volunteers.

Of the considerable advantages to be enjoyed in 'A' Wing, perhaps the best was that the IRA did not allow the screws to harass or abuse anyone. They stood up to the authorities and were, as a result, largely unmolested. There was a lesson in this for me, and I learned it well.

Not everyone in 'A' Wing was a member of the IRA. The IRA used to accept men from Republican areas, particularly those acknowledged to be innocent, and extended protection to them. Hector Young, who was not a member, was one of those allowed into 'A' Wing. As a Catholic charged with killing an ex-serviceman his life in any other part of the prison would have been difficult. As for me, the prison authorities assumed that I was IRA and brought me straight to 'A' Wing where I was taken in by the men, many of whom I knew from the Falls. There was considerable sympathy for me. By this time, it was common knowledge among the IRA prisoners that I was innocent and they knew that the conditions I had endured in England, an 'enemy' country, were much more severe than at home. On the wing, I mingled freely with the men, relieved to be away from the violence, threats and abuse and to be among people I knew.

Crumlin Road Prison had another advantage: open visits. For the first time in five months, I was able to hug and kiss Gina. For fifteen minutes a day we had, compared with what we had had to put up with at Winchester and Brixton, private time together in which we could reaffirm our feelings for one another. Gina was heavily pregnant. I assured her that things would work out. I believe she trusted me.

Stories subsequently circulated, repeated credulously by both journalists and lawyers, that I was in trouble with the IRA. It was said at the conclusion of our trial at the Old Bailey that the IRA had sentenced me to death for 'squealing'.

This story, published by a Press Association journalist, came from the police, as did a *Daily Telegraph* item that claimed I had fled from Ireland after carrying out an execution for the Provisional IRA. 'Although he was acting under orders, and the Provisionals claimed responsibility for the murder, Hill thought he had gone too far by torturing his victim and feared being "punished" by his terrorist associates.' Now the IRA was after me not because I was a squealer but a torturer.

The police who fed these fantasies to the press were simultaneously blackening me and providing an explanation of why I had, as they claimed, confessed without any undue pressure. Their explanation was that I *wanted* to confess because I was afraid of the IRA; that I would prefer to go to jail than stay outside and risk death at the hands of the IRA. If I had been sentenced to death by the IRA, what was I doing in 'A' Wing? Informers were thrown out of the wing and housed separately in the Annexe.

My supposed problems with the IRA have been repeated in both Robert Kee's *Trial and Error* and in *Time Bomb* by Grant McKee and Ros Franey. They speculate that the IRA, out of revenge, might have framed me for Guildford and Woolwich. It would, perhaps, have been helpful to my case had this been true. My lawyers could have presented the jury with the scenario that not only was I not an IRA man, but that the IRA was after me.

But it was not true. I was not in trouble with the IRA for 'squealing' or for anything else because I had not been involved with the IRA. The story started as another of the unattributable briefings given by Surrey detectives to the craven press and was repeated until, like Chinese whispers, it came back grander and with much greater credibility because so many people had heard it.

In Crumlin Road, there were men who had been on remand for over a year. Serious cases, in England as well as Northern Ireland, normally took anything from one to two years to come to trial. However, the authorities managed to try and convict me within seven weeks of being charged. Their unusual haste came from the desire to see me contaminated before I went on trial at the Old Bailey for Guildford and

Woolwich. By then, they expected, I would already be a convicted IRA man.

It took the Crown only a few weeks to proceed to committal. I was sent for trial with Hector Young and another man, Martin Monaghan, on the five charges arising out of Shaw's murder. As a prisoner committed for trial, I spent two or three weeks in Long Kesh, which the authorities now call the Maze Prison, before being brought back to Crumlin Road.

I did not have high expectations of getting justice. Since 1973 the courts in Northern Ireland had been sitting without juries (these were the 'Diplock' courts, named after Lord Diplock whose commission recommended their introduction) and so it would be a judge alone I would have to convince. It did not look promising, but part of me refused to believe that I could be convicted for something I had not done.

The trial began on 17 June 1975 before Judge Basil Kelly. Just before the proceedings got underway my barrister, Michael Lavery QC, came to see me in the cells. He told me he had spoken to the prosecution and that they were prepared to offer a deal. I listened as Lavery explained that the Crown was willing to drop the murder if I would plead guilty to the lesser charges. The Crown had not stipulated the length of the sentence I would receive (this being a matter for the judge) but, as Lavery pointed out, whatever it was it would be preferable to the mandatory life sentence that would follow a conviction for murder.

The whole practice of plea-bargaining is cynical: it has nothing to do with guilt or innocence or justice. It is a tactic employed for the convenience of the prosecution (especially when the Crown has a weak case), and takes advantage of prisoners who, unsure of what is going on around them, are vulnerable to pressure. What is a prisoner about to go on trial to think when his lawyer, the person on whom he is depending to fight to clear him, comes and says, 'Look, I know you say you are innocent but the prosecution is offering a good deal here. If you plead guilty to the lesser charges, they'll drop the murder. If you turn them down you may well get life.' What kind of advice is that? What has it got to do with justice?

All the same, it was tempting, and had I not been facing

Guildford and Woolwich I might well have opted for it – anything to avoid the awful open-endedness of a life sentence. But for me there was no real choice. I knew I could not return to stand trial at the Old Bailey with a conviction for an IRA offence. It would not simply have damned me, but damaged the chances of my co-accused: by then it was clear that the Guildford Four stood or fell together. I rejected the deal.

The prosecution case rested entirely on the confession I had signed in Guildford Police Station. The police did not have to explain why, if I was not ill-treated, I had been so ready to confess. The burden was on the defence: to be acquitted I would have to show that the confession was false, that the police had intimidated me into making it. These allegations would be put directly to the police officers concerned – Cunningham and McCaul, and the English officers, Jermey, Simmons, Imbert and others, who flew over to give evidence. However, it was extremely unlikely that such experienced hands would accept accusations of brutality or 'oppression'. Lavery's task was to discredit their evidence by pointing out contradictions and implausibilities.

One obvious flaw in the Crown's case arose from a series of photographs Cunningham and McCaul had shown me. They claimed that during an interview in Guildford Police Station on 20 January 1975, I pointed out a photograph of a man named Martin Monaghan as one of the men involved in the killing. However, the problem for them was that in my confession, which I maintained they dictated for me, I had implicated not Martin but Patrick Monaghan. The police interviewed Patrick Monaghan, but he denied any involvement. They then interrogated his brother, Martin, who made an admission to complicity and was charged. This presented Cunningham and McCaul with a dilemma. How were they to reconcile the contents of the confession with the suspects they now had in custody? If my statement was true, why did I identify the wrong man (I knew them both).

In the statements written out by the police, which I signed, references were made to several other men who were supposedly involved in Shaw's abduction and murder. Several of these men were already in custody, but the police did not even try to speak to them about this offence. One of them was in Crumlin Road Prison on another charge at the same time I was there – he confirmed to me that the police had not been to see him. Why, if my confession was true, were these men not questioned?

There were other flaws in the police evidence. Sergeant Anthony Jermey, one of the Surrey detectives who played a prominent role in the Guildford interrogations, gave evidence on behalf of the Crown. During his cross-examination by Lavery he was asked what time I was arrested.

JERMEY:	At 10.40 on the 28th.
LAVERY:	Are you sure about that?
JERMEY:	I am, my Lord.
LAVERY:	Do you see this document here?
JERMEY:	I do, yes, my Lord.
LAVERY:	And what time does that give as being the time of his detention?
JERMEY:	9.35am, my Lord.
LAVERY:	Can you account for that?
JERMEY:	I cannot, my Lord.
LAVERY:	Are any of the entries in that document in your writing?
JERMEY:	That is in my writing, that entry there.
LAVERY:	9.35am?
JERMEY:	That is in my writing.

Lavery tried to use Jermey's inability to explain the confusion over the time of my arrest to suggest that his memory was unreliable, and that since he had acknowledged getting the times wrong that he was wrong about other things.

LAVERY:	And of course it is right to say that you have already made one mistake, is that right, in the times?
JERMEY:	There is a discrepancy between the detention sheet I agree, yes.
LAVERY:	Well is there a distinction between a discrepancy and a mistake or do you accept that there is a mistake here?

106

JERMEY:	It is a discrepancy.

Lavery, after suggesting to Jermey that I had been ill-treated ('I can only term those allegations as ridiculous,' the detective replied smoothly) questioned him on his interviewing techniques.

JERMEY:	Police officer[s] merely speak to the people and you eventually try to gain their confidence so that they do talk to you.
LAVERY:	Well were you trying to gain Hill's confidence?
JERMEY:	If he knew anything about the bombings it was only right and proper that I should do my job by trying to extract from him what information I could to find out what he knew.
LAVERY:	Were you trying to gain his confidence?
JERMEY:	The question of gaining one's confidence in the police station does not cross my mind as long as he accepts me and is talking to me, my Lord.
LAVERY:	But it was you who introduced the concept of gaining a man's confidence as a means of making him talk.
JERMEY:	I beg your pardon?
LAVERY:	It was you who introduced the concept of gaining a man's confidence as a means of making him talk. Was it not you who said that a few moments ago?
JERMEY:	I did not say that.
LAVERY:	Did you not say in answer to me a few moments ago that this was a method that you

	used in trying to get a man to talk, that you set out to gain his confidence?
JERMEY:	I said that if I can sit down and talk to a man I will sit down and talk with that man to see if I can elicit what I can from him in my investigations.
LAVERY:	Are you saying that you did not say a minute ago that it was part of your technique to gain a man's confidence?
JERMEY:	I do not recall saying that.
LAVERY:	You do not recall saying it?
JERMEY:	No, my Lord.
LAVERY:	I suggest that in fact you did say that, Detective Sergeant Jermey?
JERMEY:	I say I did not.

It was at moments like this, when Jermey had so obviously been caught out, that my hopes rose. I should have been warned, however, by the judge's silence. Although Jermey had plainly contradicted himself and refused to accept what he had said just seconds before, the judge did not see fit to remind him of his testimony and allowed him to go on unmolested. Defendants and their witnesses are rarely treated with the same indulgence.

The police also insisted, improbably, that Cunningham was not informed by Surrey officers that I had been arrested on suspicion of having been involved in Guildford. All the police witnesses maintained that they had no discussion about me before Cunningham and McCaul began their interviews. Lavery pursued this point with Detective Chief Superintendent Wally Simmons who had been the officer in charge of the interrogations at Guildford.

LAVERY:	It would be an extraordinary thing, would it not, for one experienced police officer in dealing with another who was

	coming to interview a man not to say something to the effect he has not spoken yet or what the case was?
SIMMONS:	It would be extraordinary and it may well be that some person had said that he had not implicated himself but I certainly did not, my Lord.
LAVERY:	You did not say it to Mr Cunningham?
SIMMONS:	I certainly did not say it.
LAVERY:	And no one else said it in your presence?
SIMMONS:	I did not hear anyone say it in my presence, my Lord.

However, McCaul, who gave evidence after his colleague Cunningham, admitted that he had been told that I had been arrested for Guildford. Cunningham had already said no one had passed this important information on to him. It was necessary for McCaul not to let the side down.

LAVERY:	And no one told the Chief Inspector [Cunningham] about it?
McCAUL:	Not in my presence, no.
LAVERY:	You had ten or twenty minutes in the police station before you went to see him [Hill]?
McCAUL:	That is correct.
LAVERY:	Was there no opportunity then to tell the Chief Inspector he was suspected of the Guildford bombings?
McCAUL:	No.

Lavery went on to press McCaul about the extraordinary lack of interest he and Cunningham, if their evidence was to be believed, had displayed in the prisoner they were preparing to interrogate.

109

LAVERY:	I suggest to you you must have asked about him?
McCAUL:	I did not ask about him.
LAVERY:	Was that not extraordinary?
McCAUL:	Mr Cunningham was in charge.
LAVERY:	He says he did not ask either?
McCAUL:	That is his prerogative.
LAVERY:	Here were two officers going to interview him and you heard nothing when the English police had him.
McCAUL:	I gather they would have told us.
LAVERY:	Did you ask what sort of fellow he was?
McCAUL:	No.
LAVERY:	Or whether he talked freely?
McCAUL:	No.
LAVERY:	Or whether he was denying anything?
McCAUL:	No.

To counter defence allegations that conditions had been oppressive the police witnesses sought to outdo themselves in describing the conditions at Guildford. One said that the cell was 'rather comfortable', another that it was, by the standards of Castlereagh (an interrogation centre in Belfast), 'luxurious'. I was described during this time as 'well rested', 'completely calm' and 'perfectly normal'. As Lavery pointed out, the allegations of multiple murder alone, even if they were not accompanied by threats and ill-treatment, would surely be enough to upset a suspect. This led to a bizarre exchange when Cunningham pretended he was concerned about me.

LAVERY:	Would that not shock most people to be told they are suspected of a serious crime?
CUNNINGHAM:	It is a rather dangerous question.
LAVERY:	What sort of answer is that

	Detective Chief Inspector, is that intended to deter me from pursuing this line of questioning?
CUNNINGHAM:	I think you would be wise not to pursue it.
LAVERY:	Why would you be concerned about any traps I may be laying for Mr Hill?
CUNNINGHAM:	I would be concerned in the interests of the prisoner some things maybe in my knowledge would not be disclosed to his Lordship.
LAVERY:	What concern have you for the prisoner Mr Cunningham? Are you telling his Lordship that you are worried in case some harm would be done to the interests of the accused?
CUNNINGHAM:	I am being careful I do not tell your Lordship hearsay evidence.
LAVERY:	Or is this show-acting in an effort to inhibit further questioning . . . ?

Cunningham was stonewalling and it took Lavery some time to get him to answer the question. In the end Cunningham said that he did not think that being accused of a serious crime would have come as a shock to me.

But although the police contradicted themselves and each other on some points and did everything they could to bluster their way through difficult questions, they would not admit that I had been threatened or abused in custody. Nor would they agree that I had been relentlessly interrogated about Guildford prior to the arrival of the RUC men.

At that time, the defence did not know about the existence of the documents which were to prove that Surrey detectives perjured themselves about the interviews and which were eventually to clear us. Lavery, therefore, had an uphill task. The police stuck to their story. As far as the confession was concerned, Cunningham was adamant that it had been elicited without duress. He said I 'was extremely confident' while in custody. Lavery pursued the point.

LAVERY:	And you say he is confident?
CUNNINGHAM:	I didn't see any lack of confidence.
LAVERY:	But you did say positively that he was confident didn't you?
CUNNINGHAM:	Yes.
LAVERY:	And that he was confident throughout the statement?
CUNNINGHAM:	Yes, he was.
LAVERY:	Why did he make the statement?
CUNNINGHAM:	I have no idea.
LAVERY:	That was a statement putting him very close to a very serious crime?
CUNNINGHAM:	Putting him right into it.
LAVERY:	And he was not, according to you, under any signs of pressure, internally or externally?
CUNNINGHAM:	None whatsoever.
LAVERY:	Completely in command of himself?
CUNNINGHAM:	Very much so.
LAVERY:	Confident?
CUNNINGHAM:	Yes.
LAVERY:	And suddenly he comes out with all this detail to a police officer, just like that?
CUNNINGHAM:	Just like that.
LAVERY:	How does that compare with your usual experience of suspects?
CUNNINGHAM:	I never met it so easy.

In the witness box I told the court about Guildford Police Station, why Cunningham 'never met it so easy'. It fell on deaf ears.

A second, and unexpected, strand of evidence was raised. During my cross-examination, Mr Appleton for the Crown asked me what wing I was in. I told him, 'A' Wing.

APPLETON: Is that the Provos?
LAVERY: I would object.
JUDGE: On what basis?
LAVERY: On the basis that he is now being asked about something that happened since he was committed to lawful custody. He is now being asked about something which exists in prison and is a system which accused persons are entitled, if they so wish, to take advantage of, and the Crown is attempting to draw some inference or innuendo from association.
JUDGE: Well I think it is admissible on the grounds of credibility.

I was in 'A' Wing – that is, in among Republican prisoners and therefore an IRA man. Although I did not take part in the parades or other IRA activities, I was branded as a member of the organization simply by being in 'A' Wing. By the time I stepped out of the witness box, I knew I would be convicted.

In the end, Hector Young was acquitted on all counts. Martin Monaghan was also acquitted of murder but got three years for the lesser charge. The judge found me guilty and sentenced me to life. I could not believe it. To me it had seemed so clear that the police were telling lies. As sentence was passed, I could hear Gina and my mother crying. My granddad was in court and he looked so sad. Seeing my family like this made me all the more angry. As I was dragged out of the court, I shouted to the judge, 'You bastard!' A court reporter printed a story the next day in which he claimed I had said, 'Goodnight, you bastard!', which was interpreted as a threat to his life. My shout was one of impotent rage. It was 'You bastard!' and I

113

feel the same towards him today, especially because of what is now known about the police's perjury, as I felt then. I was innocent and he blithely gave me a life sentence.

As I walked for the last time through the tunnel back to the prison, now a lifer, I reflected bitterly on how easy it had been for them. I would now stand trial at the Old Bailey as a convicted IRA killer.

Chapter Nine

TRIAL

The mailbag shop, Wandsworth. I cannot think of a place more like the grave; or a cemetery, fenced in and guarded, whose tombs have delivered up their grey corpses. Zombies sit and cut the cloth, zombies stitch and sew. Grey men, with long, skull heads; balding. They had mangled mouths, chipped and broken teeth; haunted, red eyes – and my first thought on entering: 'What am I doing here?'

When I had first gone into prison, in Winchester, I knew nothing of how to conduct myself. But as time went by I learned. My brief spell in 'A' Wing in Crumlin Road had taught me many lessons, the most important of which was that at all costs I had to stand up for myself. I saw how the screws looked with contempt on prisoners who whined; I would not whine. I saw how they bullied those who showed themselves weak; I would not be weak. I saw how demeaning it was when a prisoner went to them to ask a favour; no favours.

There was fear everywhere, but it was better to take what they were going to give you in a manly way and not let them see you frightened. From the day I was brought to Wandsworth after my conviction in Belfast in June 1975, I was determined to stand up to them.

The mailbag shop is slow death. I refused to work, my first rebellious act as a convict. After an exchange of words, they left me alone. I sat in the shop and watched as men pulled the long needles through the seams. In one corner was the cutting table. There were several men slicing up the material with big, old-fashioned tailor's scissors. As I scanned the room, I saw that several of the men were looking at me, and I knew what was going through their minds. One prisoner in particular, he sat among a group of four or five, stared at me and nodded menacingly.

I thought of the scissors and the damage they could do. Irish prisoners had become the targets of men who wanted to curry favour with the screws. They knew that if they attacked Irish prisoners, no prison officer would stand in their way. And, of course, the screws loved it. I had to be on my guard all the time and I developed a special sensitivity to atmosphere. Whenever I entered a room – the TV room, the mailbag shop, wherever – I scrutinized every man and weighed up the possible attackers. Even in the silence I strained to listen, as if the violent words spoken in my absence would be carried to me on an echo.

In August 1975, six Irishmen were convicted of causing explosions in two Birmingham pubs in which twenty-one people lost their lives. The men received life sentences. One of them, Gerry Hunter, was sent to Wandsworth and, before it became generally known that he and the others were innocent, he was the recipient of anti-Irish hostility. Gerry was a slightly built and gentle man, and he was frightened by the atmosphere in Wandsworth. The screws persuaded Gerry, who had been severely assaulted by prison officers in Winson Green after his arrest the previous year, to go on what is known as Rule 43 – voluntarily putting himself in solitary for his own protection. Another Irish prisoner, Mick Sheehan, who was elderly, desperately thin, and in poor health, was also on Rule 43.

When I discovered that they were in the prison and on Rule 43, I went to Gerry Hunter's cell and asked him why he had gone behind the door (voluntarily put themselves in solitary). Gerry said the screws had been encouraging other prisoners to attack him. He was so thin and quiet; he was not the kind who would be able to stand up and fight back. Nor could Mick.

I explained to them that they would have to come out. I said that if they remained on Rule 43 they would spend the rest of their time in prison in solitary. They would have to come out sometime, face up to the threats, and show them that they were not going to be intimidated.

Gerry and Mick came out and joined me in the mailbag shop. The atmosphere did not improve and the threatening looks and gestures continued. At one point, it got so bad that I picked up a pair of scissors and slapped them repeatedly into my open palm. I was sending a message: I would sink the scissors into the neck of the man who tried to lay a finger on me or the other two. I meant it. Prison is that way.

Not all prisoners were hostile, though, and I made some friends. By and large, the 'A' men, particularly the big armed robbers, treated me well. They were part of the prison aristocracy and scorned to do the screws' dirty work for them by attacking Irish inmates.

On 3 September, I was in the mailbag shop when a screw came up and handed me a telegram. It said simply, 'Daughter born today'. The news took a while to sink in. It was indescribable. I felt restless. I could not sit there among all the prisoners in the grave of the shop and absorb what the news meant. I had to get away to be by myself. I said to the screw to put me back in my cell. He answered that I would have to wait until half past four. I said, making it plain that I wanted to go back to my cell, that he was to take me now. He saw I was serious and telephoned control. A couple of screws came in and took me back to my cell.

Once in the cell, different emotions assaulted me: a feeling of loss was the most powerful. I did not feel as if I had gained anything; instead I felt as if something was being kept from me. Then pride came. Then disappointment: I had wanted a boy. I immediately thought, 'How selfish. I have a daughter, a perfect child, and am not satisfied.' But I grew to be.

We named her Kara.

Two weeks after Kara's birth, our trial opened, on 16 September 1975, at the Old Bailey. The clerk put the charges to us (we were all charged with Guildford; Paddy and I faced charges arising out of Woolwich). Once the pleas had been made and the jury empanelled, Sir Michael Havers for the Crown began his opening speech. The media gave it great coverage, with graphic descriptions of the deaths and injuries caused by the bombs. The atmosphere in Wandsworth as I was going to and from court was very tense. One night, as I was coming back, a large number of prisoners were being led across the landing, noisily discussing the film they had just seen. They saw me. Silence. Everyone stopped to stare; I passed rows and rows of prisoners who just watched me. They started to hiss. It was the only sound in the wing. There are few feelings more terrifying than that of being threatened in prison: there is nowhere to hide, no way to escape, no one to turn to.

Going to face trial while being held in custody is an ordeal. The regime is: woken at 6.30am by screws kicking the door, slop-out, shave and wash, kit packed, taken to reception (too early for breakfast), put in a cell and left there. Perhaps a cup of tea, if someone remembers. Police arrive, forms filled in, handed over to police custody for production in court. Handcuffed and brought to armoured van. Put in horsebox, a tiny compartment too low to stand up and too small to sit comfortably. Driven through the streets at speed, overtaking, jumping lights, with motorcycle outriders, marked and unmarked police cars, lights flashing, sirens screaming. Arrive at Old Bailey and taken from van to cell below the court. No window, absolutely airless, so hot that prisoners strip. It is 9am and already headaches are setting in. An hour or more in the cell. A solicitor arrives to introduce counsel. They cannot imagine what you have been through just to get there. You don't bother even to try to tell them. They go. Handcuffed and brought to the stairs below the court. Clerk signals the screws to bring up the prisoners. Up into the dock. The judge comes in, the jury comes in. You sit there as if everything is normal. They haven't a clue about what has been happening while they were taking their breakfast.

But going to court had one advantage. I could see, even if I could not talk to, my family. It was in the Old Bailey that I first saw my daughter. Gina held her up for me to see: helpless, tiny, her eyes screwed shut; Gina proud like a mother. Gina and my mum came to Wandsworth and brought Kara with them. It was an open visit, and I was able to touch her, but it was dreadful. There were screws sitting all around us, just inches away. People who have had children know the feelings that come with seeing their child for the first time; they go so deep and are so strong. But in the visiting room, with screws all around, it was impossible to give those feelings any kind of expression. I held Kara for a moment, but could not keep her. I handed her to my mum, who asked what was wrong. My daughter was so fragile, so beautiful: but it just made me think of where I was, in Wandsworth with its violence and terrors. Holding Kara made me uneasy; I became anxious for her safety, afraid in case a fight broke out.

On the third day of the trial, I returned to Wandsworth as usual. I was taken to reception, given a kit and put into a cubicle. While changing I overheard two screws talking. I could not get all of the conversation, but I heard that someone had been attacked. A prisoner in reception came to my cubicle and whispered something – someone had been done. I tried to get more information, but the screws chased him away. The man had been trying to warn me, that was clear enough, and as I walked through the prison to my cell I was more than ever on guard. The prison was quiet.

My cell was on 'D' Wing, but the screws that night started towards 'E' Wing and the segregation block. I was frightened by this, it was something out of the ordinary. The silence, the warning of the orderly in reception, going to 'E' Wing – I knew it meant trouble. I refused to go with them. They grabbed me and bundled me down the stairs and pushed me into a cell. I banged and slapped on the door; I was very nervous.

I settled down a little and after a while began to make my bed. I saw that they had not given me any sheets so I pressed the bell and the night guard came to the cell. I explained the problem and he went away. Some time passed. I was as nervous as a wild animal, every noise caused me to freeze and strain to make out what it was, whether it meant danger or not. I heard the jangling of keys and the footsteps of two, three, four, more men. They stopped outside my cell and whispered.

119

The door opened a little, perhaps four or five inches, and a pair of sheets was thrown inside. I felt relieved; I had been worrying unnecessarily. I bent down to pick up the sheets. As I did so, they crashed against the door and knocked me down. Several screws, I do not know how many – five perhaps – rushed into the cell, punching and kicking me. I found I was in a corner away from the door and could not remember how I got there. They kept kicking me. There was nothing to do. I prayed to God they would not overstep the mark and get carried away. I prayed they are only going to beat me. I was worrying about my head, I knew what a hard blow to the skull could do. I crouched down and covered my head and let my arms take the battering.

They finished, and, laughing, left.

I was alone. I gently fingered the cuts on my face and felt the swelling. I was too frightened to get undressed. I lay on the bed but did not dare let myself fall asleep. The next morning when I heard the jangle of the keys I got to my feet. I felt giddy and sick in the stomach from nerves and lack of sleep. I prepared for another assault, in as much as getting ready to dive into the corner and cover myself can be termed a preparation.

When the door was unlocked, the screw took one look and said, 'Jesus Christ!' He asked who did it, how did it happen? I said nothing. To me, it was all a game, they were all involved. Looking back on it, I think now that this screw knew nothing of what had happened the night before. He was part of the day shift and would not have been in prison when they assaulted me. But at the time I was so paranoid I assumed he must have been in on it.

He slammed the door and disappeared. A short time later, the door reopened and I was led to the prison hospital where my arm, which was so badly bruised and swollen I could not lift it, and face were X-rayed. Some of the screws seemed concerned, but not for me, not because a prisoner had been beaten up by officers, but because I had to be produced in court. My face was going to be seen.

They need not have worried. That day's proceedings were delayed while I was in the hospital. When I arrived my lawyers were worried. But like the screws their concern was not for me or my situation or the danger I was in.

They worried because it did not look good coming to court with injuries. They were alarmed in case my bruises would make the jury think I was some kind of rough character. I was to try to appear calm, normal. I felt as if I had done something wrong in getting assaulted. I realized then that to these middle class professionals cuts and bruises were the badges of the disreputable. They reacted to them as they would to the sour wine-breath and torn coats of a tramp.

The judge could not let the fact that one of the defendants had so obviously been beaten up pass without comment. He said there would be an inquiry: I never heard how it got on.

Back in Wandsworth, they placed me once again in 'E' Wing. That night someone tapped on the wall. I got up to the window. My neighbour told me that Gerry Hunter had been attacked. Gerry was on the other side of my cell so I shouted for him. After a minute, he came up to his window and told me that the anti-Irish prisoners had interpreted the screws' attack on me as the go-ahead. Gerry had been attacked as he had been passing the recess, the area containing the toilets and sinks. Instead of grabbing the other prisoners, the screws had taken Gerry down to the block.

That weekend Gerry, Mick and I were exercised together in the yard. As we walked around, some of the prisoners in the wing threw bottles and coffee jars at us and accompanied their missiles with threats. The screws ignored it; they hoped we would be so intimidated that we would ask not to go out on exercise.

I was to appear calm, normal. It was not easy. I was trying to fight charges of multiple murder. Each day I was expected to listen to the testimony of the Crown's witnesses and help my lawyers, pointing out to them the lies and inconsistencies. But I was in bits. The strain was killing. Too frightened to sleep, exhausted by the time I reached reception, I could not concentrate on what was going on. The temptation was to shut my eyes and let it happen without me; trust in my lawyers.

Trust? Shortly before the trial my barrister, Arthur Mildon QC, came to see me in Wandsworth. I had a sense of *déjà vu*. After a few meaningless words, he got to the point. 'Your solicitor, Mr Melton, has been speaking to the Crown. They say that if you plead guilty you'll get a life sentence without any recommendation as to how long you'll have to serve before you'll be considered for parole. If you plead not guilty, the judge will make a recommendation.'

Another deal. I told him not to go on. I would not plead guilty to something I had not done. I told him and he seemed unconvinced. I was depending on him to fight for me and he did not believe me.

So, by the time we were arraigned and told to plead, I had decided it was pointless. When the clerk put the charges to me I replied, 'Your justice stinks.' Melton rushed up to the dock and asked me what was going on. I do not remember what my exact words were, something along the lines that it was all a farce and that they were going to convict us anyway. After a while, pleas of not guilty were entered on my behalf.

I had refused to plead because I did not believe we would get a fair trial, and so I was surprised to see that this was interpreted by the press as a refusal to recognize the court. IRA men at that time would not take part in legal proceedings because they considered themselves prisoners of war and maintained that the courts had no jurisdiction over them. I had made no such claim. In *Time Bomb*, Grant McKee and Ros Franey say I 'immediately made a bad impression' while Robert Kee says, in *Trial and Error*, I was following 'in the IRA tradition'. It is hard to explain the feelings of frustration and rage that gripped me as I stood in the dock, my head crowded, trying to take everything in, my senses stretched by the violence and threat of Wandsworth, enemies all around; I do not know if anyone who has not been in that position can understand.

The others, who I had not seen since I was taken from Brixton in April, had the same tautness of expression, the same look of apprehension mixed with bewilderment. For Carole it was worse than for the rest of us. She had been moved back from Risley to 'D' Wing in Brixton for the trial and I felt sorry for her, locked up by herself there. At least Gerry and Paddy had each other for company. Carole seemed the most depressed. Although the enormity of what was happening was overwhelming us, Gerry, Paddy and I, because we were Irish, could make some sense of it. We came from communities that understood injustice not as a vague concept but as an everyday reality. But Carole was English; her own people were doing this to her. How could she make sense of that?

The judge was Sir John Donaldson; he is now Master of the Rolls, one of the most senior judges in Britain. Sir Michael Havers QC appeared for the Crown. Havers was a Conservative Member of Parliament; under Mrs Thatcher he later became the Attorney General and, briefly, Lord Chancellor. His junior was Michael Hill.

The only evidence for the prosecution was our confessions. As in the Shaw trial, the defence would have to prove that these had been made under duress. As at the Shaw trial, allegations of police violence and ill-treatment would be put directly to the officers concerned. However, while I had been free to do this in Belfast I could not do it at the Old Bailey. The rule is that under normal circumstances any previous convictions of the defendant shall be kept from the jury in case it has a prejudicial effect. By the time I went on trial for Guildford and Woolwich, I had already been convicted of murder. My lawyers did not want this to be placed before the jury, fearing, not unnaturally, that it would prejudice them against me. However, the rule also is that if the defendant attacks the integrity of prosecution witnesses – by calling them liars or accusing them of violence, for example – then the defendant's character becomes an issue. The prosecution can apply to have the defendant's record placed before the court. Mildon, my barrister, would have to find a way of putting it to police witnesses that they were lying, that they had beaten and abused me, without actually saying so. This was how the Shaw conviction paid dividends for the Crown. I would have to tread a tightrope, and be very careful not to impugn the integrity of the police witnesses.

Fortunately, Gerry, Paddy and Carole were not labouring under the same handicap. Gerry's barrister, Lord Wigoder QC, accused Detective Chief Superintendent Wally Simmons of putting on 'the act of a wild man' to frighten Gerry, of making repeated threats against him and his family. Lord Wigoder put it to Detective Inspector Timothy Blake that he had assaulted Gerry, pulled his hair and squeezed his testicles.

123

Detective Sergeant Anthony Jermey was also accused of violence. Paddy gave evidence from the witness box alleging that officers had threatened and hit him. Carole's barrister put it to police witnesses that they had shouted at her and struck her.

Calmly, with just the right hint of restraint under extreme provocation, the witnesses denied the allegations. Blake, far from accepting that violence had been used, told the court that 'Hill seemed to take a liking to me'. It was more than I could bear. My good friend Blake, it was subsequently discovered, had fabricated notes of interviews which, fortunately, he was too arrogant or stupid to destroy.

But the documents Blake left behind were not to be uncovered for another fourteen years. In 1975, they and the other Surrey detectives, as well as Imbert and Nevill from the Bomb Squad, doubtless looked impressive to the jury as they gave their evidence. They were experienced witnesses, old hands at this game, careful to appear detached, unemotional, bearing no personal animosity towards the prisoners (just another day on the job). They were convincing.

It is hard to listen to lies being told about you, lies that you know will condemn you to years and years of imprisonment. There were times I could not control myself. When Blake was giving evidence, I jumped up and shouted out that he was lying. I said, 'My God, can't you see he's lying.' The trouble was, no, they could not. A couple of screws grabbed me and plunged me into my seat. The judge said that if there were any more outbursts he would have me removed from the dock and I would find myself in the cells for the rest of the trial. By then I did not care; I would have preferred to sit in the cell so as not to have to listen to this; let them get on without me. But that would have been interpreted as not recognizing the court. I would be making a bad impression.

One of their witnesses, however, let the side down badly. Havers called a young lad, Brian McLoughlin, who had volunteered information to the police after being arrested on a minor charge. McLoughlin, who knew Paddy vaguely from the North London squats, was serving a term in Borstal and he saw an opportunity to do himself some good. He testified that Paddy had tried to get him to bomb a pub. Furthermore, McLoughlin claimed, Paddy had shown him a package containing a gun and, presumably to add a dash of convincing colour, a set of rosary beads. In spite of it being such a fantastic story, McLoughlin's evidence initially caused us some alarm because it was the first time that anyone other than the police claimed to have anything against us. It was of course a complete lie. Paddy was incapable of firing a water pistol let alone a gun.

Fortunately, McLoughlin was such a bad witness that the defence lawyers were able to discredit him without difficulty. The judge told the jury in his summing up, 'The fairest thing to do would be to put McLoughlin's evidence to one side and say that it does not really help you at all.' However, McLoughlin was proof of one thing: the lengths to which the Crown was prepared to go to convict us. I do not believe that Havers, Michael Hill or the police thought McLoughlin was telling the truth. They threw him in like mud to see if any of it would stick.

An 'independent' witness called by the Crown was Donald Lidstone, one of the principal scientific officers at the Royal Arsenal Research and Development Establishment. Lidstone told the court that a description given by Paddy of a bomb was 'fairly accurate'. Under interrogation, Paddy had told the police that he had seen a bomb made from 'gelignite or dynamite sticks with a detonator attached to it with a timer wired on to it'. No matter how you looked at Lidstone's testimony, it carried little evidential weight. He was thrown in – scientific credentials and all – to impress the jury.

Another witness called by Havers for effect alone was a survivor of one of the explosions at Guildford. She had a stump of an arm and wore an artificial leg. It was terrible to see her, and a shocked hush fell on the court. The jury looked at her, her life ruined, and then turned around to look at the four monsters who had mutilated her, had wrecked her life. I felt ashamed to be where I was; these people thought I had done this. There was no necessity to hear the girl in person; her evidence could just as easily have been read to the court. No one was denying there had been bombs; no one was saying there had not been appalling injuries. But Havers wanted her there because he knew what the effect would be. I felt like saying, 'Hold on, what is going on here, why have you brought this girl to court?' But even to point out to the jury Havers' motives would have been to make myself even more of an animal in their eyes. As the girl gave her testimony, people in the public gallery snatched wicked glances at us; they wanted to see the evil freaks and monsters who had done this.

Meanwhile, the active service unit was busy. In August, it attacked the Caterham Arms in what the police described as a carbon copy of the Guildford bombings. I remember switching on the radio one morning in Wandsworth and hearing Simmons say precisely this. How odd, I thought, for I seemed to remember that at the time of our arrests the police had said that they had broken up the tightly-knit terrorist cell responsible for the bombing campaign. The explosions continued. In September, two people died in a bomb attack on the Hilton hotel.

Our barristers were not too happy about making an issue of the fact that the attacks were continuing. I raised the possibility with Mildon. He shook his head vigorously. 'No, let's not enter into other bombings,' he said.

I used to watch our barristers in court. I hated Havers and Hill for what they were doing to us. In the conventions of the English bar it is said that such men are merely advocates, doing their job; that they have no personal interest or feeling towards the defendants. That is untrue. Havers and Hill revelled in what they were doing; it was written on their faces. Yet, and at first it was odd to see, our barristers, the men fighting for us, seemed not to harbour any kind of antipathy towards Havers and Hill. Indeed, they were pally; they seemed to be more at ease talking to them than to us. I got the impression that any of our barristers could easily have gone to Havers' seat and taken over the running of the prosecution. They were no different.'

It was all going so badly. Only Carole thought we had a chance. Havers was demolishing our defences. He was astute, articulate and persuasive. He explained away the contradictions and inconsistencies in our confessions, claiming that we had been specially trained to mislead the police. In cross-examination he easily got the better of us and our witnesses – ordinary, uneducated people – and in every exchange he came out best.

My alibi for 5 October was already looking very shaky. Gina and I had, while in Guildford Police Station, picked the wrong Saturday, confusing it with 12 October when the American soldiers had been in town. Later, the police had taken me to see Gina and I got her to withdraw her alibi. She made a new statement saying that I had arrived in Southampton at 10.15pm. In the trial, we had to try to convince the jury that Gina had only said this because I told her to, and that I had told her to because the police had said they would charge her. After the way the police had given their evidence, I knew the jurors were not going to believe us.

To make matters worse, Havers was able to confuse the circumstances around the alibi. He called rebuttal evidence from British Rail to show that on 5 October there had been engineering works on the Waterloo–Southampton line and that trains from London had had to terminate at Eastleigh. The first train to be affected by the works had been the 8.42pm from Waterloo. Havers claimed that Gina had said that when I had arrived at Southampton I had told her that I had been held up by engineering works. If so, I could not have been with her, as we both insisted, at tea time. The 8.42pm from Waterloo did not get in until around 10pm. This sounded damning. But the fact is that nowhere did Gina say that I had given this as a reason for arriving late: not in any of her statements to the police and not in court. Havers got away with this. The British Rail evidence was a blind, a highly effective blind, and Havers was able to destroy my alibi. Worse, it looked as though my witnesses – Gina and her sister Cathy Crosbie – were liars.

My alibi for 7 November (the night of the Woolwich bomb) was that I had spent the evening at Anne and Frank Keenan's in Brecknock Road and had gone out only for about thirty minutes to phone Gina. Anne and Frank were called and Havers demolished them; they were just not used to court, not used to being disbelieved, and – like most truthful people who have a reputation for their integrity – did not know how to react when doubted. It was terrible to watch. The police had lied and done so well; my witnesses were telling the truth and doing it so badly.

Not all my witnesses were called. Malcolm Crosbie, Cathy's husband, had been in Stainer Close, Southampton, when I had arrived at tea time on 5 October, but he did not give evidence. He came to court and was prepared to testify in support of the evidence given by Cathy and Gina. My lawyers did not explain why they did not call him. Perhaps they saw how badly it was going and did not want to risk another witness. Similarly, Yvonne Fox, the friend of my Aunt Anne's who had been in Brecknock Road on the night of 7 November, was not called, although my lawyers had spoken to her about the alibi.

Other valuable witnesses were overlooked. In retrospect, I believe it was a serious mistake not to make more out of the fact that originally eight people had been charged with Guildford. If the police had been wrong about Annie Maguire, Sean McGuinness, Brian Anderson and Paul Colman why were they right about us?

My alibis were in ruins, but Carole Richardson had what in most people's minds amounted to a cast-iron alibi for the night of 5 October. She had been at a concert given by a band called Jack the Lad at a venue near the Elephant and Castle. She had had her photograph taken with the band so there was no doubt she was there. Before going to the concert, she had met two friends, Frank Johnson and Lisa Astin, for a drink in a nearby bar. On hearing of Carole's arrest, Johnson went to a police station in Newcastle, where he lived, to explain that they had made a mistake: Carole, he said, had been with him and could not have committed the bombings. The police were not pleased. In fact, they arrested him and flew him to Guildford where Surrey detectives detained him under the Prevention of Terrorism Act and threatened to charge him with terrorist offences. Johnson was held in Guildford Police Station for two and a half days during which time he was abused, struck and threatened. Thoroughly disorientated and worn down by their refusal to believe him, he signed a statement in which he apologized for having tried to cover up for Carole and agreed with the police that he had got the times wrong: he had met Carole forty minutes later than he had originally said.

Edward Street, near our house in Nelson Street, in the Docks as it was when I was young. *(Courtesy of Henry Bell)*

Durham Street mills, Lower Falls, 1969, with St Peter's pro-cathedral and Divis Flats in the background. *(Courtesy of the Linenhall Library, Belfast)*

Children at the corner of Currie Street and Irwin Street in the Pound Loney. *(Courtesy of Falls Community Council & Belfast Exposed)*

B-Specials occupy the Falls Library, 1923: part of the collective memory of past repression.
(Welsh collection, Courtesy of the Ulster Museum)

Making my confirmation,
1962, and looking forward to the
legendary riches.
(Courtesy of the Hill family)

Christmas at the Co-op: *Left to right, me, Janet Smalley*
(Theresa's daughter), sister Marion, and brother Martin, c. 1967.
(Courtesy of Janet Smalley)

The Cushnahan family at Cairns Street. Left to right: me, my mum holding my brother Martin, Elizabeth with Janet in front, Aunt Margaret, Granny, Granddad and Uncle Charlie, c. 1972. *(Courtesy of the Hill family)*

Me, 1974, in custody.

Gerry Conlon, 1974, in custody.

Paddy Armstrong, 1974.
in custody.

Carole Richardson, *left*, with
Lisa Astin.

Left to right: my mum, Aunt Theresa with Martin in front, Janet, Gina
holding Kara, and Marion, April 1976.
(Courtesy of Janet Smalley)

Prisoners on the roof during the riot at Hull, 1976. *(Press Association)*

Errol and Theresa Smalley with their daughter Siobhan meet Charles Haughey, the Irish Taoiseach, 1988. *(Courtesy of Lensmen, Dublin)*

Outside Belfast, High Court after release on bail, 20 October, 1989.

With Kara, the day after my release. *(Courtesy of the Smalley family)*

With Gerry, on my right, on RTE's *Late, Late Show* soon after release.

With Marion, November 1989.
(Courtesy of Sean Smith)

A final comment.

In his evidence in the trial, Johnson reverted to his original position, and he explained that he had signed the statement only after ill-treatment. He told the jury that police officers had hit him in the face, banged him against walls and lockers, threatened him with prosecution and said they would set fire to his invalid mother. The jury did not believe him. Nor did they believe Lisa Astin who supported Johnson. Carole's alibi was in the same position as mine. No one seemed to make anything of the fact that the police had arrested and detained a witness – not a suspect, a *witness* – for two and a half days. Why did they do that?

I listened to the closing speeches with a heavy heart. Havers was strong, vitriolic; he left the jury in no doubt as to what he believed. Our barristers, by contrast, seemed to be embarrassed. I remember Mildon, on his feet for his closing speech, addressing the jury. It was his chance – the best chance – to plead my case. This should have been his tour de force; instead, he stumbled through it. I vividly remember him standing there, at a loss. I see him now in my mind's eye. He is saying, 'Members of the jury . . .' He points to the dock and he stops. He cannot explain.

The judge's summing up was one-sided. In the courts of the United States judges must restrict themselves to explaining the law when they send the jury out. Yet in Britain they can tell the jury what they think. They add the rider, 'Of course, members of the jury, it is entirely a matter for you.' But who are they kidding? Most juries are influenced by what judges say. Donaldson posed the jury a simple question: 'Who do you believe? The police or the defendants?' He might as well have stopped the trial then and there. The answer was obvious. What chance did we have when it was put like that? At one stage in the trial, an issue had been made of the tie worn by Blake. It was, he said, his regimental tie. There followed a cosy exchange about club ties, school ties and regimental ties. We had no ties; we did not belong to this club.

I do not blame the jury. Had I been on the jury, at that time, in that climate, listening to the evidence, I would probably have come to the same verdict. After a day and a half of deliberations, the jury filed back. The foreman, a military looking man in a green blazer with a large badge and some tie or other, took his time. His moment had arrived and he milked it. He began to read out the verdicts. Guilty on all counts. Sometimes I think the jurors were fools; most of the time I think it was not their fault.

I looked over at Havers and Hill. They were gleeful and they congratulated each other. My mother was crying; Gina, too.

Rowe got up to say I was already serving a life sentence for the murder of Brian Shaw. Our lawyers stumbled in an effort to think of something to say in mitigation. I believe Gerry's barrister did not even try. It was a pointless exercise.

Donaldson began to speak. He said:

> Your crime was not directed at those you killed, it was directed at the community as a whole, every man, woman and child living in this country. You obviously expected to strike terror into their hearts and thereby to achieve your objectives. If you had known our countrymen better, you would have realized it was a vain expectation.

Donaldson's reference to 'our countrymen' made it clear how much he considered us to be outsiders, aliens. He continued:

> The English language is rich in words but no single one can adequately describe your crime . . . It was a completely pointless crime and one which will be remembered for its infamy.
>
> Having been sentenced to life imprisonment you may think that you can expect to be released in 12 to 15 years. That is a widely held view, but it is also a very dangerous view . . . The idea that life means 12 to 15 years dates from the days when the sentence for murder was death. Only when there were extenuating circumstances were murderers reprieved and sentenced to life imprisonment, and it was the reprieved murderers who were released after such a period. None of you three men would have been in this category. You would have been executed. The sentence of life imprisonment in your cases must be altogether different . . . it must be

doubtful whether any question of release will arise
during the lifetime of the trial judge.

Gerry was sentenced to life with the recommendation that
he serve no less than thirty years. The judge stressed the
words 'not less than'. He told Gerry, 'I do not mean by
my recommendation to give you any reason for hoping that
after thirty years you will be released.'

Paddy, who had like me been convicted of Woolwich,
received a recommendation of thirty-five years. Again
Donaldson made clear that he did not 'mean by this recommendation to give you, either, any reason for hoping that
after thirty-five years you will necessarily be released.'

Then Donaldson turned to me. I was the worst, he said,
because of the Shaw conviction, and would suffer accordingly. His words meant nothing to me. I only half heard
him; it was through a fog. My senses were so strained,
the blood was beating so hard behind my eyes, that his
words seemed to reach me from far away. I had been told
by George Ince, who was then waging a famous campaign
to show he had been framed by the police, that if I was
convicted I should get up and scream at them, tell them
they had got it wrong, protest our innocence. But I was
too dispirited; I was not sure I was hearing what the judge
was saying; I thought, 'This can't be happening.' 'Protest,'
George Ince had said. But every time I had protested
they had branded me an IRA man. What was the point?

Donaldson was saying, 'Your crime is such that life must
mean life. If, as an act of mercy, you are ever to be released
it could only be on account of great age or infirmity.' I don't
even know now if I fully took in the meaning of his words
as he uttered them: the feeling I had was unreal, as if I was
hardly a part of the real world any more.

The last thing I heard Donaldson say was 'very well.' Then
we were led down the stairs and locked in the cells.

Chapter Ten

'MAY THEY ROT IN HELL'

The day following our convictions, 23 October 1975, the newspapers sought to outdo each other in vitriol. The *Surrey Daily Advertiser* ran a front-page editorial in which we were described as 'the warped dregs of humanity'. 'The quality of mercy,' the *Advertiser*'s readers were told, 'is strained to the limit in attempting to feel anything but loathing and revulsion for those who have been convicted.' One tabloid headline ran, 'May they rot in hell'. Now that we had been found guilty, the police felt free to say anything they wanted. The reporters took it all down and spewed it back up, even the most fantastic stories. Where was the 'investigative research' journalists are so fond of proclaiming as the hallmark of their profession? Where was the scepticism? Where, for God's sake, was their common sense?

I have a low opinion of British journalism, of crime reporting in particular. Most crime correspondents seem to be dazzled by the presence of those they regard as tough, hard-drinking, hard-working, street-wise detectives. The Surrey policemen were none of these things: among the men who interrogated us were liars and thugs. Their toughness was the toughness that comes from beating defenceless prisoners; their powers of deduction and observation so lacking that the only equation they could make was Irishman equals bomber. The crime correspondents, flattered by their exciting access to this elite band of hard men, thought they were getting scoops; in fact, they were being used. Strangely, though, in spite of everything that has happened, the men and women who wrote stories about the case in 1974–75 are still around; some of them, presumably, are highly regarded in their profession.

Not that it would have troubled them, but their stories were putting us in danger by feeding anti-Irish hostility in the prison. I had just been sentenced to spend the rest of my life in prison, yet, as we were driven away from the Old Bailey, I did not feel as oppressed by the length of my sentence (perhaps the enormity of it had not sunk in) as by what was waiting for us at Wandsworth. What concerned me – and Gerry and Paddy had the same worry – was physical safety.

In the van, we were placed in separate horseboxes, but were able to shout to each other. Gerry seemed to be holding up quite well, but Paddy was in a terrible state. Gerry and I tried to rally him, saying that this could not last, that they would have to release us, we *would* get out. Every word, even as I spoke, sounded like a lie. Part of me refused to accept what had happened, but another chain of more rational thought was banging in my brain: what I had been telling everyone – Gina, my mum, my aunts and uncles, Paddy, Gerry, *myself* – could never happen, had occurred: we had been convicted.

We were all nervous about where they were taking us. No one wanted to go to Wandsworth. As I had already been there, they bombarded me with questions. In the event, Paddy was taken to Wormwood Scrubs while Gerry and I went to Wandsworth. I said to Gerry, 'Stay close. Whatever they say, don't bite, say nothing back to them.'

The atmosphere was bad. In reception, the screws glared at us and made jokes about our sentences. After we had been processed they led us to E1, the segregation block where I had been assaulted at the beginning of the trial. Both Gerry and I were very frightened; I kept thinking about the night they had stormed into my cell and beaten me up. Would they do it again?

Gerry and I were placed in separate cells. Later, the medical officer came down and offered me a sleeping draught. I refused it, and he left the cell. I watched him through the spyhole as he went across the landing to Gerry's cell. Gerry came into view for a second and then his door was closed. I was not to see him again for two years, when we appeared in the dock together for the appeal.

I can make no sense of the rhythms of violence inside prison. There seems to be no logical pattern, and this added to the strain. When you were least expecting it, the screws would jump you; when, conversely, you were certain they were coming to get you, like as not you were wrong. That night they did not come into the cell.

Early the next morning, I was taken to Bristol prison, a local jail where I would be assessed before being sent to a long-term, dispersal jail. At reception, the screws were listening to the wireless. Professor Gordon Hamilton-Fairley, the cancer specialist, had just been killed by the active service unit in a bomb intended for Hugh Fraser, a Conservative Member of Parliament. The screw with me, on hearing the report, looked up and, pressing his nose almost into my face, said, 'I am going to kill you, you fucking bastard.' I thought, 'Jesus Christ, this is reception. I've only just arrived and they're like this.'

As we prepared to go to the wing, one screw shouted, 'Hill's coming through, one on!' I was walked up a flight of stairs to a landing where there were a dozen or so screws, all of them glaring at me, muttering threats. One of them shouted, 'Where's the other half?' – a reference to my thinness. A screw who had a scar across his face (courtesy, I learned later, of a borstal boy in Reading), and who was notorious for beating prisoners on the block, took over and dumped me in a cell. The door slammed shut. I thought, 'So this is how you start the rest of your life in prison.'

Some time later, I heard a voice calling me to the door. I was a little apprehensive and at first would not approach it. The voice encouraged me.

'Where have you come from?' it asked.

'I've just been weighed off,' I said.

'Do you need anything?'

Someone was asking me this? I was a bit taken aback.

'Tea?' The voice prompted.

'They won't open the door to let me have it.'

'Leave it to me.'

A couple of minutes later, the voice was at the door once again.

'Bring your cup over to the spyhole.'

I did what I was told. The spyhole had a diameter of perhaps a quarter of an inch and I watched in amazement as the end of a makeshift funnel poked its way through. A thin trickle of tepid tea dripped into my mug. I did not often drink tea (I could not forget how it had been served up in Winchester), but I was glad of it then and drank it down. It warmed me, as did the act of kindness.

During slop-out, someone, another prisoner, banged the door and asked me where I had come from. I explained again that I had just been sentenced. He went away, got the screws to open the door and passed me sandwiches and a pint of milk. The screw looked at him as if he was deranged. As the screw closed the door, I heard him say, 'I'm fucking surprised at you, Williams. Don't you know who that is?'

'Bollocks,' Williams said.

Williams was Mickey Williams. He was older than me, a Cat. 'A' who had done a lot of time in prison ('bird' as it is known), and knew how to handle himself. I saw him the next day as we were exercised together in the small yard set aside for 'A' men. We walked separately but after a couple of laps he came up to me and said, 'You've just been weighed off then?' I told him I was innocent; it did not make much of an impression. We got to talking about other things, prison things, and after a few days came to be quite friendly.

When I got to know him a little better, I told Mickey again that I was innocent, and I think that he began to believe that maybe I was. He said that if I was going to continue to maintain that I was innocent there were some things I ought to know. First, I was not to try to convince the screws. 'Don't waste your breath on them,' he said. The same went for Welfare. He told me to keep away from them, not to let them wheedle their way into my confidence. 'They act like they're your friends, like they believe you. But they don't. They go and tell the screws everything. A man has problems with his wife and it's killing him – maybe she's seeing another man. He's upset and he tells the Welfare, asks them to get him a compassionate visit. They do and he's grateful. So the Welfare comes back and they start getting into other areas, about his case, that kind of thing. You think they keep that to themselves? Bollocks. It's all written down, nothing is confidential with them. They are part of the same system.'

He warned me not to get absorbed into the prison system. 'Don't trust them, don't ask them for anything. No favours, no understanding, nothing. Don't go to see the AG (Assistant Governor) and don't never, ever, apply for parole. That is an admission of guilt. If you want to be cleared you cannot go before a parole review. But remember what that means. Parole is the only way lifers get out – unless they prove their innocence.'

I followed Mickey's advice; more closely than he ever imagined. I liked him and was impressed by the way he conducted himself. He held himself aloof from the screws and would not talk to them. He was in prison but he seemed not to be. He knew the way they worked. Screws, he said, were creatures of paperwork. If you did not talk to them, or to the Welfare or to the priest, the only information they could get was from what you wrote to your family. 'Careful what you write. They search those letters for your weak spot.' From then on, even when I most wanted to open up to Gina or my mum, I held myself back so as not to leave them a way to get at me.

Eventually, Mickey and I were transferred to dispersal prisons. I did not see him again for fourteen years. It was in Parkhurst in October 1989. He had been taken to the hospital for treatment and I was also there. He smiled when he saw me and said, 'You've kept yourself together well. I'm pleased.' We talked a little and he slapped me on the back. 'You'll be out soon,' he said. Two weeks later I was released.

I do not think I ever came to terms with my imprisonment or my sentence, which, when Donaldson pronounced it, was the longest ever handed down in British judicial history. But it is surprising how quickly you construct as much of a life as is possible. It is the same phenomenon seen in wars and disasters. It is the instinct to survive; the alternative is to lie down and wait to die. So a life of sorts began to grow up around me, and there were small pleasures to be harvested.

The prison showed films once a week and they were a high point; and at the same time a measure of how meaningless life inside becomes. They used to show the films in the chapel or gym on a Sunday night and by Monday morning you would find yourself talking about next week's film. It was escapism and, of course, there were women to watch.

One film, *The Long Good Friday*, caused a few problems. In the film, Bob Hoskins plays an East End gangster who runs foul of the IRA. He seems to settle the score (lots of cheers from the Cockneys), but at the close of the film is captured by the IRA (lots of cheers from the Irish). The night it was shown it created a lot of tension between the IRA prisoners and the armed robbers and Cockneys.

No serious violence occurred on that occasion. But film night was often a time for settling scores. Men used to pad themselves against knife attacks with magazines which they tucked under their shirts. I used to file into the gym for the film, find a seat among people I would be safe with, and settle down. The screw would turn out the light, and the film would start. But above the soundtrack we would still hear the sucking noise of a knife entering and leaving flesh, followed by a moan and the dull thud of someone hitting the floor.

The radio was a safer and more satisfying pleasure, and soon, like all prisoners, I became an authority on the dial. I knew the location of every station and could tune into any given one at the drop of a hat. I used to listen to Radio Four a lot. I was a news addict, partly because I was convinced that something would break in our case at any time. I listened to the *Today* programme and *PM* in the afternoons. I also liked *Book at Bedtime*, *Desert Island Discs*, *Science Now* and *Weekending*. From time to time, I would find a series that interested me. I remember one on Europe's relationship with the Far East, the development of trading links and the clash of the two cultures. I was especially fond of *Kaleidoscope*, the arts programme, which I found soothing. It introduced me to a new world. I listened to the theatre and cinema reviews and imagined myself at the performance.

One day, when I was fiddling around with the dial, I accidentally tuned into Radio Tiranë. A shock! I could not believe it. At first I thought it had to be a rebel station somewhere in England, but it turned out to be an English-language broadcast from the Albanian capital. It was broadcast to Capitalism's down-trodden masses and exhorted them to rise up and cast off their chains. It gave the day's news stories a special slant and always made me laugh.

For music I listened to Radio Luxembourg. I liked a programme called *Battle of the Giants* in which people rang in with votes for the record they liked most. I was very partisan and castigated the voters for their obvious stupidity if my favourite did not win.

Contrary to popular belief, prisons are not silent. They are very noisy. But it is a monotonous noise and offers the senses nothing. This worried me. Prison runs down the mind and body. The body can be rebuilt; damage to the mind is more serious. When I was in solitary, I would almost be tempted to go and lie in the corner and not do anything, not even think; just give in and accept their drugs. There are prisoners who are addicted to the night draught, who have surrendered and want only to be left alone to get out of their heads. Even when at my lowest, I never thought of surrender and would try to keep mentally active. Sometimes the radio failed to spark my imagination – listening was too passive when what I needed was activity. So I would read.

I read Zola and Dickens – I used to like Dickens's stories at school – and was transported into worlds I did not know but whose characters were as familiar as family. I read Sholokhov's *And Quiet Flows the Don* and *The Don Flows Home to the Sea* which, in a way that was romantic and anti-romantic at the same time, dealt with the hopes of poor people in revolution. Then I started to read Shakespeare. This was a culture shock. I had always thought of Shakespeare as so English, much more so than Dickens, that there would be nothing there for me as an Irishman. On the wireless one night I heard *Macbeth* and was so entranced that the following day I went to the library to borrow the Complete Works. I got a lot from it, but in the end it defeated me and I never finished it. It was too much, I think, for an imagination that had so little to draw on day to day.

Kafka was another favourite. Again my introduction came through the radio, a dramatization of *Metamorphosis*. I was immediately captivated. The story of how the mild clerk turned overnight into an insect and lost all control over his life, was persecuted and killed had resonances for me.

I got to know Joyce. He was difficult to crack, but once inside I felt I was being taken places I had never dreamed existed. Unlike the characters I could recognize in Dickens and Zola, Joyce peopled his novels (apart from *Dubliners*) with strange men and women, but no less fascinating.

I became interested in feminism through Simone de Beauvoir's *The Second Sex*. It was an intriguing book, for me an introduction to the world as seen from a woman's point of view. Women had always been important in my life, I had always been loved by my female relatives, yet I had not wondered about how they saw their lives. It was interesting to read *The Second Sex* – it was saying things that were, to an Irish Catholic male, new and challenging.

I put poetry above fiction: to have the gift of creating an image or mood with just a few words seemed to me something close to magic. When I sat down to read poetry I could feel the hair on the back of my neck stand up. One night, I read 'The Raven' by Edgar Allan Poe. I read it by the cell's red security light and, momentarily, lived in the poem. I liked the poems of William Carlos Williams and those of the Irish poets, particularly Seamus Heaney. During my later years in prison, a writer's group in Dublin used to send me books of poems and so I had access to new work.

But it was not all highbrow. I found escapism in Harold Robbins's stories. Mostly, though, I steered clear of detective novels and crime thrillers.

Prison literature, however, was another matter. Black prisoners in the United States had been publishing some powerful accounts of their lives and struggles. The civil rights movement in Northern Ireland had drawn heavily on the black movement for equality in the United States in its philosophy and organization, and so instinctively I felt a bond between the black and Irish prisoners. *Soledad Brother* by George Jackson, who was given a life sentence for stealing seventy dollars when he was eighteen years old, was powerful and sad. Jackson handled himself in an exemplary

139

way in prison, standing up for himself and for his fellow prisoners, making no compromises, until he was shot dead by a prison guard. I also admired Jack Abbott's *In the Belly of the Beast. Frightened for My Life*, an account of deaths in British prisons, was a fascinating and powerful depiction of brutality and negligence within the penal system.

Irish history had always interested me, and in prison I read everything I could find on the subject, from accounts of the Cromwellian settlement, the penal laws against Catholics in the eighteenth century, the Catholic Emancipation movement led by Daniel O'Connell, the Fenian risings, and the 1916 Rebellion to analyses of the present day political situation. *Ten Men Dead*, about the hunger strike led by Bobby Sands, was one of the strongest books on Irish history and politics that I have ever read.

While I was in Bristol, another tragedy was being played out at the Old Bailey. In January 1976 the Maguire Seven went on trial charged with possession of explosives. During our trial, the newspapers had carried stories about Annie Maguire and her 'bomb kitchen'. Gerry's father Giuseppe also went on trial with Annie. The prosecution, since it could not produce any explosives, based its case on the Thin Layer Chromatography (TLC) test which it claimed was a reliable method of detecting the presence of explosives. This was the only evidence against the Seven and for a time they must have drawn hope from the fact that Dr Brian Caddy, the former head of the Royal Arsenal Research and Development Establishment who developed the test, came forward for the defence to testify that it was not definitive, as the prosecution claimed. In a paper written for the defence, he described as 'unscientific, illogical and pig-headed' the Crown's assertion that a 'positive' result from the TLC test proved the presence of explosives.

But to no avail. Havers, who appeared again for the Crown, would have none of it, while Donaldson summed up against the defendants. All seven, who like us had given evidence about the brutality of interrogating officers, were convicted. Annie Maguire and her husband Patrick received fourteen-year sentences; her sons Vincent and Patrick got five and four years respectively (Patrick was only fourteen years old). Giuseppe, a dying man, got twelve years.

The press called her 'evil Aunt Annie' and said she was a 'senior armourer' for the IRA, training the men sent over to London from Ireland. Vincent was to say, 'I don't think she could put a screw in a plug, let alone make bombs.'

Outside the Old Bailey, Peter Matthews, the Chief Constable of Surrey, let the mask of detached professionalism slip when he told reporters, 'These are the bastards we have been after.' The *Daily Express* ran the story under a headline that read: 'Aunt Annie's Devil's Kitchen'.

In April 1976, a screw had come to my door and opened it up. He said, 'Have you got a grandmother called Cushnahan?' I said, 'Yes.' He said, 'Well, she's dead.' He slammed the door; and that was that. I got up and I sat down, I got up and I sat down. I walked up and down. I sat down for a second. Then I stood up and started to pace the cell again. It was, strangely, the first time I had felt really confined.

They gave me no more information about my granny and I did not hear the details until some days later when I received a letter from Gina, who at that time was living in Belfast with my grandparents. She had come home one day and found my granny sitting dead on the settee. She had died of a heart attack when no one was there to help her. I had not seen my granny since I left Belfast in August 1974 to come to England. Her messages to me in prison had been brief, sad encouragements to keep up hope and that she would see me when I got home.

Years later, I read Jimmy Boyle's *A Sense of Freedom* and, later still, I saw the film of the book on television. There was one scene that made a strong impression on me. It was when they told him his mother had died. He was in a strip cell and there was nothing he could do. He stood up and he sat down, he stood up and he sat down; he just did not know what to do with himself. I saw this scene in the television room of some prison or other. Television-watching in prison is almost like a spectator sport. Men take sides and cheer and curse and make loud comments. Up until Boyle's scene in the strip cell I had been joining in – but then I fell silent. It was a weird feeling, almost as if I was in the television room alone. As I listened to the screw tell Boyle his mother was dead and watched him pacing the cell, I saw less and less of the screen. I was living through the recollection of a scene of my own,

141

the time in Bristol when they told me about my granny, when I had done exactly what Boyle was doing.

During the time I spent in Bristol, I was visited several times by solicitors and barristers who discussed the possibility of getting our case to the Court of Appeal. But, however, much they went over the papers, they could see no way to argue that we had been wrongly convicted. We had no grounds, they said, to apply for leave to appeal.

And that seemed that. No one was prepared to believe that we were innocent. Even members of our own families appeared to think we were guilty. Theresa's husband Errol, whose father had been a colonial police officer and had acted as a bodyguard to the Queen, reminded Theresa that a jury had convicted us, the law had done its work: therefore, to Errol, we must have been involved. It was not for some years that Errol became convinced of our innocence. As the truth emerged, he was so shocked at the scale of the authorities' deceit – a shock he felt all the harder because of his background – that he helped to organize a campaign to vindicate us.

While I was in Bristol, in December 1975, I heard on the radio that four armed IRA men had taken refuge in a flat in Balcombe Street. The police had surrounded them and a few days later they gave themselves up. It was Joe O'Connell, Eddie Butler, Harry Duggan and Hugh Doherty, members of the active service unit responsible for the wave of shootings and bombings in London and the Home Counties, including Guildford and Woolwich. I knew none of these men – who were not from Belfast – and, at the time, paid the news little attention. What I did not know was that Eddie Butler had talked to Jim Nevill, the new commander of the Bomb Squad, and Peter Imbert, his newly promoted deputy. According to their notes of the interview, Nevill and Imbert asked Butler about his first operation with the active service unit:

BUTLER:	My first job, someone you've already put away for it.
NEVILL:	Which one?
BUTLER:	Woolwich.
NEVILL:	You mean the bomb thrown into the pub, the King's Arms?

BUTLER:	That's correct.
NEVILL:	Who were you with on that job?
BUTLER:	I'm saying what jobs I'm on.
NEVILL:	Were you in the car?
BUTLER:	I was out of the car.
NEVILL:	At the pub?
BUTLER:	Yes.
NEVILL:	Did you throw the bomb?
BUTLER:	No.
NEVILL:	But you were there when the bomb was thrown?
BUTLER:	Correct.
NEVILL:	When you went over there did you know they were going to do a bombing?
BUTLER:	Yes.
NEVILL:	Had you been there on a reconnaissance of the pub?
BUTLER:	I was not.
NEVILL:	Who made the bomb?
BUTLER:	I'm not saying.
NEVILL:	Fair enough. Now you know that Hill and Armstrong have been convicted of the Woolwich bombing. Were you with them?
BUTLER:	No.
NEVILL:	You weren't with them?
BUTLER:	No.
NEVILL:	I see. Do you know them?
BUTLER:	Never heard of them.
NEVILL:	What about the Guildford bombing?
BUTLER:	Wasn't in London at the time. Wasn't over here at the time.

Nevill and Imbert went to see O'Connell and asked him about Guildford and Woolwich. At first, O'Connell would not talk. 'There's no point in discussing it,' he said.

NEVILL:	There is a point in discussing

	it. If Hill and company did not do it and it was down to your team, there is every reason to discuss it.
O'CONNELL:	It won't do any good.
NEVILL:	We are here to get the truth, and if a person didn't do something that's as important to us as if he did. If your team did it there is no point in Hill and company doing time for it?
O'CONNELL:	It wouldn't make any difference.
NEVILL:	Are you trying to shield Hill or Butler or members of your team?
O'CONNELL:	I'm not trying to shield Hill.
NEVILL:	I beg your pardon?
O'CONNELL:	They have been looking for them.
NEVILL:	For what?
O'CONNELL:	For passing information to the Army.
NEVILL:	Is that why Hill admitted it, to get out of the way?
O'CONNELL:	Did he admit it? They knew nothing about it.
NEVILL:	Hill admitted the Woolwich bomb to both Peter [Imbert] and me. I can assure you of that. Now why would he do that? How would he know the details of it? How would he? Was it your team? Was it? Was it your team? Were you on it?
O'CONNELL:	Our team, not me, four.
NEVILL:	Four of your team?
O'CONNELL:	Yes.
NEVILL:	And you?
O'CONNELL:	Four, me.
NEVILL:	You.
O'CONNELL:	I have nothing to say on it.

NEVILL:	Are you trying to shield your team or Hill?
O'CONNELL:	Not trying to shield anyone.
NEVILL:	Look, if it wasn't your team then I want no mucking about. If it was, the matter must be reported. We must do something about it.
O'CONNELL:	What can you do? They've been convicted of it.

It is odd that, given Nevill's protestations that 'we must do something about it', neither he nor Imbert informed our lawyers that the police now had men in custody who were admitting to offences for which we had been convicted. They did report the matter to the Director of Public Prosecutions, but there it rested. Vital information was being held back from the defence. Why? To this day no one has satisfactorily answered that question.

It was not until May 1976, five months after Butler and O'Connell first told Nevill and Imbert they had carried out the Woolwich bombing that Jackie Kaye, a woman involved in a support group for Republican prisoners in England, informed Alastair Logan of the contents of Butler's conversation with Nevill and Imbert. In June, Logan visited O'Connell in Wandsworth. O'Connell told him that neither I nor Paddy had any involvement in Woolwich. However, O'Connell insisted, he would not make a statement until another IRA man, Brendan Dowd – who had just started a life sentence for offences in Manchester – gave the go-ahead. Eventually – in October 1977 – Logan managed to get to see Dowd who was then being held in Albany on the Isle of Wight. To pre-empt any allegations of improper conduct Logan took with him James Still, a retired Fraud Squad Superintendent. In a lengthy interview, Dowd gave Logan and Still details of how he had planned and executed the Guildford bombings with O'Connell and three other IRA personnel still at large. He also described the Woolwich bombing, which he carried out with O'Connell, Butler and Duggan. After seeing Dowd, Logan and Still interviewed Butler, O'Connell and Duggan. Their accounts were different to ours in every respect: they were not the incoherent ramblings of frightened youths but the detailed accounts of experienced and confident IRA men. They specified the cars used, how the bombs were made, where they were placed. In every respect the information was coherent, precise and detailed.

It was Gina, on a visit, who told me that the arrested men had admitted to Guildford and Woolwich. That was it, I thought. Now they have to let us go.

Chapter Eleven

THE END OF THE LINE

In the prison system, Hull is the end of the line, and I got there faster than I could have imagined. In February 1976, I was moved from Bristol to Albany on the Isle of Wight where I spent less than two months before being taken back to Bristol for six weeks of solitary confinement (known in prison as a 'lie-down' because, locked in the cell all day, there is little else to do). In May, I arrived at Hull, got into more trouble, was sent to Durham for five weeks of solitary, then, at the beginning of August, shipped back to Hull.

Contrary to popular belief, most prisoners do not seek trouble. Trouble comes painfully and expensively: it is almost always followed by a beating, and it costs time spent in solitary and time added on to sentence through loss of remission. Remission is calculated at one-third of sentence: a prisoner doing twenty-one years can expect release after fourteen, seven years being remitted for good behaviour. However, infringements of the prison rules, even the most minor, lead to loss of remission. Serious breaches of the rules can result in huge losses

– 200, 400, 800 days – the equivalent of four-year prison sentences after a two-minute hearing in which the prison authorities are prosecutor, judge and jury.

These punishments (or 'awards' as the authorities call them) are handed out at 'adjudications' before the Board of Visitors (the panel of 'independent' civilian worthies who supposedly supervise the running of the prison, but who in reality rubber stamp the staff's actions). Some years ago, after cases brought before the European Court of Human Rights, the Prison Department was forced to concede certain changes in the way adjudications were conducted. In the 1970s, they were kangaroo courts. Prisoners were not allowed access to lawyers and could not challenge evidence. To do so, often prompted further charges of 'making false and malicious allegations against prison staff'. Prisoners on charges ('nicked' or 'on report') were thus caught in a double bind. If they pleaded guilty at the adjudication they would be punished; if they pleaded not guilty and contested the evidence they would receive additional punishment. Acquittals by Boards of Visitors were virtually unknown.

Many prisoners were undeterred by solitary or by the prospect of loss of remission (in my case I had no remission to lose – the judge had recommended that I never be released). These were known as 'refractory', 'rebellious' or 'subversive' prisoners, and the chances were they would end up in Hull.

By the time I got to Hull, my prison education had been completed. I was not the same man I had been on arrival at Winchester almost two years before. My behaviour was not consciously rebellious but instinctively so. I did not *decide* to be rebellious: to me the thought of 'settling down' to do my time was inconceivable; I could not come to terms with the fact that I was in prison at all. I had to maintain some kind of control over my life, in spite of where I was. I never did anything I did not want to do: that far I could be free. If I had obeyed their orders I would have been in a worse kind of prison, one that I would have half-created for myself. Inevitably, that meant saying no, and saying no was necessarily to be rebellious.

To punish me, and to intimidate me into conformity, they put me in solitary. But even in the crushing boredom I found a way to survive: it did not deter me. They could beat me.

148

But behaving 'well' was no guarantee of safety: they had assaulted me at Wandsworth when I had done nothing to them. I was to discover that the fear of being beaten was worse than the pain. When I was being attacked I merely felt numb; the pain came later, and by then the fear was gone. My only worry was that they would get carried away and not stop until they had killed me; at these times I would think of the lonely deaths of Barry Prosser and George Wilkinson.

In large part, my attitude stemmed from the behaviour of the screws. In Bristol, I had merely disliked them. I saw prison officers as crude and inadequate; men whose low self-esteem led them into acts of brutality against the people in their charge. Prison officers are usually rejects: too stupid to be accepted into the police force, too old to be in the Army, too patently lacking in courage to join the fire service. Fat slouches, they lounged against the landing rails doing nothing all day but reading pornography and locking and unlocking doors.

The day they told me about my granny's death was the day my attitude changed. I thought, 'What kind of human being can be like that? So callous.' From that day I hated them. Even if I was going to be in prison for ever, for the rest of my life, I would never have any respect for them. In fifteen years of imprisonment I can say I met very few decent screws and even they, when the chips were down, turned against prisoners and were as brutal as the rest.

The screws in Hull had, when I arrived, been notorious for some time for the beatings they gave out, and for their 'nickings'. Conditions in Hull were rapidly worsening. Cuts had been made in the prison's budget which affected the screws' overtime, which in turn meant a reduction in prisoners' association time. There were also cuts in education classes. The Irish prisoners had had their Gaelic classes stopped. The screws were becoming more aggressive and were charging men for trivial or imagined breaches of discipline.

Hull was dismal. Like all prisons it was unhygienic and lacking in adequate facilities. Prisoners worked mostly in one of the two mills. I worked in the woodmill (there was also a textile mill), a squat, three-storey concrete building in which we assembled furniture for the Shah of Iran's prisons. We worked a thirty-hour week. It was piece work. The average wage was ninety-five pence a week, but there many prisoners failed to meet their quota (the jail set the minimum at forty-two pence a week). Failure to earn the forty-two pence minimum was a chargeable offence and every week men were taken down to the punishment block for failure to reach it.

Jake Prescott, who worked in the woodmill, described conditions as they were in 1976:

> The shops are so noisy and choked with dust that a factory inspector visiting earlier this year entered each shop, stopped, wrote NOISE! DUST! on his clipboard, ordered the authorities to issue earplugs and filter masks to everyone and left. Needless to say, they only got these articles a couple of months later and they did not issue them, only reluctantly handed them out to those prisoners who persisted in asking for them . . .
>
> There was always a queue of prisoners at the instructors' office on a Friday when we got our wages, all arguing about being cheated out of our earnings . . . And out of 80 pence a week that prisoners get you have to buy tea, sugar, milk for breaks and you could not possibly work in that dust without it – so 12p a week would be spent in this way . . . The rest of the wage went like this: 10p for the film club (prisoners run and pay for one film a week); 5p a week for the people in the segregation unit [the punishment block] – there was always 20 to 25 men in there, and we all used to collect this and buy tobacco and get it smuggled down to them; 6p a week for TV (rented by prisoners); 1p a week 'common fund' (this was compulsory and was supposed to be for the buying and upkeep of recreational facilities, and the extra food at Christmas . . .). That left about 60p a week (if you were lucky) for a half ounce of tobacco and a 'canteen letter' (you're only issued with one and have to buy any extra) and a pot of jam every other week . . . The canteen was run at 10% profit . . .

Jake Prescott was serving ten years for offences arising out of the actions of the Angry Brigade in the early 1970s. When I first met him he looked like a young Karl Marx with his long hair that fell in ringlets about his neck and shoulders. He had a kind of dignified intensity about him, and was well respected. I first got to know him when I was having problems with my visits.

Since Hull was a long-term prison, unlike Bristol, I had been looking forward to open visits, but when Gina and Kara arrived we met across a wide table and were separated by a board some eight inches high. We could not touch, kiss or hold hands. We were surrounded by screws who listened to every word that passed between us. After a few minutes, I felt I could not cope. I could not stand the thought that this was how my visits were going to be from now on. Gina, who was upset to see me upset, managed to calm me down a little. I asked for Kara to be passed over the table to me so that I could hold her. But Kara, not knowing who I was, was too frightened to leave her mother and started to cry.

There were so many things that Gina and I needed to sort out. I had always felt responsible for her, but the longer I was in prison, the less I felt able to let my mind dwell on her. I could not allow myself to feel responsible for her or it would kill me. She was loyal to me in the first couple of years. She came to visit and brought me food and clothing; she wrote and sent me money. But loyalty can be crushing and can bring feelings of guilt when it cannot be matched or returned. For my own safety's sake, I was, though scarcely conscious of it, already withdrawing. At times, when I thought I would never get out, I did not want to continue our relationship. I was heart rent to think that it was not just my life being destroyed but Gina's and Kara's and I would urge Gina to start a new life without me.

Men in prison go mad, literally mad, about the women they love. They get anxious as the time for a visit approaches, and if their wife or girlfriend or lover does not come they fall into black depressions. It wrecks their lives. They might start into drugs to try to find a way out of the strain, or smash up the cell. Jealousy eats into them.

I was not jealous of Gina: I did not think she would go with other men. I do not think this was arrogance on my part but love. I was so in love that the thought that she would do that to me did not cross my mind. The distance I was slowly putting between us came not from jealousy. Partly it came from common sense – the impossibility of having a relationship in the circumstances. But, mostly, it came from a need to be free of a burden; loyalty and love can be burdens in prison.

But this did not happen suddenly. It unfolded over the years slowly, sadly, unevenly.

The inability to talk during our visits, and the feeling of being a stranger to my daughter ate into me like acid. I always had at the back of my mind a memory of bewilderment at my own father's distance from me as a child, and, when Kara cried in my arms, I thought of him as I had seen him, with a child's eyes – a strange, frightening person. Was this how Kara would come to think of me?

When I came off the visit, I was upset and angry. I was passing the centre on my way to get a PO or Chief to complain when Jake saw me and said, 'All right, Paul?' In my rage I did not notice him. He immediately guessed something was wrong and shot up the landing to cut me off. He asked again what was wrong and I told him about the visit. 'I can't stand it,' I said. 'I have a child and I can't lift my own child across to the other side of the table. I can't handle this. I'm going to hurt one of them.'

Jake said, 'Okay. Calm down. We'll go to see them. Let me do the talking.'

Jake had spent a long time inside. He was calm and principled. He would accept no abuse from the screws and they came to respect him. If Jake saw another prisoner, even one he did not know, being threatened or harassed he would intervene at whatever cost to himself. He had a rare sense of solidarity, and it was widely admired. The screws knew this and would listen to him.

Jake found a Chief and told him that the visiting conditions were unacceptable and were contributing to the tension in the jail. He and the Chief exchanged some more words on the subject. 'If you want music,' Jake told the Chief, 'we've the band to play it.' Although I was still furious, Jake's intervention calmed me down and we avoided a confrontation. Had he not come along when he did, I have no doubt that I would have landed myself in more trouble.

Part of my frustration came from the lack of developments in our case. By then it had been nine months since the Balcombe Street siege. When Gina had first told me about the admissions of Butler and O'Connell I had assumed that everything would be swiftly resolved. Any day now, I used to think, they will come to my cell, open me up and say, 'Look, sorry, we've made a mistake.' The lack of progress was so frustrating. The only thing I could console myself with was that at least there were now grounds to go to the Court of Appeal: they would have to let us go at the appeal.

I was not the only innocent prisoner in Hull. Also there were Paddy Armstrong, Paddy Maguire (Annie Maguire's husband) and Johnnie Walker, one of the Birmingham Six who, much to the amusement of the Republican prisoners, the police had claimed was a 'brigadier' in the IRA.

There were also IRA prisoners. They maintained their own discipline and command structure, as in 'A' Wing in Crumlin Road. In Hull, there was none of the tension in the relations between Irish prisoners and the rest that I had encountered elsewhere. The men at Hull were of a different mould, more 'solid' with each other, more politicized. Among the Republicans was Martin Brady, who came from the Lower Falls and who walked, like so many of the men from the district, with a tough little Belfast dander. I enjoyed the company of Belfast men for the crack, the gossip from home and for the banter or 'slagging'. It helped pass the time in that awful place.

On 31 August, Martin and I were returning from the woodmill, where we worked together, when several prisoners stopped Martin. They said that the screws had just taken a man named Marty Clifford down to the punishment block (or segregation unit) and that a cleaner had sent back word that Marty had been badly beaten up. This was not unusual; it was taken for granted that if a man was dragged down the block he would almost certainly get a beating. This used to cause much ill-feeling. In Hull, a convention or informal arrangement had grown up that the friends of men on the block could visit them to see for themselves whether there had been any assault.

Martin did not appear unduly perturbed. He told the men to keep him in touch and we continued on to our cells (which were on different wings), arranging to meet later that evening.

However, as I was eating my tea a prisoner came in to my cell and said that there was going to be a sit-down in the centre (the area that controlled movement and access to different parts of the prison) because the screws had refused to allow Marty Clifford's friends to see him. The rumour that Marty had been severely beaten up gathered strength. As we were discussing it, another prisoner rushed in to say that he had just had it confirmed that the screws had done Marty. The news spread in seconds throughout the prison. Plans were finalized for a peaceful sit-down to demand that Marty be seen.

Meanwhile, Martin Brady was telling all the Irish prisoners, both IRA men and non-Republican inmates, that if there was going to be trouble it would be best for all the Irish to stick together. The screws, he told us, would not distinguish between us and that we would all certainly be singled out for special attention. I needed no convincing, after Wandsworth; nor did Johnnie Walker who, in addition to the beatings he had received during his interrogation by police, had suffered terrible violence at Winson Green.

At about 7pm, we went with the other men to sit down in the centre. At first the atmosphere was relaxed, even jovial and the screws, instead of trying to beat us back to our cells stood around and cracked jokes with us in an effort to ease the tension. Marty Clifford's friends demanded to see him, but the screws said that there was no duty governor on that evening to give the go-ahead. The screws were told to find one quick.

More and more rumours were going around. It was said that someone had been beaten up in the gym; that another man had seen large numbers of screws dressed in civvies coming through the gate lodge carrying clubs, billiard cues and nightsticks. If true, this signalled trouble, for it meant that the prison was calling in off-duty officers and preparing for a confrontation.

While the screws were trying to contact a duty governor the atmosphere suddenly changed. A group of prisoners was spotted breaking into a room where there was a telephone. There was some jostling as attempts were made to stop them. As the situation became more tense, we realized that we were in an exposed position. In the centre (which was the join of the T-shaped building, with 'D' Wing the stem, 'A' Wing to the left and 'C' Wing to the right), we could be attacked from all sides. After a quick discussion, it was decided to make for 'A' Wing, access to which was controlled by a gate. A man named Bertie Coster went to the 'A' Wing gate and pretended that he had had enough of the protest and wanted to return to his cell. As the screw opened the gate, Bertie pushed him back and pinned him against the wall. Everyone – around seventy men – rushed through the gate and into 'A' Wing.

Once inside 'A' Wing, we made for the upper landings, the 'threes' and 'fours', where we would be safer from a sudden assault by the screws. As we milled around on the landings, a screw called Jake Prescott by name. 'Prescott! I'm giving you a direct order. Come down!' Jake ignored them, but another prisoner grabbed a fire bucket and tossed it down on the screws. That was it: the Hull riot had begun.

Men at once erupted and began to demolish the wing. Jake realized that we would have to defend the iron staircase – that was the only way the screws could gain access to the 'threes' and 'fours'. He started to organize the smashing down of cell doors for use as barricades. Cell doors are made from heavy wood reinforced with metal, but they were easy to break down. All we had to do was put a broom handle or bible at the hinges, give the door a good push and it would crack and fall in. We had more of a problem with closed doors but realized that we could break them down with the ones we had already ripped off. We crashed broken doors onto the hinges of closed ones. Once the lower hinge was displaced the door was dragged down by its own weight; the whole thing would fall in, taking the frame and brickwork with it. We tossed a couple of the doors down at the screws to keep them at bay while we constructed barricades at the top of the stairway.

As we worked on the barricades, the rest of the prisoners were destroying the wing. The pent-up rage and frustration of 300 men burst into a furious attack on prison property.

Mattresses were shredded, windows smashed, desks over-turned, lights broken. I had never seen a place demolished so fast and with such enthusiasm.

In every prison riot men make for the roof. It is almost as if they are impelled to get into the light, to breathe air, to see and be seen. As the destruction went on around us, Jake and I and a couple of other prisoners turned our attention to the roof. It was made of reinforced bullet-proof glass and rose in an apex. The authorities had earlier boasted that the glass was unbreakable. Even to reach it, we had to bring beds from the cells for use as battering rams. It did not take long to realize that the authorities were right: the glass would not break. However, the wood into which the panes were stuck was not as strong as the glass itself. We battered away at the wooden frames until the whole roof folded back like the cover of a book.

As I prepared to make my way onto the roof, Jake pulled me back. He ripped up a grey prison jumper. He tore off the sleeves, punched two holes in it for my eyes and stuck it on my head as a makeshift balaclava. It looked absolutely absurd, like a Noddy hat. However, it did the trick. Jake did not want the screws to be able to identify anyone on the roof.

I was the first person out, followed by Jake, similarly dis-guised, by Frank Conteh, the brother of the famous boxer John, and by a Scot named Jimmy McCartney. The four of us headed along the roof to the segregation unit which adjoined 'A' Wing.

The prison, which was in a working-class district of Hull, bordered blocks of run-down council flats. As we made our way towards the unit, a woman spotted us from her balcony. She called out, 'Sandra, Sandra, quick!' Sandra came out. 'Look Sandra! They're on the roof, they're escaping!' Sandra rebuked her, 'Well, keep your noise down and let them get on with it.'

'A' Wing was a volcano. As Jake, Frank, Jimmy and I edged our way along, we could hear an incredible clamour behind us. When we reached the segregation unit, we broke open the roof and peered in. Below us on the landing of the 'ones', we saw the screws decked out in riot gear. They spotted us and started up the stairway. Frank immediately jumped down onto the landing and threw fire extinguishers and anything else he could lay hold of to keep them off while we sent for reinforcements from 'A' Wing.

The reinforcements arrived at once. We made an assault on the block and, after serious fighting, forced the screws out. In their eagerness to abandon the block, they tried to escape out of an adjoining exercise yard which was fenced in by wire – a bad move on their part because they were in full view of prisoners on the roof who pelted them with slates and bricks.

After gaining control of the block, we began to smash in the doors to release the men on punishment. Everyone wanted to find Marty Clifford, the prisoner whose removal and beating up had sparked the riot. We ran around trying to find Marty's cell. Meanwhile, we also began breaking open the doors of the other cells in the block. Some men had been held there for six months or more, and were pretty confused when we came to liberate them. One of these men, whose name was Frank, could not believe what was happening. He had been in the unit so long he was a bit scrambled and found it difficult to communicate. However, once on the roof Frank recovered his powers of speech and spent almost the whole riot talking to one of the women in the flats with whom he had fallen in love.

Outside, the fire brigade had been called in to rescue the screws trapped in the exercise yard. A group of firemen hacked a hole in the fence for the screws while others turned their high-pressure hoses on the roof to keep the prisoners at bay. The screws – not being the bravest of souls – lost whatever discipline they had and dashed for the fence. It was every man for himself. They showed no pity to their colleagues. The fat and slow were mercilessly pulled out of the way and trampled on by the leaner and fitter ones. Shields, visors, sticks, helmets, jackets were abandoned as they made for the hole.

Eventually, we located Marty Clifford's cell and set about the door with a vengeance. Such was our fury to liberate Marty that we made a pig's ear of the door and it took a long time to crash it in. At last, it gave way and slammed onto the floor. Marty, the beaten prisoner, was free.

There was not a mark on him, and this presented us with a bit of a problem. A riot had started because prisoners believed

157

Marty had been beaten up. Everyone knew that when the riot ended we were going to have to face the music, that men would lose remission and have years added to their sentences, that there would be beatings and long periods spent in solitary. We could not take Marty, unmarked, back to the wing: the chances were he would be lynched. After a quick discussion, from which he was excluded, Marty was given a black eye. We took him, a bit dazed, back to 'A' Wing.

'Look what the bastards did to him!' someone shouted. A roar of outrage went up.

Once more on the roof, we made our way to the point 'A' Wing met 'D' Wing. 'D' Wing roof was about forty feet higher than 'A' Wing. There was a drain pipe all the way up, but, to hinder escapes, it had been covered with grease. Bit by bit, we wiped off the grease with towels, and eventually scaled 'D' Wing roof. There I saw a beautiful sight: a calm, sloping sea of Bangor Blues, the slates I and my friends used to loot from the Pound Loney to sell to the Housing Executive in Belfast.

At the bottom of 'D' Wing, where the roof overlooked the administration block, I found Jimmny McCartney, the prisoner who had come up on the roof with Jake, Frank Conteh and me but who had since disappeared. He was crouched down and looking intently at the gate lodge. He told us to be quiet and I tip-toed up behind him and asked him what was going on.

'If I could reach the gate lodge I could easily get over the perimeter wall,' Jimmy whispered.

'You're mad,' I said. It was eighty feet to the ground. 'You'll never make it.'

Jimmy would not be put off and stared silently at the gate lodge, weighing up his chances, looking at the angles. Suddenly, he got up and moved to the drain pipe that ran down the wall to the ground. He would break his neck I was sure.

'Jimmy! Don't do it!' I hissed.

I could hardly believe it, but Jimmy slithered down the drain pipe in a matter of seconds. However, just as he got to the ground, the gate suddenly burst open and in rushed about fifty screws who made a dash for the administration block. Jimmy was in plain view but they were so intent on getting into the admin that they did not notice him. Their brief was to secure it and its records at all costs. But at the time we did not know this and sent a runner back to tell the men that the screws were preparing to storm 'A' Wing. Jimmy, surrounded by screws, made a dash for the drain pipe and climbed back up in seconds. I had never seen such agility.

By now, 'D' wing roof was being shredded and the precious Bangor Blues used as missiles against the screws.

We quickly realized the strategic importance of 'D' wing roof because of its position overlooking the gate. As long as we held it, no one could enter or leave the prison without coming within our range. The authorities, too, recognized the importance of 'D' wing and got the firemen to try to hose us off the roof. However, we held on and after a while they gave up.

It had already become clear that the riot was not going to blow over quickly. While a few men had given themselves up, the rest were preparing for a siege. For this we would need food and water. The mains supply had been cut off, but we located huge water tanks (full of dead pigeons) in 'D' Wing roof.

Food was a more pressing problem. A decision was made to raid the canteen, and I was one of a party of about thirty formed for the task. When we reached the canteen, we found we could not break in, but noticed a circular hole high up in the wall which housed a steel fan. We removed the fan and found that there was just enough room for someone to squeeze through. I went in first, followed by two others. We started to pass out tobacco, chocolate, sweets, crisps, biscuits and cans of soft drink.

While we were inside, the screws were gathering, and, their numbers up, made several charges to clear us from the canteen. They were held off by the other prisoners, but with each charge were gaining ground. They marshalled enough strength to attack and disperse the men outside the canteen, leaving us trapped inside. We were fearful of what the screws would do if they got at us because there would be no escape. Fortunately, they had no keys and were unable to open the door; none of them seemed too willing to copy our method of entry.

It looked as if we were trapped, but the prisoners organized a counter charge and beat the screws back, enabling us to escape with more loot. As we were escaping back to 'A' Wing, one man was caught by the screws. They attacked him so fiercely that they broke his leg. He played dead until they stopped beating him. Then he jumped up, broken leg and all, and dashed for 'A' Wing and safety. He was even able to get up the staircase. Pure terror must have driven him because when we got a proper look at the leg it was clear that the injury was serious: the bone was exposed and he was in considerable pain. Although his condition worsened, he refused to give himself up. In the end, we had to bundle him into a laundry basket (against his wishes, which he expressed vehemently) and lower him down from the roof in order to get him to a hospital.

During the counter charge, the screws were finally beaten out of 'D' Wing. The fighting had been serious. Bangor Blues peppered the walls and the discarded mattresses which the screws had used as shields littered the floors.

With the fall of 'D' Wing we had control of the whole prison, apart from the wood and textile mills and 'B' Wing – a separate building which housed remand prisoners who were now also rioting. We prepared to resist the inevitable assault and set about gathering piles of slates and improving what weapons we had. I saw one man carrying a billiard cue with a kitchen knife fastened on the end to make a crude spear. Another man had converted a bullworker into a bow and had fashioned arrows of sorts. Some of these were wrapped around with inflammable material, lit and fired over to the prison mills in an unsuccessful effort to set them on fire.

Other prisoners were looking for ways to escape. There was a rumour that secret tunnels led to the nearby docks. There were earnest discussions about the most likely spots and some men went off in search of these. Over the course of the riot, which lasted from Tuesday, 31 August to 3 September, I would come across men frantically chipping away at floors and walls.

Another group of prisoners had broken into the governor's office where they found a safe. They saw it as a challenge to their skills and spent a long time trying to crack it. It was funny to watch these men, oblivious to the riot going on around them, intent on getting into the safe. After several failures their methods became increasingly primitive. They took a hammer and chisel to it. That failed. At last, they dragged it up to the 'fours' and dropped it over the side. It smashed open, and they found some money inside. It was of no use to us, of course, so we sellotaped the notes to footballs and basketballs from the gym which we kicked from the roof over the walls and into the streets where a gang of street urchins had gathered to watch the riot.

During the night, the tobacco and other goods were shared out among the prisoners. It was like Christmas, and we greedily gobbled down the sweets and chocolates. Then we sat down and reflected on our situation.

Most prisoners prefer to avoid riots: the penalties are just too grave. It was a measure of how bad things were in Hull that men so quickly, instinctively, did what they did. The deterioration in conditions, the bitterness caused by the enforcement of petty restrictions, the arbitrary 'nickings', the beatings, the bad visits, the squalor, the dread and tension, the appalling working conditions – all of these led to a spontaneous eruption of fury. The riot had not been planned; it did not have to be. When it broke out prisoners had acted as one man with one aim: to wreck the jail, to avenge themselves by fighting back. I was an unrepentant rioter. The feeling of euphoria that being on the roof gave me was matchless. I felt that by fighting back I had regained some kind of control over my life. The riot meant that I could stay up late, to wander freely around in the darkness, chat to whoever I liked, smoke as much as I wanted, look out into the night. I was going to suffer, but it was worth it. The screws called to us and told us what we could expect when we came down. Yes, it was going to be bad. But we were defiant, and gave them as much abuse as they gave us.

We set up a first-aid post where a variety of wounds – mostly truncheon wounds to the head – were treated. We organized a rota system for sleeping and posted look-outs and runners.

I sat with some lads and had a smoke and tucked into a big bag of Liquorice All Sorts. I remember looking across at the docks and the winches and I thought of my granddad and of the docks in Belfast. I saw men walking home from work, dockers. I thought, 'Wouldn't it be great just to walk down that street with those people and look up at the jail and watch the prisoners smash up the roof?' I suppose most prisoners have a fantasy about materializing in another place, a free place. When I was being transferred by van from prison to prison I used to imagine as we passed a little pond or stream that I was outside the van, sitting by the water, watching the prisoner in the van with his guards. I used to think, 'Will yourself to be there. Imagine what it would be like.'

A huge cheer went up and took me out of my dream. Jake had tuned into Radio Tiranë, the Albanian station, which had a report on the riot. He nearly fell off the roof he was laughing so much; tears were streaming from his eyes. I asked him what the matter was. 'You're never going to believe it,' he said, 'but they've just said that this is a glorious prison revolt, that the prisoners have rebelled against the capitalist system of oppression.' From then on, every time I tuned into Tiranë I used to think of Jake lying in stitches on the roof surrounded by the devastation and mayhem and by men who, in their ragged disguises, looked like they belonged under the arches. Jake had a manic laugh and it echoed through the wing: I would hear it long after I last saw him.

Our tempers worsened when a group of prisoners discovered the files kept by the screws. The men arranged them on a big table, and throughout the night runners came to the roof to page men when their files had been located. We did not get the full records, which were kept in the administration block, but a summary – a kind of introductory record – which was kept on the wing. I was reading through my file when Paddy Armstrong came up and showed me his.

It read: 'This man is believed to be innocent.' It went on to say that Paddy was not an IRA prisoner, that the IRA leaders in prison had not accepted him, that he did not possess the calibre of an IRA man and did not conduct himself as such.

Mine was different. It said that I was a potential hostage taker, that I was non-conformist, rebellious, subversive and would escape if given the chance. It contained items of gossip, including an update on the state of Malcolm and Cathy Crosbie's marriage (though the relevance of this to my situation in prison was not clear). Referring to my relationship with Gina, the file said, and this was underlined in red, 'This relationship must be ended.' No reason was given. I suppose they knew how emotionally involved I was with Gina and if the relationship could be ended I would be so much the weaker.

Other men were reading similar things, and it added to the fury. Men discovered they were supposed to be having homosexual affairs. Others were branded as 'psychopaths' or 'psychotics' (based, presumably, on the amateur observations of a screw who had perhaps read a Reader's Digest edition of *Inside the Mind of a Psychopath*). Most files contained invented accounts of conversations with screws, Welfare officers or clergymen in which prisoners 'confessed'.

Having lost control of the prison, the screws called in reinforcements of police and other prison officers to secure the perimeter. Then they settled down to wait until tiredness, cold and hunger forced us to surrender.

Over the next couple of days, organizations like PROP, the national prisoners movement, held demonstrations near the prison and encouraged us to hold out in order to focus public attention on the reality of prison conditions. The riot was certainly attracting publicity. The newspapers, which I read later, condemned the destruction of property, but asked questions about what had driven us to rebel in this way. According to *The Sunday Times*, '. . . an analysis of the official prison statistics seems to suggest that overall the prison regime at Hull is considerably harsher than in any other dispersal prison in the country . . . More than 40% of the prisoners at Hull in 1975 were put in "cellular confinement" [solitary] during the year, 10 times as many men proportionately as Wormwood Scrubs, a similar jail but nearly 5 times as large as Hull.'

Although we had a strongly fortified position, we could not hold out indefinitely. More men had given themselves up, reducing our numbers. On the second night, an armoured car appeared at the gate and while some men prepared petrol bombs to bombard it, others were clearly unnerved by its appearance. Rumours flew around: the Army was going to be brought in; they would use the SAS against us; snipers would pick us off the roof.

At last, we decided that we would have to come down. This decision came about after a full debate, during which a group of Young Turks said they would not surrender but would stay up on the roof. After a long discussion, however, they agreed in principle to surrender with the rest of us. A team of negotiators was picked. It consisted of Jake, Bertie Coster and Martin Brady. They were to negotiate with the Home Office official, Lewis, and to put forward a set of demands: that there be no brutality; that prisoners be allowed to retain their personal property, including whatever tobacco they had; that an independent doctor and the Board of Visitors be present when the surrender was made; that we be transferred quickly to other prisons ('B' Wing had been cleared for us as a short-term measure); that Hull prison officers take the surrender (prison officers had been drafted in from other prisons, but we wanted Hull screws to be present when we came down: if there were going to be attacks we wanted to be able to identify our assailants).

At about 1pm on the Friday, on the fourth day of the riot, we massed on 'A' Wing roof, joined hands and sang '*Auld Lang Syne*'. We waved to the people who had gathered to support us, to the people in the flats, and then made our way down onto the landings. That was the end of the riot.

But it was only the beginning of the real violence. We had decided against surrendering en masse, opting instead for going out one at a time. Before my turn came to leave, rumours were already reaching us that the authorities had reneged on their promises. The first men to reach 'B' Wing were shouting from their cells that the screws were confiscating personal property. Another rumour reached us that a prisoner named Billy Gould had been assaulted, placed in a straitjacket and dragged to the hospital wing. The position was very confused and Lewis, the Home Office official, assured us that if anything of the sort had happened it was because of a breakdown in communications and would be immediately rectified.

Martin Brady was the first of the Irish prisoners out, and I followed him. I did not think, as I climbed over the barricade, that we would be beaten up in Hull. I assumed that they would wait until we were dispersed and brought to other prisons. So, while I was nervous, I was not particularly frightened. We walked down a long corridor lined on either side with screws in riot gear. It was very tense and I knew that if we so much as glanced at them or muttered anything they would attack us. They were straining for an excuse to do us violence.

At the bottom of the corridor, they had spread a white sheet on the ground, on which we had to stand as we were strip-searched. I was taken to 'B' Wing, which looked bomb-blasted, and put into a cell. It was completely bare, the glass had been smashed out of the window and the bed and mattress had been removed. After about ten minutes, the door opened and a number of screws entered. They demanded my ring and a religious medallion I wore around my neck. I resisted, insisting that it had been agreed that we be allowed to keep our personal property. They pushed me into a corner, gave me a few slaps, then ripped the medallion off. They could not get at the ring so easily so they gave up and left.

I attempted to warn the prisoners who had not yet surrendered by shouting from the window that they were, contrary to promises, taking personal property. I do not know if they heard me. In any case, the surrender continued.

I peered through the observation slit in the door and saw Jake and Frank Conteh placed in cells opposite mine across the landing. More prisoners arrived; it started to get dark. As evening wore on I heard shouts from the windows. Men were warning each other, 'Don't ask to be let out to the toilets. They do you in the toilets!' I went again to the observation slit and saw that the screws were systematically going from cell to cell to beat up prisoners. Men screamed in the dark (the lights had been ripped out). I was filled with fear. There was nothing in the cell I could use to defend myself, and nowhere to hide.

For whatever reason, the beatings stopped before they got to me. I suppose it can get tiring hitting defenceless men. Later, they came round again, this time with bowls of soup. I heard Jimmy McCartney laughing out loud. He shouted, 'More soup, go on, give us more soup.' The screws had pissed in it. They opened my door, but I refused to take the bowl. They left it on the floor and the stench of urine filled the cell. I was cold and tired. That night I crouched in the corner, too frightened to fall asleep.

Early the next morning, they came and took some prisoners away, Martin Brady among them. These were the lucky ones because they missed that day's beatings. A little later, the screws went from cell to cell unlocking people, one by one, for breakfast. However, to get to the breakfast table at the end of the wing, prisoners were forced to run a gauntlet. They were punched, kicked and struck with truncheons. It was during the breakfast run that the infamous words were heard – 'Don't mark his face'. These words were used by PROP for the title of a book on the riot and its aftermath, and they were heard again more than a year later at York Crown Court when evidence was presented against twelve screws and an Assistant Governor charged with assaulting prisoners and stealing their property. (Eight were convicted and received suspended sentences.) On returning from the gauntlet, those prisoners who had bedding and mattresses found that the screws had pissed on them.

On hearing the screams and groans and the clatter of the truncheons, I was filled with a kind of paralysed bewilderment. To fight was one thing, to beat defenceless people something so low that it hardly seemed the action of human beings. My insides ached in anticipation and I found myself trembling.

I was still trembling when they came to open my door to invite me to breakfast. I told them I was not leaving the cell.

'Out!'

'No.'

Several of them – I do not know how many – jumped on me and dragged me onto the landing by the hair. The gauntlet had lined up, and they pushed me into its mouth. There was nothing to do but try to get through as quickly as possible. I tried as best I could to protect my head; my arms took most of the blows: my arms, my shoulders and back. I do not remember the blows one by one; there were so many.

I got to the table where they told me to sing 'God Save the Queen'. I refused.

'Sing it!'

'Fuck the Queen!'

'Give him some jam,' one of them said. With that, they lifted me up (a sensation more frightening than anything produced by running the gauntlet) and forced my head and shoulders into the huge bin of jam that stood by the table. The surprise alone knocked the air out of my lungs, and within a couple of seconds I was convinced I was going to drown. I started to panic, but that only made it harder to breathe.

They pulled me out, swore at me and insulted me before running me back through the gauntlet to my cell. As I passed Jake's door, I heard him banging and kicking. He could see what was happening from his observation slit and, confusing the red jam for blood, thought I had been seriously injured. 'Bastards!' I heard him scream.

Back in the cell, it took me several minutes to calm down sufficiently to be able to assess the damage. All in all, not too bad, I thought, at least nothing broken. Nothing was hurting yet; the pain would come later. I did my best to clean myself up with whatever torn rags there were lying around the cell. I wondered if that had satisfied them, or would they be back for more?

The noise told me the beatings were continuing outside. From the slit, I watched as the screws worked their way round the cells until they came to Jake. They opened up Jake's door and Jake, instead of waiting to let them damage him, flew out of the cell like a madman and laid into them. He was so badly outnumbered that they quickly beat him to the ground. Jake did not even make it to the breakfast table; they lifted him and tossed him back into the cell.

The assaults went on for some time, and then died down. The wing became silent. Occasionally, I heard men talking to each other from the windows, inquiring after their friends, asking who had been hurt and how bad.

Later, I heard them calling out Bertie Coster's name, and then my name. I assumed it was going to be another round of beatings. I was dragged out of the cell by a prison officer who punched me in the side of the head and pushed me along to the staircase. He and other screws shoved me, and I lost my balance and somersaulted down a flight of the stairs. I looked up and found myself staring at the boots of a mass of

167

screws. In the middle was an AG, arms folded, smiling at the whole thing. I was hauled up and handcuffed to Bertie Coster. They took us along to where another group of handcuffed prisoners was already standing. As we were being led out of 'B' Wing, a screw kicked Bertie who turned round and kicked him back. A scuffle developed, and the screws laid into us again until stopped by a Chief.

We were being transferred to Leicester. On our way to the van we got a brief tour of the prison. I took a lot of satisfaction from seeing the destruction. Driving away and taking a last look at Hull prison, I thought of how it had been when I had first arrived. Hull was the end of the line, the place where the prison system dumped its misfits and did everything it could to grind them down. Instead, we wrecked it.

Chapter Twelve

APPEAL

On arrival at Leicester, the screws put Bertie Coster and me in the block, where we had a hot bath. I discarded my jam-messed clothes and got into a clean kit. I ached all over from the beatings of that morning – already it seemed an age away – but felt a little better after the bath.

The atmosphere in the block was tense. When the screws saw our injuries, they knew at once that we would be making allegations against prison officers. Naturally, they were unhappy about this: prison officers, like policemen, stick up for each other when there are allegations of wrong-doing. I wanted to see a doctor to have a proper record of my injuries made. They did not like the idea, but had no choice: it is standard procedure that when new prisoners are admitted to the block they have a medical examination.

However, prison doctors are civil servants and, to all intents and purposes, part of the prison service. My 'examination' was more like an adjudication, one of the sessions of the prison's kangaroo court. I was taken from the cell and brought to the end of the block where the doctor sat behind

169

the table. Five or six screws surrounded me; two stood just in front, facing me, so that I had to stand on tiptoes to be able to talk to the doctor over the sloping wall of their shoulders. The screws had pulled their peaked hats low over their foreheads to give themselves a more menacing look, and they joined their hands at their crotches: a crude message that they would be only too happy to start a fight.

The doctor, whose gestures and tone made it clear that he considered me distasteful, asked where I was hurt. I was bruised down one side of my face and neck. The bruising continued down my body and I pulled up my shirt to show him the marks on my chest and back. I started to describe the injuries to my legs. 'Wait, wait!' he said impatiently. 'Why don't you just tell me where you haven't been hurt?' He said it with such sarcasm and loathing that I turned on my heels, walked back to my cell and slammed the door shut.

A little later, a screw came and asked if I wanted to see the medic (the medic is a screw who has done some kind of first-aid course). When we had been run through the gauntlet at Hull, medics were warning the screws to be careful not to leave visible marks. 'Don't mark his face,' they had shouted – advice which, in their enthusiasm for their job, most of the officers neglected to follow. No, I did not want to see the medic.

At that stage, we were not officially on punishment, not having been adjudicated, but on Rule 48, segregated while awaiting adjudication. In effect, it was the same as punishment. They came and told me to work – sewing mailbags. I said no. Bertie Coster also refused. So I sat in cell, all day. There was nothing to read, I had no radio. The time went very slowly.

Jimmy McCartney, the Scottish prisoner who had shimmied up and down 'D' Wing's drain pipes during the riot, arrived to join us in the block. Jimmy could not stand the boredom and agreed to sew mailbags. He had done a lot of time and could sew like a granny: he tore through the bags they threw into his cell – they were the little plastic ones, not the heavy canvas variety – and he used to put down twelve bags a day for me. In this way I had some earnings put into my canteen account.

We began to make contact with other prisoners. In the

special security wing opposite the block were men I had met in Wandsworth, and an Irish prisoner named Noel Jenkinson. Noel and the others tried to supply us with tobacco but were unable to because of the strict security. Our windows were heavily guarded; cameras were trained on them twenty-four hours a day. One day, Jimmy Hayes, a Scottish prisoner who frightened the screws because he attacked them without hesitation if they annoyed him, went to the block cleaner's cell and said, 'How are you feeling?' He said it with such menace that the cleaner could hardly find breath to speak.

'What?' the cleaner eventually squeaked.

'I said, have you got over that bit of sickness you had?'

The cleaner, who was very slow, said, 'What sickness?'

'Did you not know you were sick?'

'No.'

'Well, you are. Now get into that fucking cell, and when the screws come round to tell you to bring the food down the block tell them you're sick.'

At tea time, the cleaner did as he was told. The screws needed another cleaner so Jimmy piped up, 'I'll do it, governor.' The screws, anxious to appease Jimmy, said okay. Jimmy duly arrived with the food and the bin of tea. When they unlocked my cell to give me my food I created a little diversion, during which Jimmy tossed a package of tobacco under the bed. I then separated the tobacco into five parcels, one for each man in the block, which I took to the recess when I slopped out and hid under the toilet bowl. Word was passed round and everyone was able to get their tobacco. The screws knew that we had it, but were unwilling to cause trouble. Jimmy McCartney, who liked a smoke, had kept up a kind of guerrilla war over the denial of what he considered a fundamental human right. When they confiscated his tobacco he threw tantrums, kicked and slammed doors, shouted and screamed, and abused them with his vicious Glasgow tongue. The screws, nervous about having notorious Hull rioters in their block, were keen to placate us.

Being able to smoke a cigarette helped break up the day, and, as the weeks passed, I began to get used to the slow rhythms of solitary. Small things made the time more bearable. I was able to have conversations of sorts with the men in

171

the special wing – Noel Jenkinson in particular. We shouted
to each other from our windows, often having to compete
with other men. Because of the noise and the distance, our
conversations were frequently comical.

'Paul?' Noel would shout.

'Yeah?'

'Noel.'

'What?'

'It's Noel.'

'Yeah Noel?'

'What?'

'I said it's Noel.'

'Yes Noel?'

'Did you get the tobacco?'

'What?'

'Tobacco!'

'Do you need some?'

'No, do you want some?'

'What?'

At least it was human contact, of sorts.

In prison, but particularly in the block, the day is highly
regimented. It begins at 6.30am when a screw unlocks the
door and kicks it open. You have less than five minutes to
slop out, empty your pisspot and bucket, use the toilet, wash
and shave, fetch water, clean utensils, strip the bed and carry
the bedding, mattress and the bed onto the landing. Then
back into the cell, where you sit in a corner until the cleaner
brings breakfast, which is eaten in the cell. If you are on
morning exercise (prisoners are entitled to one hour's exercise
a day if the weather is not 'inclement' – prison officers tend
to interpret this loosely and unevenly: some say dark clouds
make the day inclement; others will let you out in a light
drizzle), you get an hour in the yard, walking around by
yourself. Then back into the cell to sit in the corner. Dinner
arrives between 11.00 and 11.30am. After 2pm the door is
unlocked and the tray removed. At 4.00–4.30pm tea arrives.
At 8.30pm you slop out again and bring in the bed. Clothes
are removed and kept in a box outside your door. At weekends, for the convenience of the screws' shifts, everything is
that much earlier: you bring in your bed at 3pm and leave
your clothes out. Saturdays were the hardest. I used to think,

'It's three o'clock in the afternoon, I'm twenty-three years old and it's time to go to bed.' I pace the cell in my underpants; I walk to the sound of a slow-hand clap inside my head. The days are like long loops; endless, slow circles of time.

One October morning, they did not unlock us at the usual time. Any interruption in the routine, however slight, was taken as a sign of trouble. Before long we were up at the windows, tapping into the grapevine for news. No one seemed to know anything, except that the screws were silent and looking worried. We began to get restless. I heard a prisoner named Brown shout to Bert from the special wing opposite the block, 'That Irish geezer bowled over in the night.'

I did not understand what the expression meant. A moment later a priest came into my cell.

'There's been a very sad incident,' he said. 'Your friend Noel Jenkinson died during the night.'

Later, we heard some details of what happened. According to one of the prisoners on the wing, Noel had rung his bell at about midnight, complaining of a bad headache. He asked to see a medic or a doctor; the screw said medical staff were not allowed in the special wing. Noel asked for some tablets, but the screw said he could not open the door (everything was operated electronically and the night staff did not have access to the controls). The screw ground up some tablets, put them on a sheet of paper and passed them through the slit of Noel's door. Nothing more was heard from Noel, and the other prisoners assumed that he had gone to sleep. When the screws unlocked the door the following morning Noel was dead.

I was deeply saddened by Noel's death. I had never seen him but, after our shouted conversations, had grown to like him in the few weeks I had been in Leicester. He was an intelligent and humorous man. To die alone in prison . . .

One day, each of the Hull prisoners was given an official form. The Home Secretary had appointed the Chief Inspector of Prisons, Fowler, to head an inquiry into the riot and its aftermath. Did we, the document asked, wish to air any grievances? Any information, Fowler assured us, would be treated confidentially. However, at the bottom of the page was a warning that any prisoner making false allegations against prison staff would be punished. So much for that.

The brutality of the screws at Hull had attracted wide-spread attention outside, and the announcement of the Fowler Inquiry failed to satisfy many of those concerned about what had happened. PROP, the national prisoners movement, organized an alternative, public inquiry chaired by John Platts-Mills QC: its members included, Monsignor Bruce Kent (later chairman of the Campaign for Nuclear Disarmament); Albie Sachs (a former prisoner of the South African regime and, at that time, a law lecturer at Southampton University, as well as a number of trade union officials. The inquiry was supported by Ludovic Kennedy, the author and broadcaster; Trevor Huddleston, the Bishop of Stepney; Jo Richardson, the Labour MP; and other prominent figures. In May 1977, it heard evidence in public and published a report condemning the violence of the regime at Hull and the screws' brutality after the surrender.

The independent public inquiry also condemned the punishments meted out by the Boards of Visitors to the Hull rioters. Some men had lost more than 800 days – adding more than two years to their sentences – after hearings that had lasted less than five minutes. The Board of Visitors 'awarded' me (the word always made me laugh – up until then I had always associated it with pleasant things, things to be proud of, like prizes or medals) 144 days' 'cellular confinement' – solitary. However, since the 'award' began from the day of adjudication – the time spent awaiting the Board of Visitors' hearing was not counted – my time in punishment did not finish until 4 May 1977, seven months after the riot. Because I had no remission to lose they could not add anything to the length of my sentence. However, the Board of Visitors said that they were going to recommend that I serve an extra two years. I laughed. I said, 'You know I am never to be released. How can you add two years on top of that?'

I was sentenced to 144 days' loss of all privileges: no books, no newspapers, no radio, no association, no tobacco, no bed, no pen, no canteen. Before adjudication, we had succeeded in squirrelling away some of these forbidden goods. Now they were to be taken away. The long loops of days lengthened.

Life on the block was slow, but it was not always dull. At night, when they put the bed in, I used to lie and listen in to Jimmy McCartney's weird conversations. Jimmy, who had a devious sense of humour, enjoyed a bit of crack and liked nothing better than to wind other prisoners up. Near the block were young prisoners, in for minor offences – taking and driving away, shoplifting, theft. When Jimmy was talking out his window to me or Bertie Coster these kids, all from Leicester, used to mock his strong Glasgow accent. 'Och aye, Jock,' they would shout. Jimmy used to fume. He plotted his revenge. He waited until he went on exercise when he noted down what cells the lads were in. After listening to them talk among themselves, Jimmy figured out who was the dominant one, and he determined to bring him down to size. He made a point of talking to the 'leader' to draw out information.

'What are you in for?' Jimmy asked.

The lad started to boast, and Jimmy pretended to be impressed. Burglary mounted on burglary, joy-ride on joy-ride. Jimmy kept him going. Then, the litany over, Jimmy said, 'I suppose you think that's clever, breaking into people's houses, ordinary working-class people – stealing what little they've got.' In prison, men sense dominance and weakness in a split-second. With this not very brilliant put-down, Jimmy was able to turn the kids against their leader.

When the kids discovered we had come from Hull they treated Jimmy with more respect. Jimmy had done a lot of time and he educated them in the practical ways of prison. He told them, for example, that if you had no matches – as was often the case – you could take the frame off the fluorescent light strip, wrap a bit of vest or underpants around the tube and, after four or five hours, it would burst into flames. Or, you could take off the panel around the light switch, get a razor blade, which you held with two dead match sticks, and press it against the wires. When the blade became hot enough you could light your cigarette. Or, you take a toothbrush handle and squeezed a flint into the hole at the end of it, melting the plastic to make it more secure. Then you shave the fluff off the blankets and gather it into a ball. You flick the flint with a razor blade until a spark fell into the fluff and ignited it. The flints could be supplied by other prisoners from their tinder lighters.

With all the education he gave them, Jimmy turned the

kids into an adoring audience. They talked all night with him and bantered out the windows. Then he made the fatal mistake of telling them how he had almost escaped from Parkhurst. Jimmy had cut a hole in the wall of his cell and made a rope out of knotted sheets. Unfortunately, the rope did not reach far enough, so he added other bits and pieces: a shirt, then underpants, then, and this was his big mistake, his socks. Jimmy slithered down the rope (as I listened, I had the image in my mind of him shimmying down the drain pipe at Hull) and made for the wall. A dog handler was patrolling the far side of the prison when suddenly his animal took off and led the screw straight to the rope. It was the smell of Jimmy's socks that had given him away. Jimmy realized his mistake too late. It is hard to remain impressed by a man with smelly feet, and the kids abused him over his socks for a long time.

One day, the screws came to the cell and told me to pack my kit. I was taken, with Bertie Coster, to Armley Prison, Leeds, where I was placed in the cell previously occupied by Martin Brady (who had been transferred to Leicester and put in my cell). In Armley the atmosphere was unpleasant, the screws more aggressive than they had been at Leicester. I asked for a 'reception letter' (one of the few rights prisoners have) so I could inform my family that I had been moved. They were obstructive, and I had to argue before they allowed me the letter. I had no pen. They said I would have to buy one from the canteen. I had lost my canteen privileges. Tough luck. I insisted so much that in the end they gave me a pen. I waited to write it until after slop out. I left the cell and went to the recess to empty my pot. When I came back the screws had taken the refill from the pen. I never did get to write the letter.

While I was on punishment, the four men arrested at Balcombe Street – Joe O'Connell, Eddie Butler, Harry Duggan and Hugh Doherty – went on trial at the Old Bailey. They refused to recognize the court, and for most of the proceedings remained in the cells. News of what was happening reached me in a roundabout way for I had no radio and no regular access to newspapers. It was in Leeds that Johnnie Walker, who had been at Hull and was also on punishment, passed me a smuggled newspaper in which there was a report about the trial. It included the news that O'Connell had claimed responsibility for Guildford and Woolwich.

This increased my optimism greatly, and helped to make the time in solitary more bearable. My letters home – on punishment I had one letter a week – struck an optimistic note.

After some weeks in Armley, I was moved to Long Lartin and then to Gartree. It was in Gartree, my punishment over, that I was brought up to date with developments by other prisoners. As word spread, men came up to me and said that they had heard that I was innocent, that O'Connell and the others had claimed Guildford and Woolwich, that it was only a matter of time before I would be freed. 'You've got to get off,' they said. Although I would still be facing the Shaw conviction after the Guildford and Woolwich charges were overturned, I did not worry about this. I knew that once Guildford and Woolwich were out of the way the Shaw charge would be cleared up. In the spring and summer of 1977 I had every reason to expect that by Christmas I would be out. By then, I would have spent three years inside: a waste, but not so long that a life could not be recovered.

Surrounded by this optimism, I became increasingly confident. I received a further boost from an unexpected quarter. Detective Superintendent Ronald Sagar of the Humberside police had been put in charge of investigation into the aftermath of the riot. Sagar's investigations were separate from the Fowler Inquiry whose task was not to prosecute individual wrong-doers, but to examine conditions within the prison and to make recommendations to the Home Secretary. Part of Sagar's task was to interview prisoners held in 'B' Wing after the surrender. This was far from straightforward. Sagar and his team encountered difficulties in tracing the men. They were, for some strange reason, being moved from prison to prison around the country, arousing suspicions that the Home Office was deliberately attempting to hinder the investigation. By the time Sagar found me, he had already been sent on several wild goose chases and was furious with the prison officials. Although we were initially suspicious of Sagar, and sceptical of his willingness or ability to bring charges against the Hull prison officers, it was as a result of his work that twelve screws and an Assistant Governor were prosecuted for serious offences arising out of the aftermath of the riot.

Sagar took a statement from me about what happened at Hull. I described events on the Friday in 'B' Wing, and gave him the names of the prison officers who had assaulted me. He noted it all down. As the interview came to a close, Sagar said that the OC (Officer Commanding) of the IRA prisoners had written a note for Sagar to show to the IRA men he was going to interview – instructions to co-operate with the investigation. The note was not for me. He said that this did not surprise him because the prisoners he had already seen had told him that I was not a member of the IRA and was innocent. Sagar, of course, had no control over my case, but he was the first person in any kind of official position not to dismiss my assertions out of hand. The truth, I thought, is at last getting through to people.

Sagar took some time to complete his inquiries, but eventually he submitted a report to the Director of Public Prosecutions recommending action against Hull prison officers. They stood trial at York Crown Court in the spring of 1979; eight were convicted of assault, theft and destruction of prisoners' personal property. I, along with other Hull prisoners, took a civil action against the Home Office and was awarded £1,500 compensation. I sent the money to Kara and my mum.

After conviction at the Old Bailey, our lawyers had decided that we had no grounds for appeal. They were of the opinion that in law there was no way to fault the verdicts. Only Carole's lawyers submitted grounds, arguing that her alibi evidence was dealt with wrongly at the trial. However, with the arrest and trial of the Balcombe Street men and the interviews Logan and Still had conducted with Dowd, O'Connell, Butler and Duggan, our lawyers now sent in grounds of appeal in which they argued for a retrial.

Several things had emerged at the Balcombe Street trial – it opened on 24 January 1977, at the Old Bailey before Mr Justice Cantley – which added to the weight of evidence on our side. First, there was the testimony of Douglas Higgs, a principal scientific officer at the Royal Arsenal Research and Development Establishment (RARDE). Higgs, a civil servant and supposedly independent, had examined the pattern of IRA bombings in 1974–75. He had drawn up an analysis for the court in which the bombings were divided into two phases. Phase One covered October 1974 (beginning with the Guildford bombs) to January 1975; Phase Two dealt with incidents between August and December 1975.

Of Phase One, Higgs told the court: 'I have examined four incidents involving five devices of which all but one detonated successfully. All these incidents had one unusual feature in common, compared that is, with all other incidents studied over the previous twelve months, that is, they were either thrown or dropped and detonated almost immediately thereafter. For this reason, and a number of other features which will be outlined, it is suggested that there is a common link connecting them as a series . . .' The Phase One bombings referred to in this 'series' were the two bombs thrown into the Talbot Arms; and the attacks on Brooks's, the Naval and Military Club, and the London home of Edward Heath, the former Tory Prime Minister.

O'Connell's barrister, Ian Macdonald, acting on instructions from his client to bring out information to show that we were innocent, was puzzled by Higgs's omission of the bomb thrown into the King's Arms, Woolwich, on 7 November since it shared the characteristics he had outlined in connection with the others in the series. He asked Higgs why it had not been included and elicited a highly interesting answer.

'In my original statement the Woolwich one was included but it has subsequently been dealt with elsewhere,' Higgs replied.

Original statement? What was this? It emerged that Higgs had made a statement dated 26 January 1976, in which Woolwich had been included in the series of Phase One bombings.

Macdonald continued, 'But you agree, do you, Mr Higgs, that the bombing at the King's Arms public house in Woolwich is linked to the other three bombs?'

'It is linked in philosophy.'

'. . .do you agree that Woolwich belongs to that set?'

'It belongs to that set, certainly.'

'And from that, Mr Higgs, you can deduce a number of

179

things . . . that the same team which did Woolwich did the other throw bombs, that is one conclusion you can draw from your linking up of the other incidents?'

'It is one that can be drawn.'

If this was true, if the same men were responsible for all the bombings in Phase One, why were Paddy and I doing life sentences for Woolwich?

Macdonald asked Higgs why he had removed Woolwich from the list. 'Were you told to?' he prompted the witness.

'I think I was . . . To the best of my knowledge I was asked to do so, or was advised to do so,' Higgs replied.

'Who asked you to do so, or who advised you to do so?'

'Well, this could only have come through the police. We don't take instructions from anyone else.'

'Through the police?'

'I presume so – acting on the advice of counsel.'

This sparked Cantley, the judge, into life. He professed himself surprised at why Higgs, supposedly an 'independent' scientist, should have modified scientific findings after speaking to the police. 'I cannot understand why you should take something out of an expert witness's statement just because someone has told you to,' Cantley said.

Higgs had no answer. 'Well, my Lord, this is perfectly true. I cannot say anything contrary to that . . .'

'Can you give me any better reason for taking it out than somebody told you to?'

'I think that must be admitted, my Lord.'

Higgs had great difficulty remembering who had instructed him to remove Woolwich. He was pressed by Macdonald. 'Now would you please focus your mind, Mr Higgs, on exactly who it was who came to you, as head of the forensic section, and said, "Will you leave out Woolwich from the throw-bomb series"?'

'I cannot say, sir, offhand.'

'You cannot say?'

'It must have been one of the members of the Bomb Squad on advice, acting on advice from elsewhere.'

Macdonald would not let Higgs off the hook. In spite of repeated insistences that he could not remember who it was who had given him his instructions he at last named a sergeant in the Bomb Squad 'presumably acting on advice from counsel'.

As the trial progressed, more evidence was heard on this subject. Detective Chief Superintendent Hucklesby of the Metropolitan Police admitted that the Woolwich bombing had been left out of the Phase One series after discussions with the Director of Public Prosecutions and Crown counsel. In other words, evidence that linked Woolwich to O'Connell and the active service unit was suppressed not by junior police officers but after a conference of high-ranking officers with senior lawyers and civil servants. The implicit suggestion was that the scientific evidence had been deliberately concealed because Paddy and I had already been convicted for Woolwich. The forensic links between Woolwich and the other throw bombs did not suit the police, the Director of Public Prosecutions or the Crown. They wanted it suppressed.

There was further scientific evidence from Donald Lidstone, another principal scientific officer at RARDE, who had given evidence in our trial. From the witness box, Lidstone now agreed that there were links between Guildford and some of the other attacks, including the one at the Caterham Arms in August 1975, nine months after my arrest. 'I think,' he said in reply to a question by Macdonald, 'the Guildford Horse and Groom could be connected, I won't disassociate myself from that.' According to Lidstone, the Phase Two bombings had been carried out by 'a single cell'.

It was obvious where this was leading. There was scientific evidence that the bombings – including those at Guildford and Woolwich – formed part of an extended series. Lidstone had agreed that they were the work of 'a single cell'. Eddie Butler and Joe O'Connell had made detailed admissions not only about Guildford and Woolwich but also many of the other offences in the series. If Butler and the others had committed these offences, then we had not. The point was not lost on the judge. Cantley, irritated by Macdonald's cross-examination of the scientists, had interjected gruffly, 'So what?'

O'Connell and the three other men put up no defence. Before the judge summed up, O'Connell was allowed to make a statement from the dock on behalf of all four. He said:

We have recognized this court to the extent that we
have instructed our lawyers to draw the attention
of the court to the fact that four totally innocent
people – Carole Richardson, Gerard Conlon, Paul
Hill and Patrick Armstrong – are serving massive
sentences for three bombings, two in Guildford
and one in Woolwich. We and another man now
sentenced have admitted our part in the Woolwich
bombing. The Director of Public Prosecutions was
made aware of these submissions and has chosen
to do nothing.

The trial of O'Connell, Butler, Duggan and Doherty ended
on 7 February 1977. By then, our lawyers had statements
from O'Connell and Brendan Dowd, arrested separately in
Lancashire, in which they admitted bombing the two pubs at
Guildford with three accomplices whom they refused to name
because they had not been arrested. In addition, O'Connell,
Dowd, Duggan and Butler had made statements in which
they, and they alone, accepted responsibility for bombing the
King's Arms in Woolwich. They all denied that Paddy, Gerry,
Carole or I had been present. Alastair Logan and James Still
asked Harry Duggan if we could have been another section
of the IRA without his knowing it?

'They could have been anything without my knowing it
. . . it is very unlikely they would have been members of the
organization. I will put it this way. They wouldn't have been
members of the organization in London because if anybody
else was doing things like that in London, we would have
known. We would have been told about it if anybody was
likely to do anything like that in London at that time.'

After two delays, a date was finally set for our appeal:
10 October 1977. I saw a sinister motive in the delays. The
authorities, I believed, were trying to find ways to discredit
O'Connell, Dowd and the others. One obvious argument
open to the Crown was that Dowd and the others were
concocting their statements in order to try to get us out.
They had already been sentenced to multiple life terms, so
they had nothing to lose. This is not a tactic used by the
IRA – it has never been done before or since – but we
knew that Havers would have to make this suggestion. It

meant the Crown would try to show that during our time in prison we had put our heads together. The trouble was that we had never been in the same prison together. Our lawyers contacted the Home Office Prison Department and requested that we be kept apart. The Home Office agreed.

Then, by the strangest coincidence, I turned up in the same prison as Brendan Dowd. I finished my punishment in Long Lartin on 4 May 1977, and was moved to Gartree where a prisoner pointed out Dowd, whom I had not seen before. I was horrified, even more so when I discovered that Dowd's cell was opposite mine. I immediately understood the danger and went to the PO's (Principal Officer) office where I demanded that they telephone my solicitor to confirm the Home Office's agreement on keeping us apart. After the conversation, it was agreed that I be moved to 'B' Wing. After a week or so, during which time I stayed away from Dowd, the authorities recognized their plan had failed and transferred Dowd to Long Lartin where, by another strange coincidence, Paddy Armstrong had just been moved from Wakefield.

Men are not moved randomly around the prison system. The authorities think very carefully before allocating Irish prisoners to particular jails. I was, and remain, convinced that it was done deliberately, so as to damage our chances at the appeal.

Our appeal opened on 10 October, and Dowd and three of the Balcombe Street men – O'Connell, Butler and Duggan (Doherty, the fourth man arrested at Balcombe Street, had not been a member of the active service unit at the time of Guildford and Woolwich) – testified from the witness box. We already knew that they had given Logan and Still details of the bombings that only the real bombers could possibly know. But I do not think anyone was prepared for the confidence with which they testified. O'Connell was able to describe in detail the interiors of the Horse and Groom and the Seven Stars, how the bombs were made, who planted them, who was lookout, who drove. His account in every way fitted with eye-witness descriptions and the forensic evidence. But, more tellingly, he and the others were able to give evidence about aspects of the attacks of which, up until then, the police had not understood the significance. O'Connell, for example, said he had worn a bush hat during the attack on the King's Arms, Woolwich, which he left behind in the stolen car they had used. At the time, the car's owner had reported the theft to the police, but since it had not been connected to the bombing it had not been thoroughly checked on recovery. Once the car's significance became known – after O'Connell and the others had talked to Logan and Still – it was traced. The owner confirmed that a hat of the type described by O'Connell had been found.

Dowd also offered something that could have been known only to the real bombers. In one of his interviews with Logan and Still, he had made a passing reference to 'two old men with shopping bags waiting for a bus' among the customers in the Horse and Groom on 5 October. Dowd could not have come across this detail in any legal document that we had access to since it had not been made known at the trial. In fact, two old men had been interviewed by the police shortly after the explosion. Their statements had never been served on the defence. How could Dowd have known this if he had not been there? Havers was unable to say.

Havers, the skilled advocate who had torn us apart in the witness box, could not shake them. In the end, he was forced to concede that O'Connell's account of Guildford and Woolwich had 'such a ring of truth' that he accepted that 'a great deal of what he says is true'. He was also prepared to admit Butler had been present at Woolwich, and that Duggan was 'convincing'. It was the detail, so precise, that made it obvious O'Connell and the others were telling the truth. It was the detail that marked their statements out as in a different class to ours.

Nor could the judges find a way around it. Roskill, who presided, said, 'We are content to assume that O'Connell's story of his presence [at Guildford] and participation may indeed be true and that Dowd may also have taken part ... It is difficult to believe that had he [O'Connell] not been present on both occasions his knowledge of the detail ... could have been wholly invented.'

Apart from the testimony of Dowd and the others, our barristers also called a forensic expert, John Yallop. He, like Higgs and Lidstone, testified to the links between Guildford and Woolwich and the series of bombings in 1974–75 committed by Dowd and the other members of the active service unit. Our case, it seemed to us, could hardly have been more compelling. After hearing the forensic evidence I wrote to my mother:

> It went really well for us. I admired the man [Yallop] for his thoroughness and honesty. He said he would stake his reputation on his findings – twenty-five years' experience. I think people are believing us now: the only trouble is that they will have to criticize the police if they clear us, and that is not something they like to do. I can't wait until it's over. I feel as if I have a ton weight on me.

But the judges did not share my view of the proceedings and the witnesses. Turning logic upside down, they used the detail provided by Dowd and the others against us. Dowd, for example, gave evidence about the cars used on the Guildford bombings. He told the court that the bombing team – he, O'Connell and three unnamed persons – had travelled to Guildford in one car which he had hired with a stolen driving licence in the name of Moffitt from Swan National's Victoria branch. His version was confirmed by the branch manager who had supporting documents to show that a car had been hired on the relevant dates by a man named Moffitt. The signature on the rental was Dowd's. Havers was in trouble. If he accepted the version provided by Dowd and O'Connell, that the bombing team had consisted of five people, there was no room for Gerry, Paddy, Carole and me. So he rewrote the scenario, enlarging the bombing team to make room for us. For this Havers needed another car. Among the records of the Swan National's Victoria branch was a rental agreement in the name of Moffat who had hired a car for a two-week period that included 5 October. Havers claimed that this Moffat was also Dowd. Based on what? The signature on the Moffat rental agreement was nothing like Dowd's. Would Dowd have tried to hire two cars in different, if similar-sounding, names from the same branch within days of each other? Would that not have been risky? Might the staff not have recognized him?

It was completely cynical. Havers needed another car to fit Paddy, Gerry, Carole and me into the new script. So he lighted on Moffat. Apart from the similarity of the names, he could not connect the car in any way to Dowd – it was a complete blind. Alastair Logan traced Mr Moffat in South Africa; he confirmed he had hired the car from the Victoria office of Swan National during the period in question. But Logan did not find him until well after the appeal; too late for us.

The evidence and arguments came to an end on 24 October. The judges then retired for a few days to deliberate. I wrote to my mother, who (after another of my father's periodic visits home), was in hospital in Belfast having just given birth to my third sister – Katrina:

> All I can do is hope that the witnesses [O'Connell and the others] will be believed. They have given details of things which could only have been known by those who committed the offences. Their evidence was so good – how can anyone disbelieve it?
>
> I hope you are all fine at home and that everyone is giving you a good rest. I'm sure the baby is really nice now – I think they look best during the first twelve months. I look forward to seeing her.
>
> Take things easy, and don't worry too much about things. I know you do worry. Give all my love to Martin and Marion, and, of course, the baby.

The judges delivered their judgment on 28 October. They did not believe the witnesses, preferring instead the explanation offered by Havers. They seized on the Moffitt/Moffat point. Roskill said, 'We feel no doubt that the former car [Moffat's], which was yellow, was hired by Dowd for the purpose of the Guildford bombings . . . It will be convenient to mention at this point that in his third statement Hill mentioned a yellow XL Granada as one of the two cars.' Moffat had hired a yellow Cortina.

The judges read a suspicious coincidence into the Moffat Cortina and my Granada. Yet they latched onto a discrepancy in the account given by Dowd of an aborted attempt to bomb the King's Arms in which he mentioned another Cortina. In O'Connell's account of this incident he referred to a Corsair. But Dowd had not been certain. He had told Logan and Still that he had been on so many bombings and shootings and had stolen so many cars that it was hard to remember all the details. The two models are similar, but the judges said that the discrepancy showed that the whole thing was a cunning conspiracy, but that the conspirators had not learned their lines. It was a case of damned if you do and damned if you don't. When the accounts from the witness box tallied, Havers and the judges claimed that it proved collusion; when the accounts differed – even in the slightest detail – it also proved collusion.

We had started out confident, it all seemed so clear. But as the appeal wore on, I knew it was hopeless. But it did educate me about one thing. Until then I had assumed that we were the victims of a simple miscarriage of justice. I could understand the jury's mistake, I could even, just, accept that the police might have thought we really were guilty and that was why they had lied and fabricated evidence. But the exchanges in the Court of Appeal convinced me that no one in authority wanted to hear evidence of our innocence. No one who listened to O'Connell, Dowd, Duggan and Butler could have doubted what they were saying was true, no one who listened with an open mind.

Lord Roskill rejected our appeal saying, 'We are all of the clear opinion that there are no possible grounds for doubting the justice of any of these four convictions, or for ordering retrials or, in Richardson's case, for quashing her convictions in their entirety. We therefore propose to dispose of all these applications for leave to appeal by refusing them.' The system of criminal justice in Britain has grown up over the centuries. Central to that system is trial by jury: it is left for juries to decide the facts of a case, to decide whether someone is telling the truth or telling lies: those things are, as trial judges so often remind members of the jury, 'entirely a matter for you'.

That is the system, that is the law. Yet in the Court of Appeal the judges took onto themselves the role of the jury. They weighed the testimony from the witness box. They decided the facts. They decided that Dowd, O'Connell, Butler and Duggan had conspired to tell lies. It was none of their business to do so. All we had been asking for was a retrial – a chance to put the evidence of the Balcombe Street men, which had not been available when we were tried and convicted – before a jury to let it decide where the truth lay.

The day after judgment was delivered I wrote to my mum from Gartree:

> Mum, there isn't a lot I feel like saying. There it is, nothing I can say hasn't already been said.
>
> I hope both yourself and Katrina are well. I'm glad she eats well and is content. I bet granddad and uncle Charlie are well pleased with her and, no doubt, my old man.
>
> Mr Melton said he'd probably be speaking to you over the weekend. He'll fill you in on everything. I don't really know myself what's going on. I shall finish now. There's not a lot more I can think to say. Lots of love for Kara and Katrina.

Chapter Thirteen

A CITIZEN OF PRISON

In reception at Gartree, a con came up and said, 'They took a liberty with you – a right liberty.' On my way to the wing, a Chief told me that everyone in the prison – including the staff – thought we were going to win. Once on the wing, the Irish prisoners offered their sympathy. Then the English prisoners came and told me to keep my chin up. They gave me newspapers – while in Wandsworth, where I had been kept in solitary for the duration of the appeal, I had not seen the papers. I read through the accounts of the appeal: they were brief, buried away in the inside pages. No one was interested any more.

I missed my family; I missed not being able to talk things over with them. Mysteriously, my letters were not being answered. I had written to my mother after the appeal, but had heard nothing back. I wrote to her again, trying to put up a brave front, joking about scraps of Belfast gossip. I was looking forward to seeing my new sister, I said. Still, no letter came to answer mine.

A few weeks later, a screw told me I was wanted by the

AG. I went to the office where there was a priest, and I knew instantly there had been a death. The priest took me into the office and said, 'I'm afraid it's very bad news, it's the child.'

Kara? I felt sick in my stomach. 'Is it my daughter?'

'No, no. It's your baby sister. She died of meningitis a couple of weeks ago.'

Katrina had died on 24 October, four days before the judges rejected our appeal. My mum had not written for fear of upsetting me. She felt bad, but had not been able to bring herself to write. She had asked the chaplain to inform me. As I returned to my cell, what I felt most strongly was not sorrow but relief. The thought that Kara had died scared me so much that it was not until later that I was able to think about my mother and my dead sister, and acknowledge the guilt about the relief I had felt. But I also felt angry at having been left in the dark. I wrote to my mum:

> I felt terrible. I felt helpless that there was nothing I could do for you. I was tempted to take something to help me sleep – I'm glad I changed my mind at the last minute.
>
> I wish you had told me sooner, about Katrina. I had to know sometime, and it only means that when I don't hear from you for a while I always start thinking the worst. Mum, no matter what happens let me know.

In a way, the death of a sister I had never known, so soon after the confirmation of my sentence, seemed to symbolize something about the stage my life inside had reached. There had been a birth and a death: a life, however brief, of which I had hardly been aware, had passed. I was losing touch with my own people; my life was diverging so sharply from theirs that I was no longer one of them.

I began the fourth year of my imprisonment unable to see any favourable outcome. Gina and I had been trying to maintain our relationship as best we could. Outside, it was understood that Gina, who had gone to live in Belfast with my mother, was still my girlfriend and I her boyfriend, and that we had a child. Insofar as that was a relationship, we had a relationship. But it was all so unrealistic and impossible to sustain through a letter a week and a visit every few months. I worried constantly about her; not knowing what was going on took a heavy toll on me. I wrote to my mum:

> Just a few lines to say I hope you are all keeping fine. I'm a little worried myself because I haven't heard from Gina in a while. I'd be glad if you would write to me and let me know if anything is wrong, mum. The reason I ask is that she always lets me know how she and Kara are. You know, I worry enough about you all and it makes it worse when I don't hear anything. Is anything wrong? Please find out and let me know, mum. It really gets me down. I worry about Kara; I do, everyday. Perhaps I'm just being paranoid and nothing's the matter, only when I'm banged up it's heavy on me.

Our best chance to communicate was during visits. But the visits, which should have been occasions of some small pleasure, were nightmares. In Armley, when I was on punishment, I waited for Gina and Kara to come to see me. It is hard to convey to people who have never been in prison what waiting for a visit means, how unsettled and anxious you become. If your visitors are late you think they have had an accident. Then you curse them for their selfishness. Or, have they got lost? Have they missed the train? You curse them for their stupidity. Have they abandoned you? You see men pacing the cells and landings, dressed up, biting their nails, waiting for their names to be called. They have no power. They are waiting for someone else, and sometimes the visitors do not come.

Visiting time ends at around 5pm. That day in Armley, 5pm came and went and there was no sign of Gina. I gave up hope, bitterly disappointed. Suddenly, at 6.30pm the screws called me down for the visit. I was upset and tense. I had been in solitary for several months and was having difficulty talking to people. A dozen or more screws crowded into the small room and watched and listened to us. Gina explained that they had been held up, something to do with a train. I wanted to try to talk sensibly to her, to get our positions

191

clear. I wanted to be sure that Kara would be all right, that no matter what happened between us, I would be able to see my daughter. But how could I say any of these things? We hardly spoke at all. Gina, who had travelled several hundred miles for a twenty-minute visit, went, bewildered, back to Belfast. I got to my cell. I was so depressed and angry that if I had been in a normal cell I would have smashed it up. But I was on punishment: there was nothing to destroy.

I could see no way out, and so I started to prepare for the inevitable. I never said, 'Look, that's it, it's over.' Nor did Gina. I increased the distance between us, not wanting to let go, but having to. Gina's letters became less frequent and different in tone. She continued to sign them with love; but if it was love, it was of a different and despairing sort.

One day, I do not recall exactly when, I had a letter from my mum to say that Gina had left the house with Kara. Gina had not said where she was going. Shortly afterwards, I got a letter from Gina's sister Cathy to say that Gina had found someone else. I had no news of her for some time and became anxious. In the end, a friend managed to find Gina and Kara and assure me they were all right. I did not write to try to change her mind.

I was saddened by how things had turned out, but it was not a devastating blow. There were times I felt angry, but in a way it came as a relief. The thought of her wasting her life waiting for me was too heavy a burden to bear.

After she moved out of my mother's house, I did not hear from Gina for about a year and a half. Then a letter came. I replied, and for the rest of my time inside we kept in touch through occasional visits and letters – irregular but warm. Gina married and had more children. That was that.

Gina gone, our appeal turned down, my granny dead, my baby sister dead: I was in prison for the rest of my natural life, never to be released. Things were happening outside I had no control over; I seemed to be far away from everything familiar to me. I no longer belonged to the real world; I was a citizen of prison. This was my life.

It is a meaningless life. The endless frustration, the hopeless sexual fantasies, the dreams and nightmares, the waste. Watching *Top of the Pops* to look at the girls, masturbating to get to sleep. The idiotic conversations with stupid men who have done too much time and know nothing about life outside prison. The fantastic exaggerations and embellishments. A con on exercise tells you a story. A week later he tells you the same story, but this time it is bigger, more fantastic. He has got nothing else to say. He exaggerates to try to convince himself that something is happening. A story that stays the same is just a story you've heard before: it has no movement, no change, therefore no life. Walter Mittys – they are everywhere. They boast about their criminal careers. A robber tells me about his life: he stole this, he stole that, he robbed a dozen security vans, a hundred banks. He has just finished sixteen years; he's back inside doing twenty-one. He is supposed to be one of the top villains in England. How can he be a top villain? He's never been out of prison, he hasn't had time to be a top villain. There is nothing happening.

I am living on my nerves. I am hanging on by my fingertips. I am afraid I am going to fall into a hole so deep no one will ever find me. I am twitchy, my speech comes in disjointed bursts, my concentration is going. I chew the inside of my mouth until it bleeds. I have nothing to look forward to. I am never to be released. I can never relax. I am always waiting for something to happen. I am waiting for the steps that will stop outside my cell. The door will open, they will say, 'Sorry, there's been a mistake.' They will say, 'Get up, wash, shave', and they will hand me a travel pass like they handed one to George Daves and to Cooper and McMahon.

I daydream about getting out. I sit in the corner of my bare cell and fantasize about it. I can picture it all down to the moment I step out of the gate. I see myself surrounded by my family. I am being hugged and kissed. It does not go further than that. I cannot see what comes next, but I do not care. I want out. I think about it all the time. I am worried about what so much solitary is doing to me. I am angry all the time. I am losing weight. I have no mirror – they are not allowed – but occasionally I glimpse my reflection – on the metal of the hot plate, in a basin of water – and I am shocked at my own image. My cheeks are hollow, my eyes sunken. I am so thin and run down. I have a permanent cold.

I think about Kara: it is 8am, she is eating her breakfast, getting ready to go to school; 9am she is in the playground.

Sunday she is at mass. In some prisons, the noise of children playing and fighting comes over the wall on the wind.

My life is becoming petty. I am obsessed with little things. I hate cockroaches. I cannot stand cockroaches. Whenever they throw me into another cell I look for traces of mice. Where there are mice there are no cockroaches; where there are no mice there are cockroaches. I am in a cell and there are no mice. There are hundreds of cockroaches, they are everywhere. I find them in the mornings on my clothes, in my shoes. I cannot sleep for thinking that one will get into my mouth. I sit there in the empty cell and fume at them. Someone tells me that cockroaches are the only lifeforms that will survive an atomic war. I am repelled by the idea that the world will be taken over by cockroaches. I plot their destruction. I wait until they come out at night. I take a shoe and I go hunting them, taking pleasure in hearing each soft, crushing noise.

But the shoe is not good enough; not thorough enough. And I am losing sleep because I know they are coming into the cell at night. I have to keep them out. I discover that they hate scouring powder. The screws keep Glitto in the recess, plenty of it. But I am not allowed it in the cell. I scheme all day – how do I get the Glitto I need? When I slop out I take my pisspot and bucket down to the recess and when the screws are not watching I steal some Glitto, putting it in my bucket. I saunter casually back to the cell, I might even engage in a bit of banter with a screw, just to put them off the scent. I am fooling them. As soon as the door closes behind me I am transformed into a cunning and bloodthirsty maniac. At night, when the screws have turned out the light, I make a mountain of Glitto at the bottom of the door. I am in bed and I hear the cockroaches. I jump up and examine my defences. Some of them did not brave the Glitto and turned back. Others stumbled through it, but they have left a powdery trail. I follow the trail to a crack in the wall. I fill the crack with paper and I set it on fire. They scurry out. I execute dozens of them.

I can never get enough Glitto. I lie awake at night and think of ways to steal more. It's never easy. They watch you when you're in the recess. You go to shit and they're watching. They watch as you clean yourself. There's no chance to get

194

at the Glitto. I am like an addict. I make bogus applications – to see the Governor, the doctor – anything so I can steal more Glitto. I'm in the recess and they're watching me and I can't get at it. 'I've got a headache,' I say. 'Get me a tablet.' The screw turns, and I swipe the Glitto.

In most punishment blocks, you only get one trip a day to the recess. I must not fail. I must plan for every eventuality. There might be three of them. One of them stays in the recess, another just outside, another across the landing: how do I cope with the first, the second, the third? What if there are four?

Everything is scheming. I smoke. Many times I wish I had never started because when I am not thinking about cockroaches and Glitto I am thinking about tobacco. I am on punishment and not allowed tobacco. In Leicester, I have a stash hidden away. Then they come in and announce that I am being moved and there is no time to get it. In Armley, I am in a cell that has just been vacated by Martin Brady. Martin smokes like a chimney, I know he will have stashed his tobacco somewhere and that, like me, he will not have been able to get to it before his ghosting. I start to hunt. I dismantle the cell. Martin will be doing the same in Leicester. I search and search, desperate for a smoke. I get up to the window. The walls are two feet thick, the ledge of the window slopes down to the outer grill and bars. It is squalid, a mass of old bits of papers, lumps of shit parcels, discarded match boxes. I go through it all until I find Martin's hiding place – an old matchbox stuffed with tobacco, match heads and cigarette papers. Matches are in such short supply that men split them. Jimmy McCartney is an expert, and I am too. I can split a match into four with the razor blade – four lights for one; it is truly the work of a master craftsman. Martin is no good at splitting them: the mangled match heads are the evidence of his botched handiwork. To get a light, I put the match head into the cigarette, nip the cigarette and strike it along the box.

Sometimes, I have no match heads. Following Jimmy's advice, I wrap a bit of vest around the fluorescent light strip. I lie on the bed and wait. I am thinking about nothing else.

In Armley, there are several of us on punishment. Johnnie Walker, Jake Prescott, Billy Gould – all from Hull. We are all obsessed; we want a smoke. We construct a crude pulley from window to window. We have tobacco, but no matches. I get extra vests from the cons at the bath house, and, as soon as I have fire, I take a light, fly to the window, knot the flaming vest onto the line and shout for the next man to pull. Smoke everywhere, I can hardly see what I am doing; there are burns on my hands.

A remand prisoner above sends me down a line. I take it and find a letter and a parcel of tobacco. He's from Derry and knows who I am. As I read the letter, the screws charge into the cell – a screw on patrol outside spotted the line and radioed in. I try to hide the parcel and the letter. They hold me down while they search. They confiscate the tobacco. The lad gets punishment.

Whenever I am smuggled tobacco I have to find somewhere to hide it. There are not many options in an empty cell. I have to be careful, and cunning, in case the burglars come round. The burglars, who wear brown overalls, are screws who specialize in searching cells. A search is called 'a spin'. It is literally a spin, because everything in the cell – a normal cell, one with a bed and a chair – will be upside down after they have left. They can give you a spin at any time.

But I am always ready for them. I have unpicked a thread from the blanket. I put the thread through the tobacco-stuffed matchbox and tie it around my testicles. The matchbox hangs behind my testicles when they strip-search me. The rules about a strip-search – often ignored – are that the prisoner should not be left at any one time fully naked. The top half comes off, then you put your shirt on and take your trousers and underpants off. With a bit of luck they do not examine my genitals too closely; the shirt tails help a little.

I have a Parker pen and some tobacco – these are my earthly possessions and they are illegal. I find a vent in the wall which I use as a hiding place. I wrap the pen in toilet paper. Of course, the screws know that the vent is the obvious place, but I have pushed everything far in, out of arm's reach. The screws can feel nothing. To retrieve my riches, I have a needle which I use to extend my reach. When they have gone I put my arm inside and stab my tobacco or the paper padding around the pen.

In one cell, I see a line of brickwork. I scrape away to

make a small hole. I hide my things there and cover them up with wet toilet paper which sets into a paper mâché the same colour as the wall.

I get a spin and they find a razor blade. I know nothing about it. (I have a blade, hidden: this is not mine.) I'm charged and brought down to the strong box to await adjudication. There is nothing in the strong box at all. After a while, I am unlocked. The screws are aggressive. The Governor wants to know why I have a razor blade. I say that before the spin it was not in the cell. The Governor says I am making false and malicious allegations against prison staff. I insist I did not have the blade in my cell. He fines me £2 (two weeks' earnings inside). I remind him I am on loss of all privileges: I have no money. He says they'll get it off me when I come off punishment and start working. I say that when I come off punishment I am not going to work – they'll have to wait a long time for their £2. We argue. They drag me to the strong box. I am there for three days – 'a cooling down period', they tell me.

The strong box is next to a room that houses the machinery operating the ventilation system. Every thirty seconds it starts and runs for five seconds. Three days and nights of noise. It never stops. There is a constant buzz in my head. After three days I am scrambled.

I am never out of solitary for long. After the appeal I am on normal location in Gartree. It is known as a liberal establishment. I wear a sweat shirt and trainers. The screws are not so aggressive. But it's no good. I can't settle in. I should not be in prison, I am innocent. I argue and demonstrate.

My Aunt Theresa comes to visit – I have not seen her in two or three years – and they take me not to the visiting room, but to the small cubicles where they listen to everything you say. I tell the screw to get out of the cubicle. He says no. I say I am going to bash him if he does not get out. I lift up the table and heave it at him. I throw the chairs at him. Theresa comes in, I have a chair in my hands. She thinks I have gone mad, she is worried about what they will do to me. I tell her I have to do this or they will walk all over me. She cannot understand what I am going through.

I read the letters I get and destroy them. I cannot leave them in my cell where they will be read by screws. With every sheet of paper I tear up, I destroy the words and memories that link me to the real world. I can carry no baggage.

There are prisoners I will not go near. I am in Wormwood Scrubs in 'D' Wing, the lifers' wing. They are mostly sex offenders, child murderers, men who have chopped up their families – nonce (from nonsense) cases. They are often attacked by the other prisoners. I do not join in this, but I will not associate with the nonces. There is a man who has murdered two children. He is hated so much that some prisoners have stolen fluorescent light strips and ground down the glass which they have put in his bowl of sugar. The other prisoners wait for the glass to shred his stomach. Nothing. He is not damaged. They steal more strips and add the glass to his sugar. Still nothing. They nickname him the Bulbeater. The Bulbeater eats fifty light strips. The prisoners get so frustrated that one of them takes a sauce bottle, goes into the cell and does the Bulbeater. The Bulbeater looks like the Elephant Man. They rush him to hospital. He reappears on the wing; a network of livid scars cover his face. They put the Bulbeater in the cell next to mine. That night I hear the noise of scraping and digging. The following morning they don't unlock us. They drag the Bulbeater away. They discover that he was digging a hole in the wall adjoining my cell to get me. The prisoner who attacked the Bulbeater is stabbed to death in another jail.

I am moved around from prison to prison so often that I am becoming disoriented. Solitary makes it worse. I come out and a con starts to talk to me, but I cannot hear what he is saying. He talks for five minutes and when he has finished I realize I haven't taken in a word. I am losing touch with people. I am getting confused.

I am crouched in the corner of a strip cell. I think, if I had not come to England this would never have happened. When the police came to Frank and Anne's looking for Patrick, why didn't I get a solicitor and go with Gina and the solicitor to the police station, and say, 'Look, is there anything you want?' Get it straightened all out. If I had known in Guildford Police Station what I know now, they would have had to kill me before I signed. I hate them. I think of the waste and the anguish, I think of the lies they told, I think of Havers, Donaldson, Roskill. I hate them; it's killing me.

Some prisoners are weird. They are into astronomy, astrology, psychology, Ouija boards, magic, dope, drink, drugs. They talk about the stars and about other lifeforms in other solar systems. Science fiction is popular. They like to read about higher forms of society that do not know what prison is. They are amazed by distance, by the concept of vastness. A prisoner explains to me about light years, about a planet they've discovered seventeen light years away. I am trying to imagine how far away it is. I am in a cell; it is five by ten. It is three o'clock in the afternoon, and they've taken away my clothes for the night.

I look at some prisoners and I see they are mad. They say there is treatment for them, but the doctors? Dr Cooper is in charge of F2 at Parkhurst where he keeps the supposedly insane – we call them Cooper's Troopers. They can have Largactyl, Mogadon, Triptosal – as much of it as they want. The screws take a little plastic cup and mix up the drugs like a cocktail. They ask you if there is anything else you want? They will not let you have tobacco, fresh fruit, vegetables, but you can have as many of their drugs as you like. The men on F2 stagger about all day out of their heads. Cooper's Troopers have knives and shifts and there is violence. The screws are happy to let it continue – it gives them an excuse for the wing's existence. They say, 'We need this wing – there are so many violent madmen.' A prisoner is stabbed to death the day I leave Parkhurst.

Another doctor dresses in a shabby old overcoat, tied in the middle with string. He wears Doc Martens boots, a deer stalker hat and granny glasses. He walks along the paved path following the silver trail of the snails. He lifts the snails up, examines them, sniffs them, then puts them on the grass. He looks up evilly at the windows and we shrink back and hope he hasn't seen us. I am playing football and fall and graze my arm. I go to the doctor for an antiseptic spray. He says, 'Lie down.' I say I just want the spray. I hold my arm and say there's no problem. I just want some antiseptic. He puts his fingers beside his head and wiggles them, as if he's a bug. I say, 'What's wrong, doctor?' He says there are bugs everywhere and we must be on our guard. I leave without the spray. I can't handle him.

What is going on in the outside world? You see a picture

in a magazine: people have changed so much. Look what they are wearing! I am in a van on my way from one prison to another. We are going through Kennington and I see a punk, my first punk: Mohican haircut and bin-liner jacket. I look at pictures in magazines and try to imagine being in the picture. I see a nice house and wonder what it would be like to live in it. Everything in the picture is clean and shiny. There is a polished sideboard. There is a platter of fruit, with grapes so fat with sweet juice they are about to burst open. There is a woman.

I am lying naked except for a bodybelt. It is like a weight-lifter's belt but with a handcuff at each side. Even to stand up requires work. I am in the bodybelt, I am locked in a strong box and left there for three days 'to cool down'. I cannot use my hands to eat so I lie on the ground and lick my food from the plate. I lap some water. I think of O'Donovan Rossa, the Fenian who spent years in British jails chained like an animal. Nothing has changed. They say that Northern Ireland is a part of the United Kingdom, that its citizens are British. I laugh to myself. I am Irish. Every time I open my mouth they say I am Irish. If I had been English this never would have happened. My Republicanism is becoming more focused, more educated. I read books on the history of Ireland. I read John Mitchell's prison memoirs, I read about the 1916 Rising, about James Connolly, Wolfe Tone, Robert Emmet, Roger Casement, about the Republicans who went to Spain to fight against Franco during the Spanish Civil War. Bobby Sands starts his hunger strike in the H Blocks; he is elected MP for Fermanagh-South Tyrone; he starves to death in an effort to force the Government to acknowledge that he is driven by a political goal and is not a criminal. Thousands upon thousands of people turn up to bury him. I am burning with the sense of injustice and anger at the waste of a life. The Government says he is a criminal. What criminal has ever starved himself to death?

In prison, everything is black and white. Prisoners all take sides. They support Bobby Sands. They support the miners during the strike, anyone who fights back.

We fight back in Gartree. A sit-down starts in 'D' Wing, and spreads to 'A' Wing. A man tells me a black prisoner has been taken to a strip cell, placed in a straitjacket and drugged.

We are all angry. The screws are astonished. 'Why are you so wound up over a coon?' they say. The MUFTI (Minimum Use of Force, Tactical Intervention – screws specially trained and equipped for riots) squad is called in and the fighting breaks out. 'A' Wing is shredded, 'D' Wing is shredded, the education classes are shredded, windows are smashed in, doors ripped off, jumpers are cut up for disguises. Some of the prisoners want to take screws hostage. They find an old screw, a decent sort. He never carries a truncheon and boasts that he has never nicked anyone in all his years in the prison service. They corner him in the TV room where he has been watching *Top of the Pops* with the prisoners, and he's very frightened. He looks ready to have a heart attack. A prisoner calms the young bloods and takes the old screw out. *Top of the Pops* is just finishing and some of the men will not join the riot until it is over. One of them is so heavily medicated he isn't even aware that there is a riot. Someone pushes the TV over and this man watches in a trance as it falls to the floor, his doped eyes fixed on the girls' legs. He continues to sit gazing at the smashed set while the riot erupts around him.

I revel in it. I wreck everything I can lay my hands on. It is one of the few times they are not dominant, when I have some control. I am fighting them. And Gartree was a liberal prison. Sometimes you have to destroy a good jail to keep it good.

We cannot get out onto the roof. They bring in the fire brigade and they turn the high pressure hoses on us. We make incendiary bombs. We build barricades with the doors and pour hot water over the screws. The MUFTI squad advance and we toss the petrol bombs at them. Their shields catch fire and they flee in panic. They bring armed men into the prison. I see one of them carrying a pistol.

Four screws are trapped in a cell. Another prisoner – he has done so much solitary he is scrambled – is locked in his cell. He hears the commotion and panics. He smashes his window and cuts his wrists. He is lying semi-conscious on the floor and a group of prisoners have to break down the door to get to him.

The next day there are negotiations. They promise no brutality. I have a sense of *déjà vu*. But the surrender turns out differently. The AG gives everyone a letter. I write to

201

my mum and assure her I am all right. I don't write much, three or four lines, because I don't think the letter will be posted. I am taken, handcuffed, with Phil Sheridan, another Irish prisoner, to a van and we set off with a police escort. One of the policemen is carrying a sub-machine gun.

We are in the West Midlands. There are 112 penal establishments in the country – I have memorized them all – from youth custody centres to maximum security jails. I know where every one of them is. I start guessing where they are going to take us. We head towards Birmingham. I say to Phil, 'Winson Green?' Phil doesn't like the idea of it – bad prison. The Birmingham Six got a dreadful beating there. But then we veer away, and the next sign I see is for Wolverhampton. I know there is only Stafford prison in that area. Too small, they would never take us there. We head south. Shrewsbury? No, too small. Long Lartin? Possibly; but then we pass Long Lartin. 'Bristol,' I say to Phil. But we do not cross the bridge; it's not Cardiff or Swansea either. We head west. This is bad – it could be Dartmoor. We don't like this because many of Dartmoor's screws are in the National Front, and they have a very bad block there. But 'A' men don't go to Dartmoor. We drive on. We arrive, at 4am, at Exeter. The block in Exeter is a subterranean dungeon. The screws are aggressive. There is one who looks like a pig, fat with a pig's nose, as if someone had sliced the nose from a pig and thrown it at his face and it just stuck there.

Exeter is awful. I tell Phil that we have to create trouble to get moved. It's only a small, local jail and if we cause trouble they will quickly move us out. I give them abuse and refuse to do anything they say. A week later they come to the cell and tell me I'm not suited to their prison. I shout goodbye to Phil and go to Winchester, a big improvement. Phil has to stay in Exeter for nine months.

I am taken from Winchester where I am in solitary to York Crown Court to give evidence against the screws who assaulted us at Hull. While the trial is in progress they put me in Wakefield. Wakefield is a bad prison and they attempt to goad me. As I am walking to 'F' Wing they kick at my ankles. They do not like it that I am giving evidence against their colleagues. But it's not all bad. A lot of the Hull rioters are here. Jake is here, Martin Brady is here. We are not allowed to associate but when Martin is on exercise I get up to the window and watch him. He is small, but can handle himself and is self-assured. He walks with a cocky Belfast dander and he is a treat to watch. I look at him from the window, careful not to let him see me. He reminds me so much of home that it takes me back to the Falls and sets off a chain of memories.

In the trial of the screws, I tell the court about the beatings, about them trying to make me sing '*God Save the Queen*'. I enjoy the shock it causes when I tell them that I refused to sing and said 'fuck the Queen.'

The jury finds eight of the Hull screws guilty and they get suspended sentences.

The days go by, I do not know how. My days are long loops, without beginning or end. I am going round in circles and I am always afraid I will fall. I feel sometimes as if I am drowning.

Throughout the fifteen years of my imprisonment, my family never let me down. I missed them, I missed Cairns Street and everyone in it. Late in 1982, Theresa wrote to tell me that my granddad was dying of cancer, though he did not know it. The doctor had told her that he had only a few months to live. Theresa said that he was coming to England to visit me.

I had always avoided asking favours from the authorities, but now I wanted one. I was in Wormwood Scrubs at the time. I explained the situation to the PO and asked if he could arrange a compassionate visit. The PO told me that I would have to get the priest to arrange it. I went to the priest and explained that this was likely to be the last visit I would have with my granddad, and that I wanted to have a little more time with him. The priest said there would be no problem. He would, he said, send the appropriate order to the screw in charge of the visits.

My granddad had been a fit, wiry man, always boisterous and cheerful, and fun to be with. I was shocked, when I saw him in the visiting room, at how he had become so shrunken and old. His meat had been sucked from under his skin and he carried no weight. His gullet and adam's apple seemed to be all there was of his throat. His eyes were far back in his head, his skin was yellow. He was painful to see.

He asked how I was getting on, and I told him everything was fine. I said he was looking well. We discussed the case, home, prison, Kara, my mum, Belfast. After half an hour or so, a screw came up and said that the visit was over. I said, 'What do you mean, I had it extended.' The screw said there was no order for an extended visit. My granddad looked upset, and to avoid an argument in his presence I took the screw aside.

'This is my granddad. He only has a few weeks to live and I am not going to see him again. I went to the priest and he told me he had arranged a compassionate visit.'

The screw was sympathetic and said he would check the paperwork.

'I'm sorry,' he said after a moment, 'there's nothing here. You are going to have to terminate the visit.'

'Look, this is my grandfather. I'm not going to see him again.'

'Nothing I can do.'

I went back to my granddad who had been watching me, a worried look on his ruined face. I said, 'That's it, the visit's finished.' He got to his feet, slowly, painfully. We hugged each other.

I said, 'Take care.'

'I know,' he said.

Then he shuffled away.

I did not know it, but by then they had told him he was dying. If I had known I would have been able to say goodbye. I wish they had told me. I wish I had had the chance.

He died a couple of weeks later.

The priest never bothered to send down the order.

Chapter Fourteen

MUTINY

In Albany Prison on the Isle of Wight, I looked from my cell window to the exercise yard where I saw a prisoner I knew. 'Come here and have a look at this character,' I said to the lads in the cell (we were on association). They came up to the window, and we watched the prisoner walk around the yard. He was formidable looking – tall, heavily built, with long, unkempt dark hair. His front teeth were missing except for two long yellow fangs. The thick, dark-tinted glasses he wore made him appear all the more sinister.

'Who is *that*?'

'That,' I said, 'is Graham Little.'

I had first met Graham in Wormwood Scrubs. I was in the recess trying to clean the limescale off my pisspot when he approached me. I took one look – and put him down as a madman.

'Are you Paul Hill?' he asked. He spoke with one of the broadest Cockney accents I had ever heard. I took a second look at him before answering. In spite of his general Rasputin-like appearance there seemed at that moment nothing aggressive in his manner. He was more like a big, tatty-looking dog waiting to see if was going to be stroked or kicked.

'Yes, I'm Paul Hill,' I said.

'I'm Graham Little,' he said, putting out his hand. 'I've just been weighed off, got a twelve for armed robbery. I was asking who there was that was sensible on this wing and they told me to talk to you. I'm very pleased to meet you.'

'Same here,' I said.

'I don't know anyone else to ask, but have you got a pen I can have for the night? I want to write a letter out.'

'No problem.' I took him along to my cell and lent him the Parker pen I had managed to keep with me through everything. He almost blushed when he said, 'Thanks, mate.' Off he trotted with my pen, promising to return it the following morning. I watched him as he went, chuckling to myself. Very odd.

The next morning, he arrived at my cell with the pen, almost choking with emotion. I asked him if he was all right. He said, 'That's the first time anyone has ever trusted me with a Parker pen.'

'Don't worry, no problem,' I said.

Some days later, there was a fracas in the chapel during service. I saw Graham being dragged out by a dozen screws and bundled down to the block. It turned out that Graham had become friendly with a con who was having problems with a grass on Graham's wing. Graham was incensed. The con drew a sketch of the grass and told Graham that he could be found in the chapel. Armed with this 'wanted poster', Graham went off to wreak vengeance. After some time on the block, he was allocated to another prison.

I did not see Graham again until I was moved from the Scrubs to Albany. A week or so after I arrived, he came to my cell – the last person I expected, or wanted – to see (although he later became a good friend). We chatted for a while. Graham became interested in some of my books on history and politics. He picked up the *Little Red Songbook*, alighting on 'The Red Flag'. The song interested him and he asked me about it. I told him a story I had read. During the Spanish Civil War, a Republican stronghold was holding out against the fascists, refusing either to surrender or flee.

Graham was at once captivated: he could be loopy, but qualities like heroism, bravery and solidarity appealed to his better nature. At last, I continued, in an early morning assault, the fascists broke into the stronghold. The Republicans resisted all the way and the hand-to-hand fighting was fierce. The last few defenders were cornered, with no possibility of escape. They knew they were going to die. As they prepared to meet the final assault, they sang 'The Red Flag' and shouted 'No pasarán!' The fascists moved in and put them to the sword.

Graham was greatly moved by the Republicans' heroism. I told him that out of respect to the men and women who fell that day, their comrades used to gather to sing 'The Red Flag' every morning – no matter where they were they would come together at 6am, the time of the assault, to sing in honour of their fallen comrades.

Time went by and, in my continuing travels around the prison system, I bumped into a friend, Ray McLaughlin, who had just come out of solitary in Bristol. Ray said he had a bone to pick. He explained that on his first morning in the block he had been woken up by the sound of manic singing. He looked at his watch and saw it was just after 6am. Ray banged the door for the screw. 'What is that noise?' he demanded. The screw began to laugh. 'It's Little,' he replied. 'You'll get used to it. He's been here for a month and every morning at 6am he gets onto his table, bollock naked, holds up a clenched fist, and sings this communist song.' Word spread around the prison system, and prisoners who had the misfortune to spend time in the same block as Graham, used to come up to me and say, 'You bastard – why did you teach that loon to sing?'

In Albany at that time – the spring of 1983 – Graham was just one of many prisoners I had come to know after more than eight years of imprisonment. I met so many. I saw men come in just after being sentenced, saw them do their time and be released, and met them again when they were jailed for some other offence. I was on an extended tour of the prison system. Since arriving in Winchester after first being remanded to jail, I had been in Brixton, Crumlin Road (Belfast), Long Kesh, Wandsworth, Bristol, Albany, back to Bristol, Hull, Durham, Hull again, Leicester, Leeds,

Long Lartin, Gartree, Wandsworth, back to Gartree, Exeter, Winchester once more, Wakefield, Albany, Wandsworth yet again, Winchester for the third time, Parkhurst, Canterbury, back to Parkhurst, Wormwood Scrubs, then Albany again.

My second stay in Albany was brief. I got into trouble and was sent for a twenty-eight-day lie-down in Canterbury, which I finished the day before my granddad died. I was then moved back to Albany for a third time. When I arrived, there was trouble brewing over the food. Everything was served up as a stewed pulp; the ingredients were unrecognizable by either taste or appearance. We used to play guessing games: is that carrot, potato or baked beans? In general, the quality of prison food is bad, and for the most part prisoners accept that it always will be; but it was so bad in Albany that we suspected the authorities were doing it deliberately, to rub our noses in it. After I helped to organize a food strike, they carted me off to Winchester where once more they put me in solitary. After a few weeks they took me back again to Albany.

Tension was high. The dispute over the food had created a lot of bad feeling. One day, word went round that they were planning to open a mailbag shop. This was unheard of in a long-term prison, and was considered an insult and an attempt to provoke the prisoners. Sewing mailbags is deadening work. It is common in segregation blocks or in local prisons where most of the inmates are doing fairly short sentences. But it was not intended for jails like Albany and was unsuitable for men serving long sentences. The news of the mailbag shop heightened tension at a time when there was already a great deal of ill-feeling.

When the authorities ordered us to work in the mailbag shop, we refused, and the whole prison went on strike. The screws went from cell to cell, giving everyone a direct order to go to work; every order was refused. The whole prison was on charges. We were taken separately before the Governor and each fined £1.50, more than a week's wages. The next day the process was repeated: everyone refused the direct order to go to work; everyone was fined £1.50. The third day it was the same again.

The finings only increased the tension. A group of prisoners decided that they were going to smash up one of the offices.

I advised them not to, telling them that they would only lose remission, and that at the end of the day the mailbag shop would still be there. I suggested a different course of action: when exercise was called they should disguise themselves, climb the mailbag shop and wreck the roof. When they had finished with the roof, they could jump down, discard their disguises, join the rest of us and pass back into the wing. That would be the simplest way to put the shop out of action and avoid punishment at the same time. I went to a friend of mine who worked in the woodmill and got him to make some truncheons, which he carved out of table legs, with which to break up the roof.

At about 6pm, the screws called exercise. The lads – there were three of them – hid their truncheons under long overcoats. Once in the yard, they sprang onto the roof and proceeded to tear it apart. An alarm sounded and the screws rushed out to the yard. We massed together to block the screws getting to the roof, and there was an uneasy stand-off. They tried to get us back into the wing, but we refused. There was nothing they could do except look on helplessly as the lads continued their work.

The mailbag shop had been the intended target, but the boys got carried away and started on the roofs of the adjacent workshops. When it was clear that they were not going to come down as planned, we filed back into the wing to let them get on with it. They worked like navvies all night.

The following day, word reached us that they intended to stay on the roof. We had to find a way of getting food to them. To our surprise, the authorities decided to allow exercise – probably in an attempt to defuse the situation. We hurriedly collected food, tobacco and matches, which we threw onto the roof. While exercise continued, we heard that prisoners in 'B' Wing were pulling the sleeves off their jerseys, a sure sign that they were preparing to riot. The slightest wrong move would set the prison off. This came after the screws ordered a cleaner in 'B' Wing to clean up excrement that had been smeared over one of the alarms. The cleaner refused; they charged him. Incensed, he took a broom handle and set about the glass on a nearby stairwell.

From 'A' Wing, a prisoner shouted to those of us on exercise that the MUFTI squad had been seen forming up nearby. That was the signal for the riot. Barricades were thrown up; tables, desks and chairs were smashed; there was glass everywhere. More prisoners took to the roof. We turned our attention to the doors. Albany is one of the newer prisons and its electronically-operated doors were more difficult to destroy than those at Hull. When they gave way, they came crashing down in a dangerous shower of electrical splinters.

In the bath house we ripped out the baths to drop on the screws on the lower landings, forcing them to scatter. They regrouped and shouted up threats, calling us out by name. They said that when they got me they were going to break my legs. We ignored them. The destruction continued.

Before we were able to erect barricades strong enough to secure the wing, the MUFTI squad organized a charge and broke through. They chased us onto the upper landings, where I found myself separated from the main body of prisoners. Ten or so screws in full riot kit came after me. There was nothing I could do, short of jumping over the landing. They crashed down on me using their riot shields, and dragged me and another prisoner to a secure cell.

The riot for me was over. The screws worked their way through the wing, beating prisoners and tossing them into cells. Those of us who had been captured during the early stages were led in handcuffs to reception where we were strip-searched. They were in a hurry to get us out and paused only to give us a brief burst of verbal abuse. Apart from a few pushes and shoves and rabbit punches, I was not harmed. They put us in a van and we set off for nearby Parkhurst. As we pulled away I could see the lads still at work on the roof. It would be a long time before the mailbag shop re-opened.

At Parkhurst, the atmosphere was more threatening. But although the screws were aggressive, there was little actual violence. The lessons of Hull – after which screws had been convicted of abusing prisoners – had not been lost on them. They threw me into a cell in the block. Before they closed the door one of them showed me a syringe with a long, vicious needle. 'If there's any trouble out of you,' they said, 'you'll get some of this.'

The liquid cosh, it is called, and it holds more terror than the worst of beatings. We were next to one of the most feared wings in the British prison system – Dr Cooper's F2, into which they dragged screaming men to turn into zombies.

I had no trouble that night. At 6.30am the following morning, they came and gave me my clothes and took me to reception where there were a number of prisoners. The atmosphere was tense. I knew that a single word or gesture would set them off, so I avoided eye contact and willed the van driver to hurry up. Out of the corner of my eye, I saw a group of men. As they approached, I made out Graham Little being dragged along by six or seven screws. Graham looked madder than usual. He had a jersey sleeve – two eye holes punched out – half-on, half-off his head, and he wore his overcoat like a cape, buttoned at the top, with his arms out of the sleeves.

Graham was the last person I wanted to see in these circumstances. I had been counting my blessings in having been through a riot without a serious beating. Graham's arrival seemed to jeopardize my chances of escaping in one piece. When he spotted me, Graham broke loose from the screws and ran to me. He shouted, 'Did the bastards do you, did they do you Paul?' I urgently tried to calm him down, 'No, no. It's no problem,' at the same time looking around at the screws to show them that there was no need for violence.

Fortunately, the driver arrived, and three of us were handcuffed and put into the van; Graham was left behind. We set off for the ferry and, once on the mainland, I played my usual guessing game of where they would take us. My hopes rose when we reached the Midlands. Long Lartin, I thought, that's not bad – Long Lartin is not a hard prison. As we pulled up outside reception, I was feeling quite pleased. Long Lartin was a definite improvement on Albany. Sadly, we were there only so the screws and the escort could have their lunch. Then it was back in the van and off again. We headed for Manchester, a gloomy prospect, for Strangeways was one of the worst prisons in the system, its block one of the most feared. As we reached the gate lodge, I heard the screws say that only one of us was going to be left there. I strongly wished this on my fellow prisoners, but the name called was mine.

At the entrance to the block, the screws had fastened a sign: 'Don't complain, you volunteered.' They brought me to a strip cell where they took my clothes. I felt very low.

However, Strangeways turned out to be a paradise of sorts. Once allocated to a normal cell on the block, I found myself below two remand prisoners – one was a man named Callaghan who was related to a family in Albert Street, Belfast. As remand prisoners, they had tobacco, chocolate and other luxuries that I had not seen in such quantities for many years. A criss-cross wire grill on my window was all that prevented me getting at the goods. It had to go. I ripped up a plastic mat – standard prison issue – and stuffed it into the grill. I then set it on fire. There was a lot of smoke and the heat was intense. I wrapped my pullover around my hand and punched the grill until I had made a hole big enough to get my hand through. From then on, the remand prisoners – Salty and Callaghan – kept me supplied with everything I wanted. They even managed to smuggle me a bottle of Blue Nun wine – I thought I was in heaven.

The block screws in Strangeways were used to having things their own way. One screw, a man named Kerr, was particularly aggressive and petty. He liked to intimidate prisoners, and screamed and shouted at them for the most trivial things. One rule they tried to enforce concerned where prisoners were, and were not, allowed to walk. The floor was tiled in white except for the area along the walls, which was black. Prisoners were allowed to step only on the black tiles. This involved making detours to the recess, the office and the hot plate – every trip was three or four times longer than it needed to have been. I ignored their rule. A PO said, 'Look Hill, this is a local nick, this is not a dispersal prison and we're not changing our ways for you.' But I was not changing for them. While I was in the block I made a point of walking on the white tiles.

Some days after my arrival, the screws informed me and Tony Clarke, another Irish prisoner who was on the block after having been moved from Albany, that we had both been charged with mutiny for our part in the riot. In addition to the mutiny charge, we faced adjudication before the Board of Visitors at which we would certainly be awarded lengthy periods in solitary. We would be informed in due course, they said, of the dates for the hearings.

I sent several letters to my family to tell them about what had happened, but received no reply. It was terribly frustrating. Although I knew my family would never abandon me, all kinds of things ran through my mind as each day passed without word from them. I confronted the screws about it, suspecting that they were deliberately withholding my mail. They, of course, denied it, but I later discovered that letters my mum sent to Strangeways were returned marked 'Not known at this address'. Several weeks went by before they let any letters through.

My transfer to Strangeways had ruined visiting arrangements I had made with my mum, Gina and Kara. Because of the difficulties they faced in coming over and because I had been moved around so much, I had not seen them for a long time. I had saved up several months of visits, and had planned for my family to come to Albany for two weeks. When we at last managed to establish contact at Strangeways, I once again urged them to come over. However, I did not want to have my visits at Manchester because visitors were separated by glass partitions, and these I refused to accept. I complained to the Governor and told him that I wanted to be moved to another prison for my visits. When they refused, I informed the PO that I would 'shit up' – smear excrement over my cell – unless some better arrangement was made. The Governor asked me not to do anything until he had a chance to sort it out. I gave him two weeks.

Until then, it was just a question of killing time. I was by then an expert in that. However, Kerr continued to give us problems and I spent a lot of time thinking of ways to get back at him. One night I heard the answer to my prayers. As I lay in bed I overheard two cons discussing Kerr.

'A real dog,' one of them said.

'Yeah. You know he lives in Stockport.'

'No?'

'Yeah.' And he repeated Kerr's address.

The following morning Kerr came to slop me out. He stood, as usual, legs apart, slashed peak pulled down over his eyes. I started whistling.

'You're very happy this morning, Hill,' he said, suspiciously.

I ignored him and continued to whistle. I filled up my breakfast bowl.

'You're not going to be too happy doing the rest of your life in prison,' Kerr added.

'I'd sooner live here than in your house,' I answered, supplying him with the address, and, still whistling, I sauntered into my cell and closed the door behind me.

A few minutes later, the PO came to the door with Kerr, who was white-faced.

'Mr Kerr has informed me that you have made a very grave threat against his life,' the PO said.

'I have made absolutely no threat whatsoever,' I replied.

'Look, we both know the connotations of this,' the PO said.

'What connotations? I don't know what you're talking about.'

There was nothing they could do. They closed the door and went away. However, Kerr was transformed. He did everything he could to get on speaking terms with Tony Clarke and me. Whenever Tony slopped out, Kerr would banter with him, call him Ginger, ask him if he wanted any more tea.

One day, the Governor came to tell me that I would be moved to Wormwood Scrubs for a month in order to have my visits. This was good news, for the Scrubs was one of the better places for visits. The rooms were reasonably spacious and the screws did not crowd in to listen to the conversation. In other jails they would be so close that it was impossible to show love or tenderness because you knew the screws would interpret it as weakness. I hated the idea of them gossiping in bars. 'Guess what Hill said to his mother today . . .' I had developed, in a way that I was conscious of but could not resist, a manner that must have appeared distant, that may have suggested lack of interest. I could not help it; it was for my own protection. When the visit was over, on the way back to the cell, I used to want to rush back and say the things I had not said. I used to think, 'Tomorrow I will say these things.' But I never did. In that way, visits were a source of sadness, a reminder of how distant I had become. I would look at Kara, wonder at how she had grown, at how much she looked like Gina, and be sad. Our worlds were so apart. How was she coping with this? What was she thinking?

I had looked forward to the visits and had protested to

get them. Yet, once they were over, I felt as if a burden had been lifted from me.

Back in Strangeways, they brought to the block a young lad called Smith. He was as thin and fragile as an ancient skeleton; his clothes hung on him; the seat of his pants fell to the back of his knees. I felt sorry for him, he was so obviously deranged. When I was given my tea that night, I put a couple of books outside his cell before they locked me up. The next morning, I found the books had been left at my door. The screw said the lad had asked who had left the books and returned them without looking at them. When Tony and I went on exercise that day we walked, as usual, anti-clockwise (in all exercise yards the flow of traffic is always one-way; no one knows why, that is just the way it is). Smith walked clockwise and kept bumping into us, so Tony and I, to avoid trouble, turned and walked his way. No sooner had we done this than he turned and walked the other way. In frustration, Tony grabbed Smith and told him not to be so anti-social.

That night in my cell I heard a dull thud and the noise of breaking glass. Someone, I thought, is preparing a weapon.

The next morning on exercise I warned Tony that Smith might have a weapon and to be on guard. We walked around the yard, keeping a wary eye on him. After a few minutes, as I was talking to Tony, I saw out of the corner of my eye a sweeping motion coming towards me. I ducked down and saw his arm sweep across above my head. I got up and punched him, splitting his nose open. While he was stunned, I twisted the glass out of his arm. He was so skinny and weak that it was not even a real fight. He staggered back, wiped his nose and inspected the blood. He said, 'Pretty fast, eh?' It was pathetic. Tony fell about in stitches. The screws came and dragged Smith away.

The next morning, the screws came to ask me to give evidence at Smith's adjudication. I refused. I told them that I would under no circumstances give evidence against another prisoner, least of all a man who was so obviously mentally ill.

Eventually, the time came for our own adjudications. Word had reached us through the prison grapevine that several men had already been awarded fifty-six days' punishment plus the usual loss of remission. At this time, lawyers were beginning to challenge the whole system of prison adjudications on the grounds that they violated the right to legal representation and contravened the principles of natural justice since, among other things, prisoners were frequently put in the position of not being able to defend themselves without making counter charges against prison staff, for which they would be punished. At the same time, another prisoner had taken a writ to the High Court to challenge the mutiny charges.

While these legal moves were in progress, the adjudications continued. I was taken to the block in Wormwood Scrubs where they had gathered rioters awaiting adjudication. The Governor and the members of the Board of Visitors sat, guarded by screws, around a table in an office off the block. One by one, men were taken from their cells to make their brief appearances before the kangaroo court. I sat in my cell and waited my turn.

Before it arrived, another prisoner was called for adjudication. As soon as his cell was opened he sloshed a bucket full of piss over the floor of the block. He had been saving it for a week; the stink was appalling. My eyes smarted and there was an unpleasant burning sensation in my nose. The adjudications were adjourned as the Governor and the Board of Visitors fled. Shortly afterwards, the mutiny charges arising out of the Albany riot were quashed by the High Court.

At around this time, I wrote to Lord Hylton, who was well-known for pursuing humanitarian issues within British prisons. I asked him to take up with the Home Office the question of my treatment in general and the possibility of repatriation to Northern Ireland. Lord Elton, a junior Home Office minister, wrote back:

Mr Hill's behaviour alone is a strong indication that he would not be acceptable to the Northern Ireland Office who, you will recall, are unwilling to take any prisoner who is not cooperating with the prison regime in this country. As you may know, Mr Hill was involved in the disturbance at Albany Prison last year and his general conduct has been far from satisfactory.

216

My general conduct did not improve.

In February 1984, after ten months in Strangeways and the Scrubs (most of it in solitary), I was moved to Gartree and put on normal location. As I was going from reception to the wing, I saw a man on the roof. It was William Hickey. Hickey had been convicted of the Carl Bridgewater murder, and inside was widely believed to be innocent, a victim of the West Midlands Serious Crime Squad – now notorious for fabricating verbal 'confessions' of the kind used to convict Hickey and the others in his case. Hickey had been on the roof for some time, sustained by prisoners who smuggled food to him. Those caught were fined £10 – a massive sum by prison standards, eight to ten weeks' wages. There were regular collections taken up to help those fined. The screws never tried to get Hickey down by force for fear of provoking a riot: there were a lot of good people in Gartree at that time, men who defended themselves and weaker prisoners.

Paddy Armstrong was in Gartree then. I had not seen him for several years. He looked much older; his hair was going, and his eyes were dull and tired. It was a reminder of how much time had passed since our arrests. Seeing him made me think back to the conversations Paddy, Gerry and I had had in Winchester in which we assured each other that the charges could not possibly stand up. And of the time in the van leaving the Old Bailey after we had been sentenced, when Gerry and I had tried to lift Paddy by telling him that everything would soon be sorted out. Conversations and conversations: they were from a decade earlier. Paddy was a bit shambolic, disorganized, but was well liked in the prison. He never had much in the way of possessions because his mother was old and ill and was unable to come over to see him very often. But there were several Irish prisoners in Gartree, Ronnie McCartney in particular, who looked after him, and used to rally him when his spirits were low.

Paddy seemed even more cut off from the outside world than me and he knew little of what was happening in our case. By then, some people had begun to express doubts about our convictions and those of the Maguire Seven and the Birmingham Six. The growing public awareness was the result of pressure from a number of sources: from the prisoners themselves, their families, their lawyers, a handful of clerics committed to seeing justice done, a small number – initially at least – of politicians, and a few journalists.

Gerry and I had – from the moment we were convicted – been writing to politicians and public figures, protesting our innocence and pleading with them to look into the case. I wrote to my mother and asked her to see Gerry Fitt, then Member of Parliament for West Belfast. Fitt, a vitriolic anti-Republican who later lost his seat to Gerry Adams, the President of Sinn Féin, refused to listen and chased my mother from his office with a torrent of abuse. In the early days, what letters I got reflected Fitt's attitude; most never bothered to respond.

Our families apart, the first people to do anything for us were two Irish priests, Denis Faul and Raymond Murray who were well-known for their work in documenting official abuses of power. They worked alongside Sister Sarah Clarke, an Irish nun living and working in London, who took, and continues to take, a special interest in the welfare of Irish prisoners in England. At the time of our committals in the spring of 1975, Sister Sarah, Father Faul and Father Murray contacted and interviewed our relatives. They also spoke to a number of people who had been arrested and questioned by the police about Guildford and Woolwich. They quickly became convinced of our innocence, and built up a dossier which they took to the Catholic hierarchy. Such was the climate at that time that they received more abuse than help from those they went to in search of support. Everywhere they were turned away; some of those they approached accused them of making pro-IRA propaganda. But they were not deterred and spoke to anyone who would hear them out. They had more success abroad, where people were prepared to listen with an open mind. Father Faul and Father Murray spoke at meetings in the United States, New Zealand, France, Germany and Italy to tell their audiences that the Guildford Four, the Maguire Seven and the Birmingham Six were innocent.

One of the few people who did listen in those days was Joan Maynard, the Labour MP for Sheffield Brightside. She replied to every letter, took up my complaints with the Home Office, and came to visit me to try to sort out problems I was having with the prison authorities. She put down questions in

218

Parliament over my treatment, forcing Home Office ministers to acknowledge, for example, the number of days I had spent in solitary confinement. At times when I was, without any reason given, put in solitary on Good Order and Discipline, she demanded an explanation. Joan Maynard worked hard for us at a time when there was no political capital – in fact, the reverse – to be made for campaigning on such issues. Clive Soley (whose South London constituency took in Wandsworth Prison) was also helpful.

After the 1983 general election, a number of other Labour MPs took up our case. One of the most notable was Jeremy Corbyn, MP for Islington North, in whose constituency I had once lived. Jeremy was tireless in his work on behalf of the Guildford Four and visited me several times in prison to discuss my conditions and the case.

We had less luck with the Labour Party leadership. In 1987 my uncle Errol attended the annual Party conference to address a fringe meeting on miscarriages of justice. He bumped into Neil Kinnock and spoke to him for a few moments about the case. Kinnock promised to arrange an interview with Errol and Theresa but nothing materialized. It made me furious when, after our sudden release, Roy Hattersley, Labour's Home Affairs spokesman, stood up in the House of Commons to express his anxieties about the system that denied us justice for so long: where had he been for fifteen years?

Many Irish politicians, in the early days, were just as bad. Partly this had to do with the state of relations between the British and Irish governments. During the administration of the conservative Garret Fitzgerald, the Dublin Government was trying to find ways to improve ties with Britain. We were among the casualties of their diplomacy, for the Irish government would do nothing for prisoners in British jails: to speak out on their behalf might have jeopardized their relations with Britain. I wrote to Peter Barry, Fitzgerald's Foreign Minister, saying that as an Irish citizen (under the Irish constitution, everyone born in Northern Ireland is entitled to Irish citizenship) I wanted him to take up my case. The letter was intercepted by the censors who told me that I was not allowed to write to a member of a foreign government.

'Foreign to who?' I asked. 'Do you mean, foreign to me or foreign to you?'

'Foreign,' the PO said.

When I protested I was given twenty-eight days' punishment.

No one in Ireland seemed to care. It took the death of Giuseppe Conlon, in January 1980, to stir consciences from their long slumber. Giuseppe's condition had been deteriorating for many months before his death because of inadequate diet and medical attention. By September 1979, his weight was down to seven stones, his nerves in his hand had been damaged, and he shook uncontrollably. Unable to digest solids, he had been living on Complan, which the other Irish prisoners chipped in to buy him. Then the authorities took away his Complan; he practically stopped eating. In December 1979, he was moved from Wormwood Scrubs to Hammersmith Hospital where a doctor described him as 'a breathless, sick man, coughing yellow sputum and blood'. Less than two weeks later, he was moved back to the Scrubs, for security reasons, they said. On 18 January they readmitted him to hospital. He died a few days later.

Giuseppe Conlon was so obviously innocent. No one who met him had a bad word to say about him; no one who knew him disbelieved his protestations of innocence. His death was a tragedy for Gerry, and for his family. Some people say that death is not always a waste, that sometimes good can come of it. Some people say that about Giuseppe's death, that it finally convinced Gerry Fitt, Cardinal Hume (who had visited Giuseppe on his deathbed) and others that we were innocent. But to me it was a waste. No one should have to die in prison, least of all a man like Giuseppe Conlon.

In an effort to focus the growing support, Errol and Theresa, helped and advised by John McDonnell, the former deputy leader of the Greater London Council and later Secretary of the Association of London Authorities, organized a campaign to press for justice in our case and that of the Maguire Seven. They talked to newspaper and television journalists who, after years of neglect, had begun to take an interest. In the first years following our trial, only the radical press – most notably the *New Statesman* and the now defunct *Leveller* – had had the integrity to stand back from the hysteria and do the job journalists are supposed to

220

do, question and investigate and tell the truth. The *London Irish Post* also covered the case particularly well, and as the years went by articles and features began to appear in national newspapers in Ireland.

Gradually, as Errol and Theresa gained in confidence, they started to make contacts with political figures. Errol spoke at fringe meetings at the annual conferences of Labour Party and the Liberal Party (of which he was a member). He and Theresa organized public meetings and spoke at trade union and public gatherings in London, Bristol, Manchester, Birmingham, Bridlington, Preston, Newport, Dublin and elsewhere. Trade unionists passed resolutions in our support at branch meetings. Leicester and District Trades Union Council sent me May Day greetings in 1987. Bolton and District United Trades Council wrote to the Home Secretary asking him to look again at the case. The Mid-Glamorgan District Committee of the Amalgamated Engineering Union affiliated to the campaign.

In Ireland, Errol and Theresa enlisted the support of a number of politicians, including Neil Blaney, the Donegal TD, and Senator Brendan Ryan from Cork. In Dublin they had an interview with Charles Haughey, the Irish Taoiseach (Prime Minister), who promised to take up the case with the British Government. Senator Paschal Mooney from Leitrim also helped, and wrote to me regularly. In June 1987, he sent me a copy of an order paper from the Irish Senate which contained a motion urging the British Home Secretary to look again at our convictions. He wrote to tell me that in Ireland there was great interest in our case, and to say that Haughey and Brian Lenihan, the Foreign Minister, also maintained a keen interest.

The Irish embassy in London, after much pressure, finally started to show signs of interest and began to send us visitors. Seán MacBride, a founder member of Amnesty International, a former Secretary-General of the International Commission of Jurists, and winner of the Nobel Prize for Peace, took up our case. He advised Errol and Theresa on how to drum up further support and introduced them to other influential people. His last public appearance before his death was in Dublin when he appeared on a platform to speak for the Guildford Four.

Errol and other campaign workers visited foreign embassies in London in an effort to raise the level of awareness about the case abroad. At the USSR embassy, Errol was surprised to find that the officials were well informed on all aspects of the case, and showed a better grasp of the essentials than did, for example, those at the Irish embassy. The Russians urged Errol to seek support among the non-aligned countries, fearing that too close an identification with the USSR could be counterproductive. They told Errol that the judicial and penal system of the USSR left much to be desired, and that anything said by the Russians could be dismissed as a cynical attempt to deflect criticism from their own shortcomings. Their frankness convinced the campaign workers that the Russians' primary interest was not to make political capital, and, as a result of the meetings, the matter was raised at a diplomatic level with the Foreign Office. Errol appeared several times on Soviet television to speak about the case, and numerous articles appeared in newspapers and magazines inside the Soviet Union.

Errol and Theresa, on behalf of the campaign, went to the United States and talked to members of congress, Irish groups, and state and city politicians. Their work, and the efforts of Sister Sarah Clarke, Father Faul, Father Murray and others, helped to open the eyes of people in the United States to what had happened. In 1989 the New York City Council adopted Resolution No 1607 in support of the Guildford and other Irish prisoners. David Dinkins, now Mayor of New York, urged the City councilmen to pass the resolution:

> The Guildford Four – Paul Hill, Patrick Armstrong, Gerald Conlon and Carole Richardson – are now serving their fourteenth year of a life sentence for allegedly bombing pubs in Guildford and Woolwich. Confessions were coerced from all four prisoners following beatings, sleep deprivation and threats. These confessions were later repudiated.
>
> Yet the four were convicted on the basis of confessions made against their will. The convictions were upheld despite the fact that four members of the IRA confessed to the bombings a year later,

providing details only those responsible for the actions could know.

Meanwhile, Father Faul was continuing to speak about our case and that of the Maguires. He had talked to Robert Kee about Annie Maguire, and when Annie was finally released from prison, in 1985, Kee interviewed her on television. Radio Telefís Eireann, the Irish national network, also made a documentary about the case. Yorkshire Television's *First Tuesday* programme, 'Aunt Annie's Bomb Factory', transmitted in March 1984, which questioned the basis on which the Maguire Seven had been convicted. Robert Kee, meanwhile, had contacted Alastair Logan and, with Logan's assistance, began researching a book on the Maguires. However, it became clear to him that our arrests and convictions were the key to the Maguire case. His project broadened and when the book, *Trial and Error*, appeared, in 1986, it carried the subtitle: 'The Maguires, the Guildford Pub Bombings and British Justice'. Although Kee made some errors concerning my past – he did not contact me – his book was a powerful indictment of the way the case had been handled. He said a grave miscarriage of justice had occurred and urged the Home Secretary to review our convictions.

Alastair Logan, who, by the early 1980s, was the only one of the original four solicitors still to be involved in the case – after the appeal he acted for all four of us; in 1987 I instructed another solicitor, Mike Fisher – was able to garner further support after his meetings with Kee. There came together a number of influential men – Cardinal Hume, Roy Jenkins, Merlyn Rees (both former Home Secretaries), and Lords Scarman and Devlin (former law lords) – all of whom publicly expressed doubts about the convictions. In a lengthy article in *The Times*, which appeared on 30 November 1988, Devlin and Scarman argued that our convictions rested on a fundamental error of law. Because of the Court of Appeal's decision in 1977 to refuse our application for a retrial no jury had heard *all* the evidence in the case. We therefore lost the 'defendant's right to have the case against him presented as a whole'. The Court of Appeal should have ordered a retrial: 'There was no way in which justice could be done except by beginning again.' The actions of the judges, they said, had worrying implications:

> Four new witnesses [Dowd, O'Connell, Butler and Duggan] appeared who had committed twenty massacres of the same type. They knew nothing of the Guildford Four. Were they lying when they said that? That was a question for a jury as it certainly would have been if the evidence had been given at the trial.
>
> The Court of Appeal judges accepted that vital parts of what the new witnesses said might well be true. If a jury thought the same, it would be for it and not for judges to put a value on the fragments that were left of the confessions and the Crown's case.
>
> Justice for the Guildford Four is now in the forefront of a larger issue. Their fate has shattered our belief that there is no one in any English prison serving a sentence of more than a year who has not been found guilty by a jury which has heard substantially all the relevant evidence. Our constitutional law on which our freedoms depend has been disordered.

The problem was, how to get the case re-opened?

Chapter Fifteen

CHANGES

The 1968 Criminal Appeal Act, under Section 17(a), allows the Home Secretary to refer cases to the Court of Appeal for review 'if he thinks fit'. In the mid-1980s, the writers and journalists who had become convinced of our innocence subjected the prosecution evidence to lengthy analysis, and, convinced that there had been a miscarriage of justice, and taking the wording of the Act at face value, believed that all that was necessary to persuade the Home Secretary to refer the case was to point out the obvious flaws in the way the matter had been handled from arrest to appeal. They, and we, were in for a shock.

The efforts of our supporters ran in tandem with those of the Birmingham Six, most notably Chris Mullin, now Labour MP for Sunderland South, whose book about the Birmingham bombings, *Error of Judgement*, appeared in July 1986. Throughout the second half of the year, speculation mounted about what the Home Secretary would do. In January the following year, I found myself in Wormwood Scrubs with Billy Power and Dick McIlkenny, two of the men convicted of the Birmingham bombings. An announcement was expected at any time: it could have been any one of a number of things – a reference to the Court of Appeal; no reference; release, even. One afternoon, Billy, Dick and I were on exercise when a message came over the tannoy. 'McIlkenny, Power and Hill to the Governor's office.' This was it. Everyone in the yard watched us as we walked towards the gate of the wing, and they wished us good luck. How far we had come, I thought, since we had first entered prison. It seemed now that the whole world accepted that we were innocent. A short time before, an Egyptian prisoner had shown me a newspaper article in Arabic, which he translated – it was about the four innocent people convicted of the Guildford and Woolwich pub bombings. Word had reached people thousands of miles away, but had it reached the Home Secretary? Dick, Billy and I made our way to the Governor's office. The screws told us to wait outside.

They called Billy first. After a few moments, he reappeared, smiling broadly, and said, 'That's it, we're going back to the Court of Appeal.' Dick was delighted, and I was too. If anyone deserved good news, it was the Birmingham Six. They were old men, grandfathers; their lives were running out. Dick went into the office and had the news confirmed. It was my turn. I went inside and I saw a woman, sitting beside the Governor. As soon as I saw her face, I knew what she was going to say. She said, 'I'm very sorry, Mr Hill, but the Home Secretary has not seen fit to refer your case to the Court of Appeal.' They told me that Douglas Hurd, the Home Secretary, had said that no new evidence had been presented in our case; accordingly, he was unable to make a reference under the Act. I said, 'Don't worry. There's no problem.' I went outside. Dick and Billy looked expectantly at me. I was so used to putting on a brave face; I put another one on for them. Disappointment after disappointment. I said simply, 'I'm not going back to the Court of Appeal,' and I wished them good luck. They said they were sorry, and I went to my cell.

It was at first a bad blow. I thought, 'Here we go again. Another knockback, another round of letters to my family beginning, "Don't worry . . ."' I was into the thirteenth year of my sentence, and although I had never once doubted that I would get justice, I was wondering, with increasing urgency, when – when were they going to give in?

I recovered from this disappointment, as I had from all the others. I had read about the Court of Appeal and its record – it was not good. Following Hurd's announcement, I saw a cartoon in a newspaper. It showed a prisoner in the Governor's office: the Governor was saying, 'You'll be happy to know that you will not be going back to the Court of Appeal.' Nevertheless, the fact remained that the Court of Appeal held the keys to the cell doors, even if it rarely felt like taking the bunch from its pocket. We had to get back before the judges. But how? Our supporters had been unprepared for the requirement of 'new evidence'. Robert Kee's *Trial and Error* and the two Yorkshire Television documentaries (the first, 'Aunt Annie's Bomb Factory', was screened in March 1984, the second, 'The Guildford Time Bomb', in July 1986) had concentrated on discrediting the prosecution evidence; they did not contain 'new evidence'. Kee had concluded his book with the words 'let Justice be done though the heavens fall'.

The sentiment was admirable, but it cut no ice with the Home Office. Those working for the Birmingham Six, on the other hand, had a higher awareness, and greater knowledge, of the mechanisms by which cases were returned to the Court of Appeal. Four of the six were represented by Gareth Peirce, who had worked on the Cooper and McMahon case. Cooper and McMahon had been convicted in 1970 in a case also known as the Luton Post Office Murder, and had received life sentences. There were serious doubts about the convictions, and the case was taken up by Lord Devlin and Ludovic Kennedy, the writer and broadcaster. Cooper and McMahon went to the Court of Appeal five times, but each time the court refused to take action. After the publication of a book by Kennedy, *Wicked Beyond Belief*, the Home Secretary used his powers to free the men in July 1980. Gareth Peirce's experience, gained from following the tortuous progress of the case through the Court of Appeal, was put to good use on behalf of the Birmingham Six.

Our own supporters were quick to learn the lesson. With Hurd's announcement, the search was on for something that would satisfy the 'new evidence' requirement. Ros Franey

227

and Grant McKee, who worked for Yorkshire Television's *First Tuesday* programme, set about making another documentary, and contacted Errol and Theresa. Theresa recalled that Yvonne Fox, a friend of Anne Keenan's, had been in the Keenans' flat on the night of the Woolwich bomb. Her evidence had not been heard in court. McKee and Franey described in *Time Bomb*, their book about the case published in 1988, what happened:

> Anne and Frank Keenan, whose whereabouts had been unknown to the Hill family for some time, declared their willingness to be interviewed. Anne Keenan confirmed that she was still in touch with her friend Yvonne Fox, who had been at the flat in Brecknock Road with Paul Hill on the night of the Woolwich bombing. Mrs Fox, who was British and unrelated to Hill, firmly corroborated the Keenans' evidence that Hill had been at home that night, leaving the flat for a short time to make a phone call to Gina and returning well before the newsflash about the throw-bomb explosion. She had been told to attend court at the original trial, but her evidence had never been heard. If she was to be believed, Paul Hill could not possibly have been part of the bombing team for Woolwich. She was, in effect, a new witness.

Yorkshire Television's third programme on the case, containing an interview with Mrs Fox in which she repeated her account of the evening of 7 November 1974, was broadcast in March 1987, and received widespread media attention. The Home Secretary indicated he would be willing to consider the new evidence. Alastair Logan took a formal statement from Mrs Fox, which, together with other material relating to Carole Richardson, was handed to Hurd on 23 July 1987, by a delegation led by Cardinal Hume; also present were Lords Devlin and Scarman, Roy Jenkins, Merlyn Rees and Robert Kee.

We had hoped that Hurd would, on receipt of the new evidence, immediately refer the case to the Court of Appeal. Instead, he ordered a police investigation, headed by Jim

Sharples, Deputy Chief Constable of Avon and Somerset, into the new evidence. To me, this was highly unsatisfactory. Why was the new evidence being investigated by the police? Surely it was for the Court of Appeal to hear? What exactly was the role of the police? Were police officers going to scrutinize the evidence and decide whether they believed it or not? Could policemen be trusted to investigate other policemen? Many of those concerned about the operation of the appeals system questioned whether a police team was the appropriate investigating body – it was time, they argued, that an independent investigative arm be established to undertake this kind of work.

Nevertheless, Hurd's decision did appear to take the case forward a little. Merlyn Rees said, 'We all felt there was something wrong with this case. I think the new evidence is the key in the lock, and I hope we'll find ourselves in the Court of Appeal.' Alastair Logan saw the reference as a way to get in front of a jury that would, unlike the jury in our trial, hear all the evidence. He said, 'If justice is to mean anything in this country, there must be a retrial. I am absolutely confident that in a retrial they will be found innocent.' An editorial appeared in *The Times*:

> Mr Hurd's decision is overdue. Even now he is not saying that he will refer the cases to the Court of Appeal. But a referral must not be delayed much longer. In January, Mr Hurd referred to the Court of Appeal the cases of the six men who have been in prison since 1975 for the Birmingham pub bombings which took place during the same period as those at Guildford and Woolwich. The doubts raised about the Birmingham convictions are similar to those raised about the others. Why refer one group and not the rest?

So the inquiry got under way.

Meanwhile, the team of lawyers involved in the case was greatly strengthened. Gareth Peirce had agreed to act for Gerry, and I, on the advice of Errol and a number of other people, had already instructed Mike Fisher, a solicitor with wide experience in the criminal law. Alastair Logan, whose knowledge of the case was, after thirteen years, comprehensive, continued to represent Paddy and Carole. By the time the Sharples Inquiry went to work, I felt we had, for the first time, a team of lawyers who were experienced, dedicated and believed in our innocence.

It was at around this time that a change – a change I had never expected – occurred in my life. Almost from the moment of my conviction on the Shaw murder, I had withdrawn, emotionally, from the people I loved. I put distance between me and what I saw as sources of hurt. Partly, I did so out of a kind of selfishness, a desire to protect myself at all costs; partly, out of simple realism. It was safer this way, but lonely. I handled it for more than ten years. But in 1986, I was beginning to doubt my ability to cope. In spite of the hopes raised by all the publicity, I was far from certain about the outcome. I looked at all the support we had received and wondered at how much things had changed. Part of me said, 'We will get out.' Then I thought about the world-wide support for Nelson Mandela. I read reports of how hundreds of millions of people were demanding he be released, how the leaders of important powers were putting pressure on the South African Government to set him free. And yet, Nelson Mandela remained in prison. If they could keep Mandela in prison, in spite of everything, they could do the same with us. Perhaps they would never let us out.

My spirits were low, the lowest, I think, in all my time in jail. My travels around the country's prison system continued. They shunted me from one establishment to the next. I never spent more than a few months in any one place, making it impossible to maintain any kind of relationship or friendship. They continued to put me in solitary; now, however, solitary was harder to do. The weight of my imprisonment was crushing – so much time was passing. My health had also begun to deteriorate. A blocked saliva duct, which had been diagnosed ten years before, caused repeated glandular infections. The membrane on my lung became inflamed – every breath was a torture. My weight dropped to just over nine stone, two stones under the norm for my height. I seemed to have a permanent cold. Theresa, distressed at my condition, urged me to try to be more co-operative with the authorities, and only succeeded in making me angry. I told her that outside she and Errol had *carte blanche* to do whatever they judged best for me, but that inside a different set of rules applied. I, and not they, understood those rules – they would have to leave it to me.

In January 1986, I was suddenly moved from Gartree where I had been on normal location and taken to Lincoln for a lie-down. It was a bad winter. The walls of my cell were damp and cold, pools of water gathered on the floor. I caught a glimpse of myself in the mirror; my skin was a jaundiced yellow. The relentless scheming that prison had taught me now focused on warmth. Cockroaches did not bother me, nor did tobacco. In Lincoln, all I wanted was to find a way to keep warm. I got into trouble and spent three days in a strip cell, naked except for a body belt. I shivered day and night. Every time I took a breath of air, I felt a sharp pain in my chest. When I tried to take a deep breath, I was cut off by the pain. Dozens of people die every year in prison; some die from pure neglect. The pains frightened me.

Letters were one of the few comforts. Since 1983, I had been writing to a woman named Mary Ellen Cantland who lived in New York. I had come into contact with her through Kara who had been on a trip to the United States, organized by a community group in Northern Ireland. During her time there, she made friends with Mary Ellen, who she told about me. After Kara returned home, Mary Ellen wrote to tell me about the visit. I knew Kara so little, and the letter let me into parts of her that I had not seen. It was exciting and satisfying to hear another person's appreciation of my child. The letter lifted me, and I wrote back in thanks. It was the beginning of a regular correspondence.

My mail came in fits and starts, depending on the censor's frame of mind. It was not uncommon for several weeks to pass without a single letter arriving. So I did not think anything was amiss when I had not heard from Mary Ellen for some time. Then one day, when I was in Lincoln, a screw came to my cell and handed me a dozen or so letters. It was like a party. I rolled a couple of cigarettes and settled in for an afternoon with my friends. One envelope had handwriting I did not recognize. When I read it, I discovered that it was from a friend of Mary Ellen. The letter explained why Mary Ellen had not written for some time: her father had died and

231

she had taken it very badly. The writer was Marion Serravalli and she lived in New Jersey. It was a formal letter and I wrote back, in the same formal way, to thank her for being so good as to write to me with the news. I wrote to Mary Ellen with condolences.

To my surprise, a letter from Marion arrived in response to mine, asking how I was, telling me that she had spoken to Mary Ellen about me and about the case. I wrote back, and we began to exchange letters regularly. The letters were friendly and had to do with everyday things. I described a bit of my life inside prison, and she told me something of her life. We discussed Kara, my case, the campaign, the prospects of getting out. She had a very direct way, and I quickly came to see that she was level-headed, not in the least giddy or silly. She came from a background that to me seemed quite conservative; she was an American, proud of her country; proud, too, of her traditional values. She was serious about her work, as a buyer for a big paper mill. I liked her maturity, and was impressed by the way she went about her life. I had not encountered anyone like her before.

The ghost train started up again. I was suddenly moved from Lincoln to Hull. I hated it. The authorities had promised, following the beatings after the riot, that I would never be moved to Hull again. I hated the cold and damp, the latent threat everywhere. The screws remembered me. I had given evidence in court that helped to convict eight of their colleagues. They did not like me. More and more, I looked forward to Marion's letters and the pleasure they brought me. We were now writing to each other two or three times a week. The letters were changing in tone, and she was beginning to let me into a corner of her life. She told me little things about her personal life, about joys and pleasures, and problems. She asked my advice on one problem. It seemed strange that someone should ask me, a man with almost no experience of the real world, for advice. For what it was worth, I gave it.

After a few months in Hull, I was ghosted to Wormwood Scrubs. It was in letters that followed me there that the first expressions of love were made. It had been present almost from the start, undeclared and lurking, probing for expression. I was thirty-two years old, but the only experience I had to draw on in this kind of situation was that of a teenager. I did not know how to go ahead, how to express myself. I feared Marion's response; I was terrified of mine. I did not trust either her or myself, and so I shadow-boxed, with ambiguous words whose true meaning outsiders spot in an instant. It made me feel like nothing so much as a fifteen-year-old boy. I felt uncertain, without points of reference; I was on the edge of something I was not sure I wanted to relive after Gina. I had seen so many men in prison destroyed by the failure and break-up of their relationships that I tried to hold myself back. I was terrified by the idea of having to cope with desertion. I was not being entirely selfish. I did not want to get hurt, but neither did I want to cause hurt. Later, when we were married, I was to tell Marion that hers was the bigger commitment. She had choice, and the choice she was making was to become involved with a man serving the rest of his life in prison.

The idea of a visit came up: I put it this way, passively, because such was our shadow-boxing that even now I cannot say with whom the idea originated. It surfaced, like the love we declared, clumsily. But once broached, we found we both liked the idea. Marion made arrangements to take time off work. As the time for the visit approached, I became apprehensive, nervous; I worried about what could go wrong. There were moments when I felt like writing to cancel the whole thing.

She arrived. The moment I saw her, I felt as if I had known her all my life. My nervousness vanished, and I was completely at ease. Marion talked freely, about her life, her job, her family, America, what she lived for and believed in. We talked about the case, about prison, about Ireland, about my family and Kara. And we discussed things that I had never talked about to a woman before – feelings, desire, sex. Sex. There is sex of sorts in prison. There is homosexuality in prison, but not as much as people believe; for most prisoners, sex is lonely and desperate, and brings neither pleasure nor warmth, only more loneliness. But the desire I felt for Marion brought hope.

I had saved my visits, and we had a week of seeing each other every day. Every morning, I woke up with a strange, vague feeling of happiness. I lay in bed and searched for its source, and was warmed when I identified it. I felt different; I possessed a happiness that came from having something to look forward to in the day, that came from the presence of a person who loved me. It was something I had not experienced in many years.

I wanted to give Marion a present. In prison, there is a miniature industry in soft toys and bits and pieces of woodwork. I never gave these out to my visitors. I had a morbid dread of coming home to find the house full of these awful things. But it meant that I had nothing to give. During one visit, Marion said she had seen a Claddagh ring, so I gave her the money to buy one. The Claddagh ring is an ancient wedding ring. Shadow-boxing, childish stuff, fencing. Marion asked how real was this for me. I said it was real. We said we should get married.

I was far from certain that I was ready for the emotional burden that marriage would bring. Our decision to marry happened at a time when everything else seemed to have been taken from me. By giving me something to believe in, it helped to rescue me. Errol had reservations, and told me about them. But I had made up my mind. I needed Marion. I wanted the warmth that the relationship brought. It was a line to the real world, a glimpse of another life.

Marion returned to America. We continued to exchange letters and she came twice more to visit me. We set a date for the wedding in November 1987. I was still in the Scrubs. Previously, prisoners needed the Governor's approval to get married, but a case brought to the European Court changed that. The court confirmed the right of prisoners to marry. However, they did not make it easy for me. Days before the wedding, I was suddenly moved from the Scrubs to Long Lartin. This altered the bureaucratic residency requirements for Marion, and we had to put the wedding back to 12 February 1988. I had to submit to the Home Office the names of the guests for vetting. Among those I wanted to invite was Sister Sarah Clarke, the Irish nun who had worked so hard for us. The Home Office refused to approve her for unexplained 'security reasons'. A Conservative MP said the Governor of Long Lartin should be sacked for having allowed it to go ahead. On the morning of the wedding, the *Sun* ran a story headlined 'IRA Pig to Wed', and attacked a group of

Labour MPs, including Jeremy Corbyn and Tony Benn, who had signed a motion to congratulate me on the wedding.

The ceremony took place in the chapel at Long Lartin. The guests were outnumbered by screws and Special Branch men. In these circumstances, it held no magic for me and I was keen to get it over with as quickly as possible. After the vows were exchanged, I was taken back to my cell for a couple of hours while the screws had their lunch. At 2pm I was unlocked and taken to the reception. Among the guests were members of my family, and people who helped Errol and Theresa with the campaign – Tom Barron, John McDonnell, Gerry Fitzpatrick, Conor Foley and Richard Wize. It was the first chance I had to talk to them and thank them for the work they had done. Jeremy Corbyn was also present, something the gutter press noted with glee. The reception lasted for two hours. At 4pm I was separated from my wife and guests, and taken back to my cell. I lay on the bed and thought of Marion driving back to London. Some friends of mine had brewed up a batch of hooch, and that night I got drunk. I was glad; it wiped out the feelings I had about the day's proceedings. They were not happy ones.

I never said to Marion during that time, 'It won't be long now.' I never tried to deceive her or fill her up with false hopes. I explained the situation to her, and I let her make up her own mind about the responsibility she was taking on. I loved her, and wanted to be married to her; but if she had said, 'I can't handle this' I would have understood.

In February 1988, when she came over to marry me, Marion had more reason than ever to doubt that I would soon be free. The appeal of the Birmingham Six had opened at the Old Bailey in November 1987. Many people, including some of the Six, believed that it was all over bar the shouting. Gareth Peirce and Chris Mullin had amassed a huge amount of new evidence. Central to the conviction of the six men was the claim that they been had beaten while in police custody. The defence produced two witnesses, former police officers, to testify that there had been beatings. Compelling new forensic evidence enabled the defence to challenge the prosecution's claim that the men had been handling explosives before their arrest. The appeal lasted several weeks, and the judges retired to consider the evidence. On 28 January

1988, the judges delivered their verdicts. Once again, the Court of Appeal took on itself the task of finding fact – the three judges, Lord Lane, the Lord Chief Justice, presided, said they did not believe the new evidence and dismissed the men's appeal. As supporters of the Six said after the judgment, the test as set out in the 1968 Act is whether the evidence is worthy of belief, whether it is credible. It should be for a jury to determine where the truth lies.

The Birmingham decision shocked many people. It appeared that the Court of Appeal was more concerned with upholding the reputation of British justice than with seeing justice done. Lord Denning said on BBC television that he would prefer to set aside the cases of injustice raised by television rather than call into question the reputation of the system of criminal justice. Denning was the first establishment figure to say publicly what we had known all along.

The Birmingham decision did not augur well for us, and I told Marion so. Nor did the Sharples team appear to be making much progress. Witnesses interviewed by the Avon and Somerset officers complained that the detectives seemed more eager to disprove the new evidence than investigate it. Their attitude added to the belief that they were not truly independent. After several months, we heard that Sharples had reported to the Home Secretary and that on the basis of this report Hurd was inclined to turn down requests to reopen the case. Only another visit, in November 1987, from Cardinal Hume's delegation, armed with further new evidence, persuaded the Home Secretary to extend the inquiry's life. Hurd instructed Sharples to look again. I was relieved when the news came through, but I could not help thinking about the system of justice that depends on access to an old boy network. We were the lucky and unlikely recipients of the attention of men who enjoyed some credit with the establishment. But what of other innocent people in jail, how do they get justice?

Sharples and his team went back to work. Finally, on 16 January 1989, the Home Secretary made an announcement. Under Section 17 of the Criminal Appeal Act, he was asking the Court of Appeal to look again at the case.

Now was the time to organize our defence. Mike Fisher came to see me and we discussed which counsel to instruct.

For leading counsel we settled on Lord (Tony) Gifford QC, an experienced Court of Appeal hand who had appeared for two of the Birmingham Six before Lord Lane. Helena Kennedy, who had appeared in the trial of the Balcombe Street men, was instructed as Tony's junior. We then had to sort out the thousands of documents generated by the case over the years. Helena and Tony Gifford came to visit me and asked me to go through the paperwork to point out the various inconsistencies in the confessions and so on. Talking to them I became increasingly confident. They believed I was innocent – not just as professionals, but as human beings – and they were determined to prove it. I could sense warmth and trust. They treated me like a person, someone with something to say, and not just as a prisoner trying to wriggle out of his predicament. They were so different from the lawyers who had represented me in the trial in 1975 and the appeal in 1977.

I remember during the spring and summer of 1989 feeling quite optimistic. We had such a good case, I thought, that the Court of Appeal could not possibly turn us down. Perhaps I was deluding myself, desperate to have a reason to hope after having been so long without hope. In July, Paddy's lawyers asked the Court of Appeal to put back the date of the hearing, which had originally been set for the autumn, because they had not had sufficient time to prepare. Gerry, Paddy, Carole and I were not in court for this, but I heard afterwards that the Crown, represented by Roy Amlot QC, had been unhappy about the application, and that the judges had only grudgingly conceded it. The news of their attitude brought me down to earth; I was falling into the trap that some of the Birmingham Six's supporters had fallen into.

But still, it was hard to keep my hopes in check. Things did appear to be improving. I thought of my marriage – a real marriage now seemed possible. I could not help but fantasize about being out, free to be with Marion. I wrote to her, and although I was careful not to build her hopes up, there were times when my optimism burst through. And afterwards I felt guilty, as if I had deluded her. And then I would feel stupid, for having deluded myself, for believing that the judges would set us free. I was reminded of the time I spent with Gerry and Paddy on remand in Winchester, when it dawned on me that to prove our innocence we would have to make serious allegations about the police. How much more serious the allegations would have to be now, after nearly fifteen years during which time judges, Home Office officials and Government ministers had all had a hand in the case. In 1975, we had called in question the reputation of policemen; now we were challenging an entire system.

Prison life continued as before. But there was an odd, unsettling, quality to it now. By the beginning of 1989, my life had changed. The case was moving, and I had a relationship which for the first time since entering prison I wanted to preserve instead of destroy. After years of nothing, something was happening. I would wake up, with that vague, indistinct feeling of happiness that I had experienced when Marion came to visit me. But then the cell door would open, and I would go outside. There is nothing that deflates happiness so quickly as the failure of other people to acknowledge it. As soon as I was on the landing, I realized my life had not changed so much after all; how precarious was my optimism. Prison life – day-in, day-out – continued as it always had for me.

It was to get worse. While I was in Albany the IRA bombed an Army base at Deal, causing massive casualties among the young Army bandsmen. The following day, I was playing football on Albany's all-weather pitch. Without warning, a prisoner named Blackett came up and punched me hard on the side of the face. I realized at once that I was seriously hurt. I felt my face; the cheek bone was smashed. I was in pain, but I was also furious. I knew that if I started a fight there and then, the screws would see us, break it up and take us both down the block. I knew what I had to do. I took off my pumps and walked back to the wing. I was taken to the hospital at Parkhurst for first aid, but refused to stay to have an operation because I wanted to stay on the wing, within reach of Blackett. In the hospital, I bumped into Mickey Williams, the prisoner who had helped educate me about the ways of prison after I had been sentenced and sent to Bristol. Talking to Mickey, remembering all he had told me, made me more determined to deal with my attacker.

I had had no problems with prisoners since the very early days. After fifteen years inside, I was known as someone who stood up for himself, and that reputation was important to me. I had worked and fought to get the reputation I had, and I was not going to let it go because of this man. I sat in my cell and thought about how to do it. A friend brought me a long, vicious knife. I looked at it. It would do the job, but it would probably do it too well. I wanted to hurt Blackett, but I did not want to kill him. I thought, 'No, I'll do exactly what he has done to me.' I went out on exercise and I prised up one of the kidney stones, like cobble stones, from the path, and smuggled it back to my cell.

A friend of mine told me that he had heard that Blackett and a friend of his had stolen a pair of scissors, which they had broken in two – he and his pal had a weapon each. Several Irish prisoners asked me if I wanted help. I said, 'No, I'll deal with it.' During the course of the week, the screws said to me, 'You've too much to lose. Don't bother with him.' I said, 'It's forgotten.' I went out to watch Blackett playing football, trying to figure out where he had his weapon. He wore overalls, and I noticed that every time he emerged from a tackle, he put his hands down inside the right leg of his overalls, as if he was readjusting something. That was where he had the scissors.

Satisfied, I returned to the wing and waited for him to come in. Once the game was over, I allowed him time to clean up and settle down in the TV room, where I knew he would go. I put my stone inside a sock, twisted the end of the sock, took a firm grip, draped a bedcover over it and walked out onto the landing, pretending to look for the man who did the washing. I went into the TV room where I saw Blackett and his minder. Blackett was sitting in a chair against the wall, watching the television. He had not noticed me. I went up quickly, took my weapon out and swung it into the side of his face. It hit him with a great crack and I knew at once that I had smashed his cheekbone. His leg shook and twitched. He managed to get up, he was shaking, in shock, in pain. I knew I had to stop him getting to his weapon, so I grabbed the back straps of his overalls and gave him another couple of blows, not too heavy – I did not want to damage him too badly – to stun him. He was heavier and bigger than me, and he recovered faster than I expected. We got into a clinch and went over a row of chairs. I hit him another couple of times until he was out of it. Then, slowly, he got up and made his way out of the TV room. Someone shouted that the screws were coming. I sat down on one of the chairs, and started to watch television. The screws looked inside, saw everyone calmly looking at the TV, and left.

The next day, Blackett was taken to the hospital and then to the block. A screw came up to me and said, 'You won me five quid. I bet them all down in the mess that you'd make a swift return.'

'I don't know what you're talking about,' I said.

Chapter Sixteen

AMONG MY OWN AGAIN

On the morning of Tuesday, 17 October 1989, I was, as usual, unlocked for breakfast. I took my plastic bowl, plate and mug, and went out onto the landing. I returned with the food to my cell, and the door was locked behind me. I ate, drank a cup of tea and settled down to study some of the legal documents my lawyers had sent for my comments. I studied the large charts, which I had drawn up and attached to the wall, showing the inconsistencies and contradictions in the prosecution evidence. Our appeal was scheduled to open in three months: this time I wanted to be ready for them. I checked the transcripts, depositions and statements, noting down whatever was useful. Then I was called for work.

I was on normal location in Albany, and my job was to look after the kit: overalls, shirts and so on. It was not a bad job, no strain and some perks – those who wanted an extra shirt put up a little tobacco or chocolate. I was sorting the kit when a screw walked up. He said, 'Paul, pack your gear.' At first, I was angry. I assumed I was being ghosted again. But then, something struck me as odd: normally, they

241

wait until you are locked in your cell – before breakfast, after dinner or late at night. And then they come in strength, ready for trouble.

I asked what the problem was. The screw said he did not know, that security had simply told him to tell me to pack a kit. I shrugged my shoulders, dropped the shirts I was sorting, and went to the cell, where I started to collect my legal papers and other personal belongings. I packed a small case and went down to reception. Something very odd happened here. Normally, they put you straight into one of the reception cubicles until they are ready to take you away. Instead, they sat me down at a chair beside a table. A screw came along and gave me some cycling magazines – I was interested in the subject because of the recent success in the Tour de France of the Irish cyclists Roach and Kelly. Then a screw asked me if I wanted a cup of coffee.

My suspicions hardened. 'Look, what's going on?' I said.

'Do you take sugar?'

'What?'

'Do you take sugar in your coffee?'

It was getting more and more bizarre. 'Yes, two.' The screw stirred in two spoonfuls of sugar. An AG passed. 'What's going on?' I asked. He said he did not know. I saw a security officer named Black. I asked him what was happening. Black said, 'I can't say much, except now I understand why you've given me nothing but aggravation for fifteen years.'

'Look, you're talking in riddles here.'

'This looks like it could be the big one.'

'What are you talking about?'

Black said nothing, and went on.

A screw came up and handed me three ounces of tobacco. 'Here you are Hill, the lads have sent this down from the wing.'

I said, 'You know I can't have three ounces of tobacco. I'm only allowed two ounces. If I try to take all that with me, there'll be a confrontation over it when I arrive at the next prison. There'll just be aggravation.'

'I assure you there'll be no aggravation whatsoever at the prison you're going to.'

This attitude, so new to me, only succeeded in making me more unsettled. There was a hold-up with the transport. They

242

were almost apologetic when they told me the van wouldn't be arriving for another couple of hours.

At last, the van arrived. No one would tell me where we were going. The operation began to take on the usual characteristics of a ghosting – armed police in the van, the usual escort – so I assumed all was normal after all; I was simply being moved to another prison. I settled down to watch the road signs and start my guessing game. Were we going to Parkhurst, the other dispersal prison on the Isle of Wight? No. We headed towards the ferry. A mainland prison, then. Then it was north towards London – the Scrubs or Wandsworth; or, perhaps a prison off the M1 – Gartree? Lincoln? Hull? We reached South London: Wandsworth was looking a distinct bet and I began to feel very gloomy. We approached the prison – resignation mixed with anger – but drove past the gates. I felt relieved, but bewildered. Where could they be taking me? We reached Brixton Hill and turned into Jebb Avenue – Brixton. This was odd. Brixton is a remand prison; they do not keep lifers here.

At reception, I heard one screw say to another, 'Oh you've got Hill there?' They led me towards a reception cell. They unlocked the door and I went inside. There was Paddy Armstrong. Paddy was very tense. He said, 'Something's happening, something's happening. They've just taken Gerry through. Gerry's just gone through reception.'

Like Paddy, I was infected with some wild hope, straining to burst through. In fifteen years, nothing as unusual as this had happened to me. Something was definitely afoot. But I did not want to let my mind run riot or let my hopes grow out of control. I said to Paddy, 'Hold on. Let's not get carried away.' *This looks like it could be the big one*, Black had said. I was too frightened to believe it. I began to tremble, Paddy and me both. I searched for a rational explanation of what was happening, something that fell short of what we could not bring ourselves to say out loud but were both thinking. 'It might be a pre-appeal hearing. They might have just got us here for some kind of hearing,' I said.

After a while, the screws took me from the cell to be processed. They took my address book. 'We'll put that in your property, and you can have it when you go to court on Thursday.' That was the first time anyone had mentioned

243

going to court. I asked them what was going on, but they would not answer. They took me to 'D' Wing, where I saw a couple of prisoners on the landing, one of whom I knew from another jail. He said, 'Well, that's it. You're going home Thursday.'

I was stunned. I leaned against the wall and looked at him to see if I could tell if he was having me on. I said, 'No, no, it can't be true.' He said it was, that it had just been on the wireless. I started up the stairs to my cell when another couple of prisoners approached me and shook my hand. 'It's honest, it's honest,' they said, 'you're going home on Thursday.' I wanted to believe it, I knew they were not making it up, but part of me refused to take it in. I was locked in my cell. I could not sit still. I got up and sat down, paced the cell, sat down for a second and got up again. My mind running riot. There was no logical progression in my thoughts. Marion? Did she know? Kara? My mum? What the fuck had happened? Why doesn't someone just tell me what the fuck has happened? I checked the time. It was just after 4.30pm. I tuned into Radio Four and waited for the news at 5pm.

Before the news came on, they unlocked the door. 'Get your tea, Hill,' the screw said. I was shaking so much I spilt the tea all over the place on the way back to the cell. I saw Gerry. Gerry said, 'I can't believe it, can you believe what's happening?' I said, 'No, I can't believe it.' I asked Gerry if he had heard it yet on the wireless and he said no. For a moment, I thought that there had been a mistake. But Gerry said, 'It must be genuine, it must be.'

I got to the cell, sat down on the bed and forgot about my tea. I waited for 5pm. I heard the pips – I had not noticed before how many there were. What were they going to say? It would have to be the first item. If it was not the first item, it meant we would not be getting out. The pips went on. Then I heard Marion – the first thing I heard was my wife's voice. I lay down on the bed and stared at the ceiling, and listened to Marion tell me how she felt about me getting out. Her words came slowly, hesitatingly; she was as stunned as I was. Then I heard cheering. Prisoners were whooping and screaming from the windows, banging their doors and shouting the news from cell to cell. The radio carried the story all night. I listened to every broadcast. It said that the Crown had sought a

244

hearing in the Court of Appeal to announce that evidence of corruption among Surrey detectives who investigated the case in 1974 had come to light which made it impossible to oppose the appeals. The Guildford Four were to be freed on Thursday, 19 October. It was all over, it was all over.

I slept. I do not know how, perhaps because the strain had exhausted me; but I slept.

I woke up fearing the worst. Had they changed their minds overnight? I jumped up and switched on the wireless. There it was again, the first item: the Guildford Four will be released tomorrow. It was all over. The day went surprisingly quickly, for I had a succession of visitors. Errol and Theresa, as stunned as I was, came. They were no sooner in the visiting room than they whipped out a tape measure to get me fitted for a suit. I asked about Marion. They had spoken to her on the phone. 'What did she say?' I asked. Errol and Theresa hesitated and then exchanged a glance. Errol said, 'What is everyone saying?'

Mike Fisher arrived, scarcely able to believe the news. My one concern now was the Shaw case. Were they going to drop that, too? He said that was unclear. 'But they can't keep me in,' I said. 'I said for fifteen years that they framed us. Now they're discredited.' Mike said we would have to wait and see. The reports of the wrong-doings by Surrey detectives were too vague. We would have to wait to hear what the Crown said in court. 'So, what's going to happen?' Mike said, 'It looks good.'

Jim Hennessey, an official from the Irish embassy, arrived; he could hardly speak. He was in a kind of daze, and just kept shaking his head. 'I can't believe it,' he kept repeating. Neither could I. There was not much else we could say to each other.

Before lock-up that night, I shared out among the prisoners bits and pieces of things that I would no longer need. Then I lay down. Sleep was slower in coming that night. Anxiety was overtaking my other emotions. Would I walk free tomorrow?

On Thursday morning, the screws called Gerry, Paddy and me from 'D' Wing. As we left, the prisoners shook our hands, and wished us good luck. At reception, the screws gave us the boxes that contained our belongings. I watched as Paddy opened his box and took out the clothes he had been wearing when he had been arrested. He had bell bottom trousers and shoes with platforms four or five inches high. Our spirits were high and we slagged Paddy about his clothes. But I secretly studied the clothes; nothing reminded me more powerfully of how much time had passed since we had first entered prison.

We did not know what was going to be said in court – the news reports had been vague, and our own lawyers had heard only rumours about the fabrication of evidence. We speculated about what this could be. More doubts arose in my mind: would they quash Guildford and Shaw, but leave Woolwich against me?

At around 8.30am, we were driven from Brixton to the Old Bailey. As we approached the court, I saw hundreds of people massed outside; an Irish Tricolour hung from the scaffolding on a building opposite the Old Bailey. I could hardly believe my eyes. I thought of the crowd that had gathered outside Guildford Magistrates' Court when Gerry and I appeared together for the first time; of the woman waving the Union Jack, of the banners calling for our deaths. We had come full circle.

It was about 9am when we were led from the van along the passage to the cells area under the Old Bailey. As we walked, images kept fighting their way into my mind of the last time we had been in the passage, just after sentence. Prisoners shouted from the cells, 'Are you the Guildford Four?' We said we were, and they banged their doors and cheered.

We were put into a cell, and a little while later a screw arrived with the suit Errol and Theresa had got for me. Gerry was called out for a legal visit with Gareth Peirce, and he returned with carnations, which we fixed into our lapels. I was called out for a visit with Mike Fisher and Tony Gifford. I was beginning to doubt everything now, and needed reassurance. Mike and Tony said they knew now exactly what was going to happen – Guildford would definitely be quashed. What about Woolwich? Woolwich too. Shaw? They said they were working on that – the trouble was that Shaw was in a different jurisdiction, and the Court of Appeal did not have power to deal with it.

'But don't worry,' Tony said, 'it's collapsing. Things will be clearer once we get into court.'

After the visit, I was taken back to the cell. A quarter of an hour or so passed before they unlocked the door and led us up the stairs into the dock. Carole, who had been held separately, joined us in the dock – she looked stunned. I had never known Carole and there was nothing I felt I could say to her. Paddy, her boyfriend of a decade and a half ago, spoke to her. I turned to see Roy Amlot, the Crown counsel, and it was my deepest regret that we did not have Havers or Michael Hill there to hear them eat their words. The press crowded the benches, the public gallery was full. The judges – Lords Lane, Glidewell and Farquharson – came in. It was just after 10.30am. Amlot got to his feet.

My Lords, it is my onerous duty to have to inform this court that since the referral in January this year evidence of great significance has come to light. That evidence throws such doubt upon the honesty and integrity of a number of the Surrey officers investigating this case in 1974 that the Crown now feels unable to say that the conviction of any appellant was safe or satisfactory. That is why the Crown has requested a hearing today when, as your Lordships know, the appeal was fixed for 15 January of next year.

If your Lordships will allow me, I will take a little time in dealing with the trial in 1975, the appeal in 1977 and the Home Secretary's reference before I come to the reasons for the Crown's attitude today.

The case against each appellant depended entirely upon confessions to the police. There was no other evidence. Each appellant was arrested and interrogated over a number of days. Each made more than one statement in writing. Each was interviewed by units of two or three officers from the Surrey Constabulary. A total of 12 Surrey officers was involved in the interviews. Armstrong and Hill were also interviewed by officers of the Metropolitan Police about the Woolwich bombing, and Richardson made limited admissions to those officers about the Guildford bombing. In each case this occurred after they had already been interviewed by the Surrey officers and in each case the interviews took place during the period they were held at Guildford Police Station.

During the trial serious allegations were made against the Surrey interviewing officers by each appellant. There were allegations of brutality, threats, intimidation, inducements and the concoction of evidence. All these allegations were denied by the officers and it is clear that the jury acted upon those denials and relied on the integrity of the officers involved.

Amlot then summarized the confessions for the judges. He pointed out that 'there were many discrepancies between the accounts of the four appellants on Guildford and between Hill and Armstrong on Woolwich', but that in the trial the jury 'considered all these matters and obviously relied upon the integrity of the officers in considering the Crown's explanations for the inconsistencies. That explanation was that the defendants either deliberately misled the police or minimized their roles out of self-interest.' He went on to discuss the alibis. 'Each appellant put forward an alibi which was carefully analysed and considered during the trial. It is right to say that no alibi was so destroyed that the learned trial judge felt able to direct the jury that it supported the Crown case against any appellant.'

Amlot then proceeded to the evidence uncovered by the Sharples Inquiry.

After the Home Secretary's reference in January [1989] the time came when Avon and Somerset officers started a close inspection of the vast amount of documentation generated by the Guildford case, the Balcombe Street case and the application [to the Court of Appeal] in 1977 – all likely to feature in this appeal.

I should emphasize that the Guildford case

papers had remained with the Surrey police until they were collected by the Avon and Somerset officers at the beginning of their inquiry. A close scrutiny of all the papers became necessary after the referral this year. Amongst the papers that had been kept by the Surrey police, the Avon and Somerset officers discovered the following documents: first, rough draft notes of each of the three interviews of Armstrong over three days. The notes were typewritten with a large number of alterations in manuscript. They have been identified by the three Surrey officers concerned . . . In their altered form they match almost word for word a separate set of manuscript notes of interview used by the officers in the trial. In the trial the officers claimed that the manuscript notes were made during each interview as contemporaneous notes. If that were so, it is difficult to see why the set of draft notes was brought into existence. It is impossible to see why the draft notes take the form they do unless they were made before the manuscript notes. If they were, the manuscript notes cannot have been made during the interviews, nor can the officers offer a satisfactory explanation now. The inescapable conclusion is that no contemporaneous notes were made of each interview, as indeed was suggested by the defence at the trial, and that the officers seriously misled the court.

. . . The Crown says that not only did the officers, all three of them [the ones who interrogated Paddy] – and not just junior officers – mislead the court, but that because of the way the notes had been prepared, and because of the statements that those officers made in 1974 for the purposes of the trial [ie their depositions], it is clear that they agreed together to present their notes to the court in this fashion.

What the discovery of the typewritten notes with the alterations in manuscript and the 'separate set of manuscript notes' suggested was that certain police officers had sat down together at a typewriter in advance of interrogating Paddy and decided what Paddy was going to say. As they pored over their invented confessions, they decided to make amendments – possibly improvements – which they added in their own handwriting. In the taking of confessions, the practice was to record them by hand contemporaneously – as the suspect spoke. Accordingly, the officers copied out by hand the draft they had typed, with the amendments, and produced them in the trial, claiming that they were true contemporaneous records.

Amlot continued:

> My Lords, secondly, the Avon and Somerset officers discovered a set of manuscript notes relating to an interview with Hill. The notes have been identified by one of the officers concerned. The interview as revealed by the notes was never tendered in evidence and had not been disclosed to the Director of Public Prosecutions or to prosecuting counsel. It relates to relevant and significant matters. It is clear from the content of the notes that it took place two days after Hill had been charged and led to his fifth statement under caution. It is clear that these officers also seriously misled the court. The content of the notes bears no resemblance to the evidence given by the officers as to the way in which they claim Hill 'volunteered' to make his fifth statement. The inescapable conclusion is that the true interview was suppressed and a false version given by the officers in court in order to circumvent the rule that a suspect once charged must not be interviewed except under special circumstances. Hill's fifth statement was of considerable significance in the trial because in it he was the first to name Carole Richardson. During the trial the officers denied defence suggestions that there was an interview that day. The manuscript notes are inconsistent with that denial . . . one is driven to the inescapable conclusion that this piece of evidence was concocted . . .

This piece of concoction arose out of the need to implicate Carole Richardson. By the time it took place, Carole was in custody but had so far not featured in any of my four previous confessions. Certain officers evidently decided that I should implicate her. Their problem was that I had by then already been charged. The Judges' Rules do not allow police to continue to interrogate prisoners after they have been charged 'except under special circumstances', for example if the prisoner initiates the interview. Thus, the officers concocted a statement, my fifth, in which I named Carole Richardson.

Amlot's sorry story continued:

> Other records have revealed disquieting aspects of the case. The detention sheets for each appellant (which do not appear to have been either required or made available in the trial) – and they record the suspect's movements around the police station – reveal a disturbing difference between the number and times of interviews according to the sheets, and the number and times of interviews according to the officers in evidence. Interviews are shown on the sheets which were never given in evidence or revealed to the Director of Public Prosecutions or prosecuting counsel. Interviews are shown on the sheets as taking place at markedly different times from those given in court by the interviewing officers, and the discrepancies apply to each appellant ... In the case of Hill ... at 1315 [on 30 November 1974] he was removed to an interview room on the second floor for six hours to 1950. Then he was seen by the Metropolitan police officers at 2015. No accounting was made in the trial or in statement form for some nine hours of interview that day by any officer, no statements, no account of the interviewing submitted to the Director or to counsel, and one is bound to say, at a vital time early on in the interviewing process and, as it happens, just before he was seen by the Metropolitan officers that evening.

It had always been my contention that I was interviewed for lengthy periods that did not show up in the official records. The police had always denied this to be the case. The Sharples team had uncovered evidence to show that interviews lasting several hours had not been recorded.

Amlot drew to a close:

> It is therefore the Crown's considered view that the recent discovery in the Surrey Police files of the material I have analysed with your Lordships throws such a doubt now upon the honesty and integrity of that part of the investigation which led to the confessions that it would not be right for the Crown to contend that the conviction of any appellant was either safe or satisfactory.

Amlot sat down. He had just perpetrated a last injustice, the kind that is the special preserve of his profession. His speech had been cool, mechanical even; a summary of . . . what? Did I hear a word, a phrase, a sentence about the lives destroyed by 'the material I have analysed with your Lordships'? Where was the shame and rage? They tell me that in legal language there are conventions and formulae: one of these, apparently, is to describe convictions as 'unsafe and unsatisfactory' when they mean to say that the people before them are innocent and have been framed. They say that justice needs calm; that voices must be controlled. I say that is in itself an injustice: to fail to speak with rage about injustice is another injustice.

Gerry's barrister reminded the court that there was still more evidence, not mentioned by Amlot. In the trial, Havers had said that no alibi witnesses had come forward for Gerry. However, it had been discovered that 'there were statements in police custody from two witnesses, both taken in January 1975, who in fact provided him with an alibi. He [Gerry] always maintained he was fast asleep at the hostel [Hope House in Quex Road] at the time and unbeknown to him he had been seen asleep by a witness whose name was known to certain police officers.' Why were these statements kept from the defence? Who took the decision to do so? Did the Director of Public Prosecutions know about them? Did Sir

Michael Havers? Did Michael Hill? In the normal course of things, Crown lawyers would be aware of statements of this sort.

For me, Tony Gifford said, 'It is a tragedy that it has taken fifteen years before the material can be brought before a court of justice but the consciousness of that tragedy is perhaps tempered by the shuddering thought that these defendants would have been executed fifteen years ago if capital punishment had been authorized by law.'

The law grinds slowly. Even after fifteen years and after the Crown's admissions of wrong-doing on the part of the police, there was to be no undue rush in setting us at liberty. The court rose until 2pm. During the recess, Mike Fisher and Tony Gifford came to see me in the cells. They said they were not waiting for the judgment but leaving immediately to catch a flight for Belfast where they would make an application for bail, and apply for leave to appeal against the Shaw conviction. Helena Kennedy, my junior counsel, would represent me during the judgment.

At 2pm, the judges returned. Lord Lane rehearsed the facts and arguments, and, in a reference to the evidence of corruption by the Surrey officers, said: 'It is some comfort to know that these matters are now in the hands of the Director of Public Prosecutions with a view to criminal proceedings being brought. We earnestly express the hope that nothing will be allowed to stand in the way of a speedy progress of those proceedings.'

There remained only the formal pronouncement:

> This morning each of the appellants through their learned counsel has addressed us. They have indicated that there were other arguments and other pieces of evidence that they would have advanced in support of their appeals had not the matter been, so to speak, pre-empted by the latest revelations explained by Mr Amlot. We note what they say, but so far as this court is concerned these appeals are allowed and the convictions are quashed.

That was it; it was oddly anti-climactic. I looked over at Amlot, at the judges, at the police in the court. No one had made even the slightest acknowledgement of our sufferings and the sufferings of our families. No one mentioned the sixty years stolen from us. The judges had referred only to 'this unhappy matter'; something, it seemed to me, they would rather forget as quickly as possible. I waved to Kara who was in the public gallery and who was leaning over to catch my eye, looking down on a father she had only ever known as a prisoner. I took a last look at the judges, turned and walked down the steps to the passage below the court.

I was led with the others to be processed for release, though I knew I would be immediately rearrested. Paddy, Gerry and Carole gave me their tobacco. Carole said, 'For fifteen years I blamed you for giving my name to the police. Now I know it wasn't you.' I heard some discussion about taking Gerry, Paddy and Carole to a hospital, but Gerry said he was not going to any hospital, that he was going to walk out the front door. It was not until some days later that I saw on video his triumphant exit from the Old Bailey; it was a truly moving and altogether fitting reappearance into the world of a man unjustly imprisoned for fifteen years.

They called me first to be processed. I do not remember if I said goodbye to the others. I was led down a long corridor, holding cells to one side, a wall on the other. The screws kept six or seven paces behind me. For a moment I thought they were going to let me walk out of the court. I remember getting half way down the corridor when I glanced around and saw a man in civilian dress suddenly come up from behind. He had a microphone in his ear and spoke into a tiny transmitter. He said, 'The man is coming to you, the man is coming to you.' I continued on, walked down some stairs at the end of the corridor, and arrived at a desk where a screw gave me a form to sign for my property. The plainclothes man was still behind me. As I was signing, a door opened and a man walked over. He said, 'Paul Hill, I am arresting you. Anything you say will be taken down and may be used in evidence against you.'

I had a fit of panic. I thought, 'They are charging me with something else.' Or, was I being arrested under the Prevention of Terrorism Act? I was handcuffed to a screw. I asked them where they were taking me – I thought perhaps it would be Wandsworth or Brixton – but they did not say. We got into a van and set off west. I thought perhaps it could be the

Scrubs. But we kept going until I saw signs for the Royal Air Force base at Northolt. We drove onto the runway. A number of RAF personnel had gathered to watch, and they glared at me as I was led onto the airplane, a small jet. We took off.

The flight took about one hour. We touched down at Aldergrove airport, Belfast, where they put me into another van. I was driven to Maghaberry prison and taken to reception. I received a shock there: the screws, far from being aggressive, were engaged in a conversation about the corruption of the English police. As they processed me, there was some discussion about what authority they were holding me under. Just then, an AG rushed in waving a piece of paper, which had just been telexed through and which he said allowed them to detain me. The screws, laughing, said they were putting me on the 'Yuppie Wing' – the wing for men coming to the end of their sentences and who, for that reason, were not about to cause trouble. Once a kit had been sorted out, I followed the screws up to a cell on the wing. They did not lock the door. I dumped my things on the bed and sat down. It was around 5pm, and I half-expected to be called for court at any minute. My mind was racing, refusing to slow down, going endlessly over the possible outcomes: release on bail tonight, tomorrow, next week? Perhaps they were going to deny bail?

I was not left alone with my thoughts for long. The cell quickly filled up with prisoners who came in to congratulate me and ask me about what had happened. One man shook my hand. He said, 'I hope you don't mind.' I said I didn't. He said, 'I'm a Protestant. I'm in for a sectarian murder.' We looked at each other. There was a time, more than fifteen years ago, when I would not have talked to him. Now we shared a common identity as prisoners. He said, 'It was wrong, it was all wrong.'

I sat down, surrounded by the prisoners, and chatted and smoked, glad to be distracted from my thoughts. I was talking to one of the men when out of the corner of my eye I saw a prisoner coming along the landing. He walked with a cocky little Belfast dander, feet pointing out, shoulders swaying. I recognized him even before his face came into view. He said, 'What's all this I heard about you getting out then? I hope

255

you'll stop all your crying now.' It was Martin Brady, who I had met in Hull just before the riot. I thought, as I watched him approach, of the times I had hauled myself up to the cell window in Wakefield, and sneaked looks at Martin dandering around the yard. We hugged each other and bantered a bit more. We talked. Martin pointed to my smashed cheek bone and I told him the story about Blackett. Martin was due to be released quite soon. He had been inside since 1973. But I found it hard to concentrate on the conversation. In the cells below the Old Bailey, Tony Gifford had said that he would be up to see me before 7pm that night. I kept waiting to be called for a legal visit.

When association time was over, we were locked up for the night. The time dragged terribly. Later, a screw came to tell me that Errol had telephoned with the news that I would be appearing in the High Court the following day. I asked the screw what the time was. He said it was 10pm. I reconciled myself to another night inside.

The next morning, I went down to breakfast with Martin. But I could not settle down. I was worried in case they had found a way to keep me in. By 10am no one had come to take me to court. This was very unusual because court productions are normally taken at around 8am. Then, the screws suddenly put an end to association, saying there was going to be a search of the prison. This made me deeply suspicious. I thought they were locking us up to avoid trouble if I did not get out. I was locked in my cell, becoming more and more paranoid. My heart was thumping.

The door suddenly opened. Two screws took me to see the Governor who told me that the Northern Ireland Office wanted to know my views on having the Shaw conviction dealt with by Peter Brooke, the Secretary of State for Northern Ireland. I immediately said, 'No.' To encourage me, they said the matter could be dealt with immediately, I would be released at once. I said, 'No. I'm innocent. I'm not going to do anything that implies guilt.'

'Does that mean you will not co-operate with the parole board?' the Governor asked.

'I am not asking for parole. I have never asked for parole. I will never ask for parole. I do not want parole.'

I was furious. They were offering to release me at once if

I would accept parole; accepting parole entailed accepting guilt. I was aware, as I was speaking, of making my way to the door. I found myself storming back to the cell and pulling the door behind me. I was more agitated than I remembered having been for a long time. The pain from my broken cheek bone was getting worse, my eye smarted and I had developed a twitch where a nerve had been trapped in the break of the bone.

I paced up and down. I was so close to getting out, my hopes were so high, and now the authorities were manoeuvring to try to salvage something from their debacle. I later discovered that our hearing, which had originally been set for 10.30am, had been put back until 1pm. When Tony Gifford asked the reason for this, the court authorities blamed a heavy schedule of divorce cases. Perhaps fifteen years inside had made me cynical, but I smelt a rat. The 'divorce schedule' was an excuse to give them an opportunity to try to persuade me to accept parole. They could have squeezed me into court any time. They were trying to minimize the damage: they could say, 'Well, look, one of the Guildford Four was guilty of something.'

At around 11am, the screws came to my cell and took me down to reception. I assume that they had realized that I had meant what I had said about not accepting parole. I was seen briefly by a doctor before being placed in the van and driven to the High Court in Belfast city centre. In the back of the van, I examined the marks prisoners had scratched into the metal: names and the sentences they had just received – fifteen years, eighteen years, life, life, life: ten thousand years scratched into the van.

We pulled into Belfast High Court. As I stepped out, I was surrounded by uniformed RUC men. My optimism had risen again and I was smiling. The RUC men glowered at me. My hands were cuffed in front of me and a screw led me by the chain between my wrists through the building's main hall. There were people sitting on the benches on either side and, as we passed, they came up and wished me luck and slapped me on the back. A woman ducked between the police and screws. She said, 'Have a drink on us, son.' Later, I found four ten pound notes in my pocket. The woman had probably given me all she had

257

had in her purse. I remember thinking, 'I don't even know her name.'

I saw Tony Gifford, Mike Fisher and Oliver Kelly, a local solicitor who had been instructed to act for me in Belfast. Mike was grinning. He pulled out some plane tickets. 'You're going home,' he said. 'This is your ticket.'

I was taken to a small detention room to wait for my case to be called. At last it was. I was led to the court, passing friends and family who had gathered. They came around me and kissed and hugged me. Kara, a happy grin on her face, was there and I smiled and winked at her. I saw Gina, too. The judge asked for the Crown's attitude to the bail application. The Crown lawyer said it was neutral. The judge asked what he meant by neutral: he said it meant that he did not oppose bail. It was just a formality. Errol and Jeremy Corbyn, who had flown over for the hearing, put themselves forward as sureties. The judge set bail of £4,100, pending an appeal application, and attached no conditions. I would be free to travel and would not have to report to the police. It was over in minutes.

I was led from the court still in handcuffs to a foyer where they unchained me. Mike and Tony led me, followed by a crowd of family and friends, towards the entrance of the court. They saw that my cheek bone was causing me problems and said the first priority was to get it sorted out. The crowd made me nervous about my injury and about my eye, which was partly dislodged and which I kept having to nudge back into its socket. A lad I knew from school, Paddy Mulligan, rushed up and hugged me. My cheek bone cracked and I felt it in the roof of my mouth. The pain was awful.

I made my way through the crowd towards a car Mike and Tony had arranged. I was surrounded by people cheering and shouting. Kara and my mum were hugging me. I saw Gina in among the crowd. I was too happy – and confused – to think; I just let myself be carried along. I did not have to look out or keep guard. I was free, and once more among my own.

As I was stepping into the car I took hold of Kara. She was coming with me.

Chapter Seventeen

STOLEN YEARS

I came out to a world that was familiar, but also strange, and there was a lot to get used to. People for one thing. During my years in prison, I was often alone. It was not just the time spent in solitary – more than five years – because, even on normal location, I was for most of the day by myself. For the first few weeks after my release, I found it hard to concentrate when I was in company; I was confused by the criss-crosses in the flow of the conversation, and my mind would wander; I would be distracted, by someone walking past, by a telephone ringing, by the clinking of a teaspoon stirring sugar into a cup. In prison, there is so little for the senses to feed on: it takes time to readjust to the barrage of noise, smells and sights of the world outside. Sometimes, it gets a little frightening. Sometimes, in the middle of a social gathering, I feel like jumping up and running away to a quiet place.

Nor was it easy to get used to *how* people are outside. In the black and white of prison, I knew where I stood with the men around me. In prison, it is all up front. Outside,

I find I have to get used to subtleties. I sometimes have difficulty in discerning what it is people are really saying, and in interpreting the signals and movements and looks they employ to tell me who and what they are. It is hard work. Perhaps my difficulties have more to do with a Belfast upbringing than with prison. Belfast people tend to say what they say bluntly. With English people, especially middle-class English people, I have not yet learned to distinguish between what they say and what they mean.

I find now that I am expected to plan ahead. People ask, 'What are you going to do?' I do not know, I honestly do not know. Perhaps it is because the Shaw conviction has not yet been dealt with – the complexities of the case, its links with Guildford, mean that no date has yet been set for a hearing of the appeal. Soon after my release, I was informed by letter that I had been granted parole for Shaw. I was furious. I had never applied for parole, and I do not accept it.

But I think it is not just the Shaw case. I seem to have lost, temporarily or permanently I do not know, the capacity to plan ahead. In prison, you learn to blank out the future when you have nothing to look forward to and have no control over your life. In prison, you can think no further than tomorrow. The future, having a future, is a new concept.

Beside these difficulties, the little strangenesses I encountered on coming home were of nothing. At first, the richness of food outside made me feel dizzy and sick, and my jaws ached after having to chew it – chewy food, it was so long since I had had anything other than pulp. The London traffic made crossing the road a nightmare: I would watch in amazement when I saw people making suicidal dashes in the face of oncoming cars. Then there were microwaves, videos, computers, clothes, money, keys, drink.

Still, it is surprising how quickly you get used to these things. Having a home helps. On release, I went to live with Errol and Theresa in London, and they have provided a stability that has done much to help me readjust. Still, I sometimes wake up in the middle of the night frightened, not knowing where I am. It is then I realize that one of the most important things I have lost is being part of a community, knowing where I am, where I belong. It is something that cannot be recovered. To be part of a community requires anonymity: it is one of community's strictest rules that its members be ordinary. As one of the Guildford Four, I am no longer ordinary. To that extent, I feel displaced. I feel as if I have always – perhaps even in prison – been looking for a substitute for the community I grew up in. I am realistic enough to know that it cannot be found in its original form, and that the search will take me – has already taken me – in other directions.

One direction was marriage. When I had originally told Errol about my plans to marry he wanted to know if I was sure about what I was doing. I said I was, and he accepted my decision and did everything he could to sort out the arrangements. When, the day after I was moved from Albany to Brixton, I saw Errol and Theresa and asked them about Marion, I immediately suspected from their reaction that something was not right. But I was too preoccupied, and excited, by what was happening to dwell on it.

Marion had not flown over straight after my release, pleading family and work demands. We wrote and spoke by telephone, and after a few weeks she came to see me in London. I had been unable to meet her at the airport because of an engagement with MPs of the European Parliament. Marion's flight touched down at Heathrow just as mine was taking off from Strasbourg. When I got home to Errol and Theresa's, Marion was already there, surrounded by pressmen who wanted pictures of the two of us together. Mike Fisher, who had come to the house after a call from Theresa, kept the photographers and reporters at bay while I went to speak to Marion – our first moment together in freedom. To get rid of the press, we agreed to have some photographs taken, then we could be by ourselves.

It was clear Marion had doubts, and I did not have time enough to dispel them. Marion had to return after only a couple of days. She flew back to New Jersey, and when she went I was no clearer in my mind about where I stood. We agreed that I would, as soon as I could organize it, fly to the States so that we could sort things out.

Meanwhile, there was much to do about making sure that the lessons of Guildford had been well learned. I gave interviews and addressed rallies and meetings to remind people that the Birmingham Six were still inside, that the system that had failed us for so long continued to fail them, that what had happened must never be allowed to happen again.

In the days following our release, the papers had been full of stories about the Guildford Four. Leader writers and columnists were appalled at the revelations about the corruption of investigating officers and at the failure of the system for so long to right an obvious wrong. The country was shocked at the scale of the injustice. In our trial in 1975, Havers had told the jury that if we were telling the truth then a gigantic conspiracy to pervert the course of justice had taken place. Now the courts had freed us. What did that mean for Havers' conspiracy? How big was it? Who was involved?

There were immediate demands that the whole matter be thoroughly investigated. If the system was corrupt, then something had to be done to clean it up. On this there was total agreement, even from the right-wing press. A leader in the *Daily Express* ran: '. . . the process of establishing their innocence took far too long. And those responsible for robbing them of fourteen years must be punished.' Peter Jenkins in the *Independent* described the law as 'an enemy of justice'. He concluded, 'Plainly, after what has happened, radical changes are required in the whole system of police interrogation and in the law relating to confessions. But not only that, the shocking history of the Guildford Four shows that justice must not be left to old men in wigs sitting in judgment over themselves. The authority of the Court of Appeal is in ruins . . .'

The Home Secretary set up an inquiry under Sir John May, a retired judge, to look into the whole affair, and he ordered the Avon and Somerset officers to investigate wrong-doing by Surrey police. The hope was expressed that action would speedily be taken against any officers who had behaved improperly. One difficulty was in getting officers involved in the original investigation to talk. On 4 December 1989, Sir Patrick Mayhew, the Attorney General, announced that witnesses who gave evidence to the May Inquiry would be offered partial immunity, in that statements made to the inquiry would not be used in any subsequent criminal proceedings. Our lawyers were sceptical about the value of this: Mike Fisher said that without complete immunity the truth about what happened in Guildford Police Station might never come out. He feared that junior officers under suspicion would be scapegoats. 'Scapegoating is more likely to conceal than reveal,' he said. Alastair Logan wondered whether Mayhew's announcement would tempt officers to say nothing to the Sharples team, but wait to give evidence to the May Inquiry, or simply stay silent. Others suggested that May's powers were inadequate to meet the task in hand. Without the authority to compel witnesses to attend or to subpoena documents, May will inevitably depend on the co-operation of men and women who, some of them at least, will have no direct interest in being forthcoming.

Inevitably, shock wears off. Since our release, something of a pendulum swing has begun. Some of those in positions of authority are saying enough is enough, arguing that police morale must not be further undermined by harping on about the case. The revelations made by Amlot in the Court of Appeal came at a time when public confidence in the integrity of the police was already low. That confidence has been reduced still further by the continuing concern about allegations of widespread corruption in the West Midlands force, the appearance of police officers in court on a variety of serious charges, and the recent payment by the Metropolitan police of record damages to a black man who claimed to have been planted with drugs. Brian Hayes, the Chief Constable of Surrey, in his annual report, has complained of the effect the Guildford Four case has had on the morale of his officers. Imbert has been reported as saying that he still sees no reason to doubt our original convictions.

All of this has engendered suspicions about the authorities' willingness to see justice done. Anxieties have been expressed about what exactly the Sharples team is doing. They were instructed by the Home Secretary to investigate evidence of wrong-doing by Surrey detectives. However, documents of Surrey's Police Committee which have come to light suggest something else. These documents record that the Avon and Somerset officers required assistance in 'helping prepare evidence for the defence of the Surrey force'.

The danger is that there are senior judicial, government and police officials who appear to believe that public confidence in the system of justice can best be maintained by keeping quiet about wrong-doing. If this attitude is as widespread as I fear, I am not optimistic about the truth of what happened in Guildford ever coming out. And if the truth remains hidden, if the authorities bury their heads in the sand, then Guildford can, and will, happen again. All the ingredients are still there: the Prevention of Terrorism Act – found to be in contravention of the European Declaration on Human Rights but still on the statute book; pre-trial investigative procedures that rely entirely on the willingness and capacity of the police to ensure that suspects are treated properly; and a judiciary that appears reluctant even to consider the possibility of miscarriages of justice.

In March 1990, I took a flight from Dublin to New York. I was on my way to a Congressional hearing in Washington, as a guest of Congressman Joseph Kennedy, into miscarriages of justice in Britain at which Gerry, relatives of the Birmingham Six and a number of lawyers and politicians were going to give evidence. I was looking forward to the trip. I wanted people in the United States to know that in England, the closest ally of the United States in Europe, standards of justice were lacking, and that although we had been freed, justice was still being denied to the Birmingham Six and to the Maguires. But I also had a more personal motive in going. I hoped to be able to sit down and talk to Marion once I had finished with the Congressional hearing. I still did not know how things stood between us.

The hearing went well, and I was encouraged to find that there were people prepared to listen with an open mind. In Britain, such is the prejudice about Ireland, that the question of justice in cases like ours inevitably gets bound up with the politics of the war in the North. In America, it was refreshing to meet people who wanted to know the facts, and who could understand how bias can stand in the way of justice – at least in someone else's country. But that is always the way – the mote in the eye.

I met Marion in New York. I knew as soon as I saw her that it was over. She had her reasons, and they were straightforward enough. There were those at the time of our marriage who said we were trying to live out a fantasy. Perhaps they were right. But if we were, it was a fantasy that brought with it hope and warmth when I most needed it. Marion and I are no longer man and wife, I do not know if we will be friends. But I hold no ill will.

On the flight back to London I had time to sit quietly and reflect on my life. I looked back at my stolen years, back to Docks, back to the Falls, to my grandparents' home, to Gina. And I looked back to the life Gina and I shared, and I wonder what would have happened had I not been arrested. I cannot tell. It is so long ago; that time belongs to another age, and to another man.

I think about the bombs and the lives they destroyed, of the maimed girl who came to give evidence in our trial. I think of the ex-Loyalist in Maghaberry who told me he was in for murdering a Catholic. 'It was wrong,' he said, 'it was all wrong.'

I think, too, of my confessions. When I made them I was broken, I had no will left. I agreed to what they said and lost fifteen years of my life. Other people suffered as a result: the police started a ball rolling that did not stop until it had crushed many other innocent victims: Gerry, Carole, Paddy, Anne and Paddy Maguire, Vincent and Patrick their sons, Sean Smyth and Patrick O'Neill; and, in the case of Giuseppe Conlon, the ball did not stop until it had crushed his life from him. There are times when I cannot help but think that if I had had greater resistance, if I had been able to hold up to the violence and threats, none of this would have happened.

I hear people mention the word catharsis, the instant emptying out of the poison so that once again you are ready to be filled up with normal things. Perhaps there is such an experience, or something like it, but I think that, if it exists, it is not the dramatic event they tell us about, but slow and uneven, and spread over time. I have not had that 'cathartic' experience. Readjustment, I suspect, will be a long and difficult process. It involves rebuilding relations – with my daughter most of all, whose young life I have missed out on – whose first communion I never saw and whose tales of growing up I only ever had snatches of. It will also involve discarding, when everything has finally been settled, the identity I have as one of the Guildford Four. For I am not yet Paul Hill. That man has not yet fully emerged from prison.

CHRONOLOGY

1954
13 August   Paul Hill born

1964
28 September – 2 October   Divis Riots

1968
April   Paul's first visit to England
5 October   First Civil Rights march, Derry

1969
June   Paul leaves school
July   Paul goes to England to work, stays
                                       in London with his aunt and uncle,
                                       Anne and Frank Keenan

1969
14-15 August   Falls attacked by B-Specials and
                                       Loyalists

1970

c. January   Paul returns to Belfast

1971

9 August   Introduction of internment without trial

November   Paul's third visit to London to find work. In summer 1972 he returns to Belfast where he spends some months with his family before going back to London

1973

December   Paul returns to Belfast

1974

20 July   Body of ex-soldier Brian Shaw discovered in Arundel Street, Belfast

23 August   Paul, Gina Clarke, Liz and Joe Kane, arrive at Heysham. Paul and Gina go first to stay in London, then move to Stainer Close, Southampton. While in Southampton they meet Gerry Conlon

20 September   Paul and Gerry leave Southampton and move to Hope House, Kilburn. Gina stays with sister in Southampton. Paul makes four visits to Southampton between 28 September and 19 October

5 October   IRA active service unit led by Brendan Down and Joe O'Connell plant time bombs at Horse and Groom and Seven Stars, Guildford. They explode, killing seven and wounding many more

19 October   Gerry Conlon returns to Belfast. Paul leaves Hope House and moves to Anne and Frank Keenan's flat

7 November   Joe O'Connell, Harry Duggan, Eddie Butler and Brendan Dowd attack

21 November	King's Arms, Woolwich: two killed. Two IRA time bombs explode in Birmingham pubs: twenty-one die, scores wounded. Six Irishmen arrested and charged with murder
28 November	Surrey detectives arrest Paul in Southampton and take him to Guildford Police Station
29 November	Prevention of Terrorism Act becomes law
30 November	Gerry arrested in Belfast and brought to Guildford. Sean Mullin arrested. Active service unit throws two short-fuse bombs into the Talbot Arms, London: five wounded
1 December	Paul charged with murder arising out of Guildford bombings
2 December	Paul's first appearance at Guildford Magistrates' Court
3 December	Annie Maguire and family arrested with Guiseppe Conlon, Gerry's father, and subsequently charged with possession of explosives. Paddy Armstrong and Carole Richardson arrested. Paul Colman arrested
4 December	Paul and Gerry appear together at Guildford Magistrates' Court and remanded to Winchester Prison
7 December	Paddy, Carole, Annie Maguire, Paul Colman, Sean McGuinness, Brian Anderson charged with Guildford murders
1975	
3 February	Charges of murder dropped against Paul Colman, Brian Anderson, Sean McGuinness. Explosives charges dropped against Sean Mullin
24 February	Charges of murder dropped against Annie Maguire

268

17 March	Committal proceedings open at Guildford Magistrates' Court. Paul, Gerry, Carole and Paddy sent for trial
15 April	Paul charged with murder of Brian Shaw
17 June	Paul goes on trial in Belfast with co-defendants Martin Monaghan and Hector Young, before no-jury 'Diplock' court, accused of Shaw murder
23 June	Paul convicted of Shaw murder. Sent to Wandsworth Prison to begin life sentence
10 July	Brendan Dowd arrested in Manchester
27 August	London Active service unit bombs the Caterham Arms, Caterham, in 'carbon copy' of the Guildford time bombs
3 September	Kara, Paul's daughter, born
16 September	Trial of Paul, Gerry, Carole and Paddy opens at the Old Bailey before Sir John Donaldson
22 October	Paul, Gerry, Carole and Paddy convicted on all counts. Carole ordered to be detained at Her Majesty's Pleasure; the others each receive life sentences. Judge tells Paul 'life must mean life'
12 December	IRA active service unit members Joe O'Connell, Eddie Butler, Harry Duggan and Hugh Doherty captured after siege at Balcombe Street. During questioning by bomb squad officers James Nevill and Peter Imbert, Butler and O'Connell make admissions concerning Guildford and Woolwich
1976 January-March	Trial of Maguire Seven: all convicted

269

16 April	Paul's grandmother, Margaret Cushnahan, dies
11 May	Brendan Dowd convicted, receives life sentence
31 August	Hull prison riot breaks out. Paul, with other prisoners, beaten by prison officers after surrender. Moved to Leicester Prison and placed in solitary
October-November	Alastair Logan and James Still interview Dowd, O'Connell, Butler and Duggan

1977

January-February	Trial of the Balcombe Street men before Judge Cantley. They refuse to recognize the court, but O'Connell makes a statement from the dock claiming responsibility for Guildford and Woolwich, and stating that Paul, Gerry, Carole and Paddy were not involved
3 October	Paul's sister, Katrina, born
10 October	Lawyers for Guildford Four make application for retrial before the Court of Appeal, Lord Roskill presiding, on basis of information supplied by Dowd and Balcombe Street men
24 October	Katrina dies
28 October	Court of Appeal rejects application

1978

October	Riot at Gartree prison breaks out, Paul moved to Exeter and placed in solitary

1979

February-April	Trial of prison officers from Hull at York Crown Court on charges arising out of 1976 Hull riot: eight convicted

1980

23 January   Guiseppe Conlon dies

1982

3 December   Charlie Cushnahan, Paul's grand-
                              father, dies

1984

6 March   ITV screens *First Tuesday* documen-
                              tary 'Aunt Annie's Bomb Factory'
                              about Maguire Case

1986

January   Paul begins correspondence with
                              Marion Serravalli while in Lincoln
                              prison

1 July   *First Tuesday* documentary, 'The
                              Guildford Time Bomb' on Guildford
                              Four case transmitted

7 October   Lords Devlin and Scarman write to
                              The Times questioning pre-trial pro-
                              cedures in Guildford and Maguire
                              case. They submit legal opinion to
                              Home Secretary arguing Court of
                              Appeal judges erred in law in 1977
                              Guildford appeal

13 October   *Trial and Error* by Robert Kee
                              published

1987

7 January   All-party delegation of MPs urges
                              Home Secretary to reconsider cases
                              of Guildford Four and Birmingham
                              Six

20 January   Home Secretary Douglas Hurd refers
                              case of Birmingham Six to Court of
                              Appeal. Hurd turns down requests
                              that Guildford Four case be reopened

3 March   *First Tuesday* transmit 'The Case
                              That Won't Go Away' in which
                              Yvonne Fox is interviewed about

	Paul's alibi for the Woolwich bombing
23 July	Cardinal Basil Hume, Lords Devlin and Scarman, Roy Jenkins, Merlyn Rees and Robert Kee meet Douglas Hurd to urge him to review Guildford Four case. They hand over statements with new evidence
14 August	Hurd appoints Jim Sharples, Deputy Chief Constable of Avon and Somerset, to lead investigation into new evidence
2 November	Appeal of the Birmingham Six opens at Old Bailey. Lord Lane, Lord Chief Justice, presides
18 November	Cardinal Hume's delegation meet Home Secretary and press for review of Guildford case
1988	
28 January	Court of Appeal rejects applications of the Birmingham Six and upholds convictions
12 February	Paul marries Marion Serravalli in Long Lartin prison
March	The Sharples team completes its investigations and reports to the Home Secretary
30 November	*The Times* publishes article by Lords Devlin and Scarman arguing there has been a denial of justice in Guildford case
1989	
16 January	Hurd refers case of Guildford Four to Court of Appeal. He asks the Sharples team to continue investigations
20 July	Lawyers for Paddy apply to have hearing of appeal put back to January 1989. Application granted

19 October	Hearing in the Court of Appeal on request of Roy Amlot QC for the Crown before Lord Lane. Amlot says Crown cannot oppose appeal. Judges quash all convictions. Gerry, Carole and Paddy freed. Paul taken to Northern Ireland pending hearing on his conviction for Shaw murder
20 October	Paul freed on bail by Belfast High Court pending appeal

Index

Albany Prison, 146, 147, 205, 206-10, 211, 238, 241-3, 261; mailbag shop, 208-9; riot, 208-10, 212, 216

Aldergrove Airport, 255

Amlot, Roy, 58, 237, 247-52, 263

Amnesty International, 221

Anderson, Brian, 85, 86, 88, 90, 128

Angry Brigade, 151

Antrim Glens, 19

Appleton, Mr, 113

Argenta, 34

Armley Prison (Leeds), 176-7, 191-2, 195, 207; brutality, 176

arms smuggling, 37

Armstrong, Paddy, 265; sentence, 1-4; 'confession', 2, 57, 75, 87-8, 93, 250; character, 50, 87; PH meets, 50; on remand, 50, 85, 86; PH names, 72-3; arrested, 74; PH confronted with, 75; Rondu Road, 88; PH hardly knows, 89; legal representative, 91; no trace of explosives, 93; committal, 96; Brixton, 96-7; trial, 117-31; Wandsworth, 122-3, 237-8; fears for safety, 133; Wormwood Scrubs, 133; Hull, 153; prison file, 162; O'Connell clears, 182; Wakefield, 183; depressed, 217; Winchester, 217; Gartree, 217; American support, 222; legal representative, 230, 237;

appeal (1989), 58, 237, 245-58; freedom, 243-58
Army: deployed in Belfast (1969), 38; hostility to, 39; brutality, 40; fires on Turf Lodge, 41; intelligence, 94
Association of Legal Justice, 40, 70
Astin, Lisa, 128-9
'Aunt Annie's Bomb Factory', 223, 227
Auxiliaries, 32
Avon and Somerset Police, 229, 236, 248, 249, 250, 262, 263

B-Specials, 30, 32; brutality, 33, 36, 42; disbanded, 39
Balcombe Street siege (1975), 53, 87, 142-6, 153, 176-7, 178, 181, 183-4, 237, 248
Barron, Tom, 235
Barry, Peter, 219
Bata, 41, 79
Belfast: Albert Street, 21, 32, 37, 42, 212; American Bar, 11, 14, 27; Andersonstown, 17-18; Antrim Road, 99; Ardoyne, 15, 21; Arundel Street, 69, 99; Bellevue Zoo, 20; Botanical Gardens, 20; Bow Street, 27; Broadway, 17, 100; Cairns Street, 7, 10, 17, 23, 28, 33, 37-8, 101, 203, 265; Castle Street, 7, 17, 39-40; cinemas, 21; College Square, 38; Conway Street, 37; Cooper Street 21, 43; crime, 10-11; Crumlin Road Prison, 7, 15, 39, 40; Cyprus Street, 37; Dermott Hill, 17; devastation, 36-7; Divis Flats, 27, 44, 50, 90, 100; Divis Street, 17, 18, 33-4, 37;

Docks, 5-15, 17, 18, 19, 24, 25, 30, 162, 265; Donegal Road, 30; Dover Street, 36; Dunville Park, 44; Durham Street, 37; Eliza Street, 19; English Street, 27; Falls Library, 34; Falls Road, 7, 10, 17, 20, 21, 22, 24, 27, 30, 31, 32, 34, 36, 38, 43, 47, 102, 265; Glen Road, 17, 25; Glengeen Bar, 44, 100, 101; Grosvenor Road, 8, 24; Hamill Street, 38; Irwin Street, 27; Kelly's bar, 41; Leeson Street, 21, 37, 44; Lord Street, 7; Lower Falls, 17, 71, 153; 'Lower Wack' 18; McDonnell Street, 32; Matilda Street, 7; mills, 18, 30, 37, 38; Milltown Cemetery, 17, 18, 21; Mooney's, 100, Nelson Street, 9; New Barnsley, 17, 41, 42; New Lodge, 25; Norfolk Street, 36; North Howard Street, 24, 30, 31; Palace Barracks, 40, 41, 95; Percy Street, 36; Pilot Street, 9; Pound Loney, 27, 38, 158; Raglan Street, 25; Riddle's Field, 27; Roden Street, 30; Royal Victoria Hospital, 24, 30, 34; Sailortown, 5-15; St James, 17, 24; St Joseph's Catholic church, 9; St Louisa's school, 26; St Peter's pro-cathedral, 8, 39; St Peter's primary school, 25; St Peter's secondary school, 25, 26, 48, 55; Sandy Row, 7; Shankill Road, 32, 36, 37, 39, 43; Shore Road, 9, 16; Spinner Street, 28; Springmartin, 41; Springfield Road, 18, 41; Turf Lodge, 17, 19, 28,

37, 40-1; unemployment, 30, 35; Unicorn Bar, 100; West Belfast, 7, 17, 30, 99; Whiterock, 17
Belfast Celtic FC, 9
Belfast Crown Court, *see* Hill, Paul
'Belfast dander', 18, 203, 255, 256
Belfast Lough, 19
Benn, Tony, 235
Best, George, 11
Birmingham, 36
Brimingham bombings (1974), 116-17, 153, 217, 218, 225-6, 227, 229, 235-6, 237
Black, Officer, 242, 243
Black and Tans, 32, 42
Blackett, 256
Blake, DI Timothy, 66, 68, 74, 75-6, 123, 124
Blaney, Neil, 221
Board of Visitors, 148, 164, 174, 212, 216
'bomb factories' 88
Bomb Squad, 180
Boyne, Battle of the (1690), 8
Brady, Martin, 153-4, 164, 166, 176, 195, 202-3, 256
Bray, 25
Bridgewater, Carl, 217
Bristol Prison, 136-46, 147, 149, 207, 238
Brixton Prison, 50, 81, 89-90, 96-7, 98, 122, 207, 261; conditions, 101, 102
Brooke, Peter, 256
'Bulbeater', 198
Butler, Eddie, 87, 153, 176-7, 178, 181, 182, 183-4, 187, 188, 224

Caddy, Dr Brian, 140
Callaghan, Hugh, 212

Canterbury Prison, 208
Cantland, Mary Ellen, 231-2
Cantley, Mr Justice, 178, 181
Carolan, Father, 50, 72-3, 74
Carrickfergus, 16, 34
Casement, Roger, 200
Category 'A', 84-5, 93, 135
Caterham Arms, 126, 181
Catholic Emancipation, 140
Central Criminal Court, *see* Hill, Paul
'Choppers', 26
Christian Brothers, 42-3
civil rights movement, 30-1
Civil War (1919-21), 32
Clarke, Cathy (*Gina's sister-in-law*), 56
Clarke, Cathy (*Gina's sister*), *see* Crosbie, Cathy
Clarke, Gina (*girlfriend*), 28, 38, 48, 87; PH's girlfriend, 43; accompanies PH to England (1974), 44, 46, 47, 94; in Southampton, 47, 52-3, 55; and Conlon, 48-9; PH's letters to, 51; miscarriage, 52; in Greenwich, 53-4; living with Keenans, 54; pregnant again, 55, 62, 67, 102; arrest, 61, 67, 68; interrogated, 62; PH's alibi, 75-6, 127, 228; visits PH, 80-1, 89, 92, 102, 118-19, 151, 191-2, 213, 214; Kara born, 117; and Old Bailey verdict, 130; death of PH's grandmother, 141; and Balcombe Street gang, 146; breaks with PH, 151-2, 190-1, 233; marriage, 192; PH's release, 258
Clarke, John, 46, 55-6, 60
Clarke, Mary, *see* Hammond, Mary

Clarke, Sister Sarah, 222, 234
Clarke, Tony, 212, 214, 215
Clarke, Tracey, 56
Clifford, Marty, 153-4, 157-8
Colin Glen, 25
Colman, Paul, 74, 85, 86,
    90, 128
Conlon Gerry, 265; 'confession',
    2, 57, 75, 85, 87-8, 93,
    250, detained by Army, 47;
    character, 48-9, 87; gambler,
    48-9, 87; at Hope House,
    49-50, 252; returns to
    Belfast, 54; PH names, 72-3;
    arrested, 74; PH confronted
    with, 75; remanded, 77; legal
    representative, 91; no trace of
    explosives, 93; committal, 96;
    Brixton, 96-7, Old Bailey trial,
    117-31; Wandsworth, 122-3,
    133, 134, 237-8; Blake's
    alleged assault, 123, fears
    for safety, 133; O'Connell
    clears, 182; Winchester,
    217; approaches politicians,
    218; death of father, 220;
    American support, 222; appeal
    (1989), 237, 245-58; freedom,
    243-58; in USA, 264; verdict
    and sentence, 1-4
Conlon, Giuseppe, 74, 85, 86,
    87, 96, 140, 265; death, 220
Connolly, James, 34-5, 200
Conteh, Frank, 156-64, 165
Cooper, 193, 227
Cooper, Dr, 199, 211
Corbyn, Jeremy, 219, 235, 258
Coster, Bertie, 155, 164, 167-8,
    169, 170, 175, 176
Coventry, 64
'crack', 18-19, 30
Criminal Appeal Act (1968),
    225, 226, 236
Crosbie, Cathy, 47, 48, 62, 89,

92; marriage, 49, 53, 163 and
    PH's alibi, 127-9
Crosbie, Malcolm, 47, 48, 62,
    92; marriage, 53
Crumlin Road Prison, 78-9,
    98-114, 115, 153, 207;
    conditions, 101-2
Crusaders FC, 9
Cunningham, DCI Albert, 69,
    98, 105, 108, 109, 110-12
Cushnahan, Annie, see Keenan,
    Anne
Cushnahan, Charlie, jnr (uncle),
    19, 20, 26
Cushnahan, Charlie, snr
    (grandfather), 9, 10-11,
    40-1, 43, 46, 47, 113; and
    daughter's marriage, 14; PH
    living with, 17, 19, 37-8,
    101; character, 19-20; refuses
    to believe PH, 21-2; death,
    203-4, 208
Cushnahan, Elizabeth (Lily), see
    Hill, Elizabeth (Lily)
Cushnahan, Margaret
    (grandmother), 20, 40-1, 43,
    45; takes PH to cinema, 21;
    PH living with, 37-8; death,
    141, 149
Cushnahan, Theresa, see
    Smalley, Theresa

Daily Express, 141, 262
Daily Mail, 86
Daily Telegraph, 94, 103
Davey, Mrs, 74-5
Davis, George, 193
Deal bomb (1989), 238
Denning, Lord, 236
Derry, 31, 36
detention-sheets, 63-5, 106
Devlin, Lord, 223, 227, 228
Dinkins, David, 222
Diplock courts, 83, 104

Docherty, Tony, 40
Doherty, Hugh, 87, 176-7, 182, 183-4
Dolan, 34
Donaghey, John, 23, 24, 25, 26, 38, 42
Donaldson, Sir John, 1-4, 121, 123, 129, 130-1, 136, 140, 198
Donegal Gaeltacht, 20
Dowd, Brendan, 53, 178, 182, 183, 185, 187, 188, 224
'Drango Kid', 31-2
drugs, 199, 210-11
Dublin, 25, 34-5, 221, 264
Duggan, Harry, 87, 142-6, 176-7, 178, 182, 183-4, 187, 188, 224
Dundalk, 25, 43
Dunville Park murder (1974), 44, 69, 71
Durham Prison, 87, 147, 207

Easter Rising (1916), 21, 34, 140
Eastleigh, 76, 127
Eire, see Republic of Ireland
Elton, Lord, 216
emigration, Irish, 36
Emmet, Robert, 200
Error of Judgement (Mullin), 225
Essex Flour and Grain, 35
European Court of Human Rights, 148, 234
European Declaration on Human Rights, 264
European Parliament, 261
Exeter Prison, 202, 208

Farquharson, Lord, 247
Faul, Fr Denis, 218, 222, 223
Fenians, 140, 200
Fermanagh-South Tyrone, 200

Fianna, 42
First Tuesday, 223, 228
Fisher, Mike, 229, 236-7, 245, 246, 253, 258, 261, 262-3
Fitt, Gerry, 218, 220
Fitzgerald, Garret, 219
Fitzpatrick, Gerry, 39-40, 235
Flags and Emblems Act, 33
Foley, Conor, 235
football, 9, 11, 12, 15, 24-5, 31-2, 35, 41
Foreign Office, 222
'Forty Coats', 23
Fowler Inquiry, 173-4, 177-8
Fox, Yvonne, 54, 128, 228
Franey, Ros: Time Bomb, 95, 103, 122, 228
Fraser, Hugh, 134

Gallagher, Eddie, 93
Gartree Prison, 177, 183, 188, 189, 197, 208, 217, 231; riot, 200-2
general election: (1964), 33-4; (1983), 219
'ghostings', 78
Gifford, Lord (Tony), 237, 246, 247, 253, 256, 257, 258
Glasgow Celtic FC, 9, 11, 24-5
Glasgow Rangers FC, 9, 25
Glentoran FC, 9
Glidewell, Lord, 247
Gould, Billy, 164, 195-6
Great Famine (1840s), 12, 36
Greenisland, 16-17
Guildford bombings (1974), 22, 52-3, 61
Guildford Four, see Armstrong, Paddy; Conlon, Gerry; Hill Paul; Richardson, Carole
'Guildford Time Bomb, The', 227
Guildford Magistrates' Court, 73, 77

Guildford Police Station, 60-1,
  65-6, 90

H Blocks, 200
Hamill, Geordie, 34
Hamill, Margaret, *see*
  Cushnahan, Margaret
Hamilton, Fairley, Prof.
  Gordon, 134
Hammond, Louis, 53-4
Hammond, Mary, 53-4, 61
Harland & Wolff, 11
Hattersley, Roy, 219
Haughey, Charles, 221
Havers, Sir Michael, 2, 87-8, 95,
  96, 118, 123-31, 140, 182,
  184, 185-6, 198, 247, 252-3
Heath, Edward, 53
Hennessey, Jim, 245
Heysham, 46, 95, 101
Hickey, William, 217
Higgs, Douglas, 178-81, 184
Hill, Bobby (*uncle*), 15
Hill, Elizabeth (Lily) (*mother*),
  45; marriage, 7; Paul's first
  communion, 13; husband
  ill-treats, 14-15; husband
  in prison, 15; move to Turf
  Lodge, 17, 19, 28, 37, 40; in
  mills, 18; wants PH to return
  to England, 40; bullet-riddled
  home, 41; visits PH, 43, 119,
  213; and Belfast verdict, 113;
  and Old Bailey verdict, 130;
  and PH's compensation, 178;
  and Gerry Fitt, 218; and PH's
  release, 258
Hill Elizabeth (*sister*), 9, 17,
  28, 37, 46; in London, 47;
  arrested, 94-5
Hill, Granddad, 7, 8
Hill, Katrina (*sister*), 186, 190
Hill, Marion (*sister*), 17,
  28, 37, 47

Hill, Marion (*wife*), 232-4, 236,
  238, 244, 261-5
Hill, Martin (*brother*), 28, 37
Hill, Michael, 2, 96, 125, 123-
  31, 247, 253
Hill, Patrick, (*brother*), 17, 28,
  37; absconds, 42-3, 55, 95;
  'Benny Hill', 55, 74, 94-5, 198
HILL PAUL,
  Early Years and Family Life:
  born (1954), 9; baptized
  Catholic, 8; childhood, 6-15,
  16-28, 83-4; school, 12,
  29-30, 55; first communion,
  13; first confession, 13;
  confirmation, 14; love of
  football, 9, 11, 12, 15,
  24-5, 31-2, 35, 41; move to
  Greenisland, 16, 25; living
  with grandparents, 17;
  films, 21; attitude to death,
  23-4; detained by police in
  Stranraer, 25; girlfriends, 26;
  and pop music, 27, 41-2;
  Bangor Blues, 27, 38, 158,
  159; father refuses to help,
  30; visits Dublin (1966), 34;
  first trip to England (1968),
  35; moves to London (1969),
  35; back in Belfast, 37, 43;
  detained by police in Belfast,
  38, 39-40, 95; throws rocks,
  39; in Crumlin Road Jail,
  40; television interview, 40;
  returns to England (1971),
  41; going steady with
  Gina, 43; living with Keenans,
    43, 54; returns to England
  with Gina (1974), 44, 46,
  47, 141; detained by Army
  in Belfast, 47; friendship
  with Conlon, 7-8; detained
  by police in Southampton,
  48, 92; London and Hope

House, 49-50, 53, 54, 72;
meets Paddy Armstrong, 50;
remand, 50, 77, 78-96, 237-8;
letters to Gina, 51; meets
Carole Richardson, 51; 'Benny
Hill', 54-5, 74, 94-5; return
to Southampton with Gina,
55; daughter Kara born, 117;
first sees Kara, 118-19; ill
health, 136, 230-1; death of
grandmother, 141, 149; break
with Gina, 151-2, 190-1;
sister Katrina dies, 190; death
of grandfather, 203, 208;
marriage to Marion, 232-3,
233-5, 236, 237, 238, 244,
261-5; living with Smalleys,
260; return to Belfast
(1989), 5-6
Legal Battle: 'confesses', 2,
57, 64, 70, 72, 77, 87-8, 90,
93, 99, 101, 103, 105, 123,
250; police interrogation, 2,
22, 51, 111; arrested (1974),
56, 57, 60-1; no trace of
explosives, 62, 93; alibis, 63,
75-6, 92-3, 127-8; clothes
taken, 67; intimidation,
65-6; assaulted by police,
66, 68, 77; denied food, 68,
80; names others, 72, 85;
and Dunville Park shooting,
69, 71; and Leeson Street
murder, 69, 71; and Brian
Shaw murder, 69-70, 72,
98-114, 123, 131, 177, 230,
246, 256-7, 260; Prevention
of Terrorism Act, 73; does
not name Carole Richardson,
74, 254; confronted with
Gerry and Paddy, 75; denied
solicitor, 75; confronted with
Annie Maguire, 77; anxiety
over Gina and mother, 83;

prays, 83-4; depression,
84; and 'bomb factories',
88; committal, 96, 218; 'in
trouble' with IRA, 102-3;
Belfast trial (1975), 63-5,
98-114, 116, 123, 177, 230,
246, 256-7, 260; branded
member of IRA, 113; offered
deals, 104-5, 122; Old Bailey
trial, 1-4, 22, 103-4, 105, 114,
117-31, 262; Balcombe Street
gang, 142-6, 153, 176-7, 178-
82, 183-8; appeal (1977), 182,
183-8, 189; approaches to
politicians, 216, 218; instructs
Mike Fisher, 229, 236-7;
appeal (1989), 58, 63, 245-58;
freedom, 243-58; rearrested,
254; in USA, 264
Prison Life: Albany, 147,
205, 206-10, 211, 212, 216,
238, 241-3, 261; Armley,
176-7, 191-2, 195, 207;
Bristol, 50, 81, 96-7, 98,
134-46, 147, 149, 207,
238; Brixton, 122, 207,
243, 261; Canterbury, 208;
censorship, 219-20; changes
PH, 148; compensation, 178;
conditions, 80, 101-2, 172,
174-5; Crumlin Road, 78-9,
115, 207; Durham, 147, 207;
effects on PH, 259-60; Exeter,
202, 208, family support, 203;
file, 162; films, 137; Gartree,
177, 183, 188, 189, 197, 200-
2, 208, 217, 231; Hull, 147-
68, 207, 232, 256; Leicester,
168, 169, 173, 195, 207;
Lincoln, 231-2; Long Kesh/
Maze, 104, 207; Long Lartin,
177, 183, 208, 211, 234-5;
Maghaberry, 255, 265;
obsessions, 194-6; Parkhurst,

136, 199, 208, 210-11;
radio, 137-8; razor blade,
197; reading, 138-40, 200;
riots, 155-64; 173-4, 177-8,
200-2, 208-10, 212, 216,
256; routine, 172, 174-5;
sex, 192-3, 233; solitary
confinement, 147, 148, 174,
198, 217; Strangeways,
211-14, 215-16, 217; strip
cell, 82; strip-searches, 196;
strong box, 197, 200; threats
and assaults, 81, 89, 116-17,
119-21, 122, 133, 149, 154,
167-8, 169-70, 178, 202,
210, 238-40; Wakefield, 202,
208, Wandsworth, 115-34,
149, 154, 171, 189, 207, 208;
Winchester, 50, 77, 115, 135,
148, 202, 207, 208, 217, 237-
8; Wormwood Scrubs, 198,
203, 205, 206, 208, 214-15,
216, 217, 225, 232, 234
Hill, William Norman (father):
marriage, 7; merchant navy,
7, 14; ill-treats wife, 14-15; in
prison, 15; leaves home, 15,
17; brief return, 28; refuses to
help PH, 30
Hilton Hotel bomb, 126
Holyhead, 87
Home Office, 79, 93, 183, 216,
218, 219, 227, 234, 238
Home Rule, 34
Horse and Groom, see Guildford
bombings
Hucklesby, DCS, 181
Huddleston, Trevor, 174
Hull Prison, 147-68, 207, 232;
brutality, 149, 174, 202;
conditions, 149-50; riot, 173-
4, 177-8, 210, 256
Hume, Basil, 220, 223, 228, 236
Hunger strikes, 200

Hunter, Gerry, 116-17, 121
Hurd, Douglas, 94, 221, 223,
225, 226, 227, 228, 236
Hylton, Lord, 216

Imbert, Det. Supt Peter, 2, 64,
68, 105, 124, 142-6, 263
Ince George, 131
inconsistencies in confessions,
75, 87-8, 90
Independent, The, 262
insanity, 199, 211
International Commission of
Jurists, 221
internment introduced (1971),
39
Irish News, 33
Irish Republican Army, 32, 34;
blows up Nelson's Column,
35; grows, 37; begins attacks
on Army and police, 38;
Fianna, 42; young couriers,
42; active service unit, 53,
54, 90, 142; and Brian Shaw,
100-1; prison organization,
102, 153, 154; PH 'in trouble'
with, 102; bombing pattern,
178-81

Jack the Lad, 128
James Mackie's, 30
James II, 8
Jenkins, Peter, 262
Jenkins, Roy, 223, 228
Jenkinson, Noel, 171-3
Jermey, DS Anthony, 61-2,
63-5, 66, 67, 69-72, 105, 106-
8, 123-4
Judges' Rules, 58-9

Kane, Joe, 46, 94
Kara (daughter), 191, 233; born,
117; visits PH, 118-19, 120,
151, 191-2, 213, 214; PH's

compensation, 178; in USA, 231-2; PH's release, 258
Kaye, Jackie, 145
Kee, Robert, 228; television, 223; *Trial and Error*, 63, 99, 103, 223, 227
Keenan, Anne (*aunt*), 19, 20, 21, 34, 41, 47, 50, 94-5, 101, 127, 128, 198, 228; marries, 35; PH staying with, 43, 54, 92-3; arrested, 73-4
Keenan, Cathleen, 26-8
Keenan, Frank 35, 41, 47, 50, 94-5, 127, 128, 198, 228; PH staying with, 43, 54, 92-3; arrested, 73-4
Kelly, Basil, 104
Kelly, Oliver, 258
Kennedy, Helena, 237, 253
Kennedy, Joseph, 264
Kennedy, Ludovic, 174; *Wicked beyond Belief*, 227
Kent, Bruce, 174
Kerr, Officer, 212, 213-4
King's Arms, *see* Woolwich bombing
Kinnock, Neil, 219

Labour Party, 219-20
Lane, Lord, 58-9, 236, 237, 247, 253
Lavery, Michael, 64-5, 104-14
Leeson Street murder (1974), 44, 69, 71
Leicester Prison, 168, 169, 173, 195, 207
Lenihan, Brian, 221
Lennon, Kenneth, 67-8
Leveller, 220
Lewis, Mr, 164
Liberal Party, 221
Lidstone, Donald, 125, 181, 184
Lincoln Prison, 231-2
Linfield FC, 9, 32

'liquid cosh', 210-11
Little, Graham, 205-6, 211
Little Red Songbook, 206
Liverpool, 35, 36
Logan, Alastair, 91-2, 145, 182, 183, 184, 186, 187, 223, 228, 229, 263
London, Algernon Road, 86; Azov Street, 53-4, Brecknock Road, 54, 127, 128, 228; Brixton, 88; Brook's 179; Camden Road, 54; Cricklewood 86; Elephant and Castle, 128; Greenwich, 53-4; Hilton Hotel, 126; Hope House, 49-50, 53, 54, 72, 87, 252; Irish embassy, 221; Irish immigrants, 36; Kentish Town, 54; Kilburn, 50, 53, 86; Liverpool Road, 35; Naval and Military Club, 179; Oxford Street, 41, 79; Quex Road, 50, 72, 87, 252; Rondu Road, 86, 88; Russian embassy, 222; Wormwood Scrubs Prison, 15; *See also* Balcombe Street siege *and* Woolwich bombing
London Irish Post, 221
Long Kesh/Maze Prison, 39, 104, 207
Long Lartin Prison, 177, 183, 208, 211, 234-5
Loughran, 'Mad' Vinty, 23
Loyalists: attack Falls Road, 36, 38; attack Shankill Road, 36, 39; snipers, 41; death squads, 43
Luton Post Office murder, 227

McAreavey, Danny, 23, 24, 42
MacBride, Seán, 221
McCartney, Jimmy, 156-64, 165, 170, 171, 175-6, 195

McCartney, Ronnie, 217
McCaul, DC John, 69, 98, 108, 109-10
Macdonald, Ian, 179-81
McDonnell, John, 220, 235
McGuiness, Sean, 85, 86, 88, 90, 128
McIlkenny, Dick, 225-6
McKee, Grant: *Time Bomb*, 95, 103, 122, 228
McKinney, Joe, 23, 38, 42
McLaughlin, Ray, 207
McLaverty, Michael, 12
McLoughlin, Brian, 124-5
McMahon, Michael, 193, 227
McMillan, Liam, 33-4
Maghaberry Prison, 255, 265
Maguire, Anne, 89, 128, 153, 217, 218, 220, 265; arrested, 74; PH confronted with, 77; charged, 85, 86; Brixton, 89-90; cleared of murder then rearrested, 90
Maguire, Francis, 74
Maguire, Hugh, 72-3, 74
Maguire, Kitty, 74
Maguire, Paddy, 74, 86, 140, 153, 265
Maguire, Patrick, 86, 265
Maguire, Vincent, 86, 140
Manchester, 46, 47, 51
Mandela, Nelson, 230
Matthews, Peter, 141
May, Sir John, 262
Mayhew, Sir Patrick, 262-3
Maynard, Joan, 218-19
Maze Prison, *see* Long Kesh
Meehan, Martin, 40
Melton, David, 90-1, 92, 97, 121-2, 188
Mildon, Arthur, 121, 123, 126, 129
Military Reaction Force, 101
missionary priests, 12

Mitchell, James, 200
Moffitt/Moffat, 185-7
Monaghan, Martin, 104, 105, 113
Monaghan Patrick, 105
Mooney, Paschal, 221
Moore, Butsy, 39-40
MUFTI, 201, 209-10
Mullin, Chris, 235; *Error of Judgement*, 225
Mullin, Sean, 86, 90
murder squads, 32, 43
Murphy, Canon, 39
Murray, Fr Raymond, 218, 222

National Council for Civil Liberties, 67, 90
Nationalists, 34, 35
Nevill, Chief Supt Jim, 64, 124, 142-6
New Statesman, 220
New York, 231, 264; City Council, 222-3
News at Ten, 54
no-go areas, 38
Northern Ireland Civil Rights Association, 30
Northern Ireland Office, 41, 256
Northolt, 255

O'Connell, Daniel, 140
O'Connell, Joe, 53, 54, 87, 142-6, 153, 176-7, 178, 183-4, 187, 188, 224; statement from dock, 181-2
O'Neill, Patrick, 86, 265
O'Neill, Terence, 31, 33
Observer, 101
Old Bailey, *see* Hill, Paul
Orange parades, 8

Paisley, Ian, 33-4
Parkhurst Prison, 136, 208, 210-11, 243; F2, 199, 211

Pat, 97
patches, 79
Peirce, Gareth, 227, 229, 235, 246
Peoples Democracy, 30
Platt-Mills, John, 174
potato blight (1840s), 12, 36
Power, Billy, 225-6
Prescott, Jake, 150-1, 152-3, 155-64, 165, 167, 195-6, 202-3
press campaign, 93-4, 99, 102-3
Prevention of Terrorism Act, 73, 128, 254, 264
Prisons Department, 148, 183
PROP, 163, 166, 174
Protestant Ascendancy, 8

Quigley, Jimmy, 23, 42

radio, 137-8; Radio Four, 137; Radio Luxembourg, 138; Radio Free Belfast, 37; Radio Telefis Eireann, 223; Radio Tiranë, 138, 162
railway repairs, 51, 52-3, 76
'Red Flag, The', 206-7
Rees, Merlyn, 223, 229
religious antagonism, see sectarianism
remission, 147-8
Republic of Ireland, 20
republicanism, 21, 26, 34; see also Irish Republican Army and Sinn Féin
Rice, Bunny, 22-3
Richardson, DI Brian, 60-1, 94
Richardson, Carole, 265; Old Bailey trial, 1-4, 117-31; 'confession', 2, 57, 75, 87-8, 93; PH meets, 51; charged, 85, 86; and WRACS, 87; PH hardly knows, 89; Brixton, 89-90, 122-3; no trace of

explosives, 93; committal, 96; Risley, 96, 122, 123; optimism, 126; American support, 222-3; alibi, 128-9, 228; O'Connell clears, 182; legal representative, 229-30; appeal (1989), 237, 244-58; freedom, 241-58; naming of, 250-1, 254
Richardson, Jo, 174
Risley Remand Centre, 96, 122
Robert Hart, 43, 50
Roman Catholics: discrimination against, see sectarianism
Roskill, Lord Justice, 184, 186, 187-8, 198
Rossa, O'Donovan, 200
Rowe, Christopher, 86, 130
Royal Arsenal Research and Development Establishment, 124, 140, 181
Royal Enniskillen Fusiliers, 7
Royal Green Jackets, 99
Royal Ulster Constabulary, 31, 36, 257; sectarianism, 31, 33; hostility to, 32; brutality, 33, 36-7, 40; and Loyalist attacks, 39
Rule 43, 116-17
Rule 48, 170
Ryan, Brendan, 221
Ryan, Father, 50

Sachs, Albie, 174
Sagar, Det. Supt Ronald, 177-8
St Denys, 76
'Salty', 212
Sands, Bobby, 140, 200
Scarman, Lord, 223
sectarianism, 8-9, 17, 30-1, 36, 43, 82-3
Serravalli, Marion, see Hill, Marion

Seven Stars, *see* Guildford
  bombings
Shankill Butchers, 43
Sharples, Jim, 228-9, 230, 236,
  248, 263
Shaw, Brian, 44, 69-70, 98-114,
  123, 130, 131, 177, 245, 246,
  253, 256
Sheehan, Mick, 116-17, 121
Sheridan, Phil, 202
Simmons, DCS Walter (Wally),
  63, 69-72, 74-5, 77, 105, 108-
  9, 123, 126
Simpson, Tommy, 22
Sinn Féin, 33, 34
Sisters of Charity, 26
Skillen, Martin, 23, 44
Slater, Caroline, 66, 68, 73
Smalley, Errol, 44, 50, 72, 94;
  PH stays with, 47, 260; and
  NCCL, 90; convinced of PH's
  innocence, 142; mobilizes
  opinion, 219-22, 231; and
  PH's marriage, 234, 235, 261;
  and PH's release, 258
Smalley, Janet, 47
Smalley, Theresa (*aunt*), 19, 20,
  21, 50, 72, 94, 101, 142, 203;
  PH stays with, 47, 260; and
  NCCL, 90; visits PH, 197;
  mobilizes opinion, 219-22,
  231; and PH's health, 230;
  and PH's marriage, 235; and
  PH's release, 245, 246
Smyth, Sean, 86, 265
Soley, Clive, 219
Southampton, 101, 127;
  Aldermoor Avenue, 55-6,
  61, 66; Butts Road, 51,
  52-3; Eagle, 52-3, 63; King's
  Arms, 47, 61; Palmerston
  Road, 52; Shirley Road police
  station, 48, 61, 92; Sholing,
  46; Stainer Close, 48, 49,
51, 52-3, 92, 128; Target,
  52-3, 63
Spanish Civil War, 200, 206-7
Special Branch, 46-7, 70, 93, 95,
  101; brutality, 40
Special Powers Act, 30
Still, James, 145, 178, 182,
  183, 184
Stormont Castle, 31, 36, 39
Strangeways Prison, 145, 211-
  14, 215-16, 217
Stranraer, 24-5
strip cells, 82
strip-searches, 196
Sun, 234-5
Sunday Mirror, 53
Sunday Times, 163
Surrey Daily Advertiser, 132
Surrey Police Force, 58-9, 132-3,
  252, 253, 262, 263
Swan National, 186-7

Taylor, Harry, 40, 70
Thatcher, Margaret, 123
Thin Layer Chromatography
  (TLC), 86, 140
Time Bomb (McKee/Franey), 95,
  103, 122, 228
Times, The, 94, 223, 229
TLC, *see* Thin Layer
  Chromatography
Tone, Wolfe, 200
trade unions, 221
Trial and Error (Kee), 99, 103,
  122, 223, 227
'Troubles' (1969), 8

Ulster Linen Company, 30
Underwood Det. Supt Ronald,
  60, 62, 63, 64-5, 66, 67-8
Unionist Government, 32, 36,
  39
United States of America, 222-3,
  231-2, 264

Wakefield Prison, 183, 202, 208
Walker, Johnnie, 153, 154, 176-
7, 195-6
Walsh, David, 91
Walsh, Joe, 22, 45
Wandsworth Prison, 115-34,
149, 154, 171, 189, 207,
208, 243; mailbag shop, 115-
16, 117
Waterfoot, 19
West Midlands Serious Crimes
Squad, 217, 263
'Whistler', The, 23
Wicked beyond Belief (Kennedy),
227
Wigoder, Lord, 123
William of Orange, 8
Williams, Mickey, 135-6, 238
Winchester Prison, 50, 77, 78-
96, 115, 135, 148, 202, 207,
217, 237-8; conditions, 80,
81, 101, 102

Winson Green Prison, 116,
149, 154
Wize, Richard, 235
Woolwich bomb (1974),
22, 53, 54
Wormwood Scrubs Prison, 133,
163, 198, 203, 205, 206, 208,
214-15, 216, 217, 220, 225,
232, 234, 243

Yallop, John, 184-5
York Crown Court, 166,
178, 202-3
Yorkshire Televison, 223,
227, 228
Young, Hector, 99-101, 102,
104, 113